"Pastoring part of Christ's flock is a glor̶i̶o̶u̶s̶ ̶b̶u̶r̶d̶e̶n̶.̶ ̶Y̶o̶u̶ ̶w̶e̶e̶p̶ those who weep and laugh with those who laugh. Willhite and Malphurs provide pastors with rich counsel and effective models on how to do both with sensitivity and skill."

—HADDON ROBINSON

"Nothing here is written in stone. All is offered to be edited to your personal taste. Creative is the order of the day. So, go ahead, add your best ideas to theirs. Shorten, lengthen, mix, and match. Engage your walk with Christ and stir in generous portions of creativity. Your corner of the kingdom is about to be blessed."

—CALVIN MILLER

"Weddings and funerals provide some of the most significant opportunities for ministry in the life of any pastor and ones for which we are usually the most poorly prepared. I highly recommend this resource as a tool for pastors everywhere to fulfill their calling with greater effectiveness and with spiritual accuracy."

—CHIP INGRAM
President, Walk Thru the Bible
Teaching Pastor, *Living on the Edge*

"As a pastor, I know how important it is to find contemporary ideas that aren't stale or hackneyed or outdated. I love the breadth of this book and I appreciate the wide range of suggestions. Ministers of all ages and backgrounds will find it indispensable. Aubrey Malphurs and Keith Willhite have performed a service to the whole body of Christ. If you are in the ministry, buy this book and keep it handy because you'll need it sooner or later."

—RAY PRITCHARD
Senior Pastor, Calvary Memorial Church
Oak Park, Illinois

"This valuable resource is packed with ideas and examples for leading these frequent moments in the life of a church, along with other events like ordinations, child dedications, and many more. This useful tool will find a valued place on the shelves of pastors everywhere—although it's not likely to sit on that shelf for any length of time."

—MICHAEL DUDUIT
Editor, *Preaching*

"The breadth of subjects and depth of help is truly stunning."

—DR. DON SUNUKJIAN
Professor and Chair
Department of Christian Ministry and Leadership
Talbot School of Theology

"Willhite and Malphurs put at our fingertips the passionate, Spirit-empowered words of seasoned partners in ministry."

—DAVID B. WYRTZEN
Senior Pastor, Midlothian Bible Church

A Contemporary Handbook

for Weddings & Funerals

and Other Occasions

A Contemporary Handbook for Weddings & Funerals

and Other Occasions

Aubrey Malphurs
& Keith Willhite

editors

Kregel
Academic & Professional

A Contemporary Handbook for Weddings & Funerals and Other Occasions

© 2003 by Aubrey Malphurs and Keith Willhite

Published by Kregel Publications, a division of Kregel, Inc., P.O. Box 2607, Grand Rapids, MI 49501.

Unless otherwise indicated, Scripture quotations are from the *Holy Bible, New International Version®*. NIV®. © 1973, 1978, 1984 by International Bible Society. Used by permission of Zondervan Publishing House. All rights reserved.

Scripture quotations marked TLB are from *The Living Bible,* © 1971 by Tyndale House Publishers, Inc., Wheaton, Illinois 60189. Used by permission.

Scripture quotations marked KJV are from the King James Version of the Holy Bible.

Scripture quotations marked NASB are from the *New American Standard Bible.* © The Lockman Foundation 1960, 1962, 1963, 1968, 1971, 1972, 1973, 1975, 1977, 1995. Used by permission.

Scripture quotations marked NKJV are from the *New King James Version.* © 1979, 1980, 1982, Thomas Nelson, Inc. Used by permission.

Scripture quotations marked NLT are from the *Holy Bible, New Living Translation,* © 1996. Used by permission of Tyndale House Publishers, Inc., Wheaton, Illinois 60189. All rights reserved.

ISBN 0-8254-3186-7

Printed in the United States of America

03 04 05 06 07 / 5 4 3 2 1

To Dr. Keith Willhite,
loving father and faithful friend to so many,
who after a life-long journey of serving the Savior,
went home to be with Him on April 16, 2003.

Contents

When Death Is Untimely or Unexpected

Funeral Services by Family Members

Perspectives on Death and Dying

PART 3: OTHER OCCASIONS

Preface

FEW OCCASIONS OFFER PASTORS the opportunities to minister to and with a family as do weddings and funerals. Often on such occasions, people open their hearts to God and to others in new ways, and the pastor can be there to give direction and encouragement.

THE NEED FOR THIS BOOK

This book grew from a stated need and aims to address that need. The manager of the Dallas Seminary Book Center approached us with the fact that he receives many requests from pastors for resources for weddings, funerals, and other occasions. Younger pastors might not have performed these duties, and even seasoned pastors might want to freshen "that same old service." Although a few such resources are in print, most of them are rather dated and reflect the era in which they were written. Hence, we have sought more contemporary resources and resources that will be helpful in specific situations.

OUR APPROACH

Our approach is that of the "colaborer" or "pastor to pastor." The materials in this volume have been shared by pastors for pastors. We intentionally sought materials that have been used in fruitful ministry with the hope that others might use or adapt them for more fruitful ministry in similar situations but different contexts. Hence, this volume contains very little sense of "Well, you might consider doing this." Rather, the resources in this book have been shared on the premise that "We found this to minister effectively." We are very grateful to the people who have been willing to share these materials.

While our aim has been to offer an up-to-date, culturally and personally relevant resource, we learned some interesting things along the way. First, from churches with very "contemporary" ministries we heard an echoing theme: "When it comes to weddings and funerals, our people often want the more traditional." Hence, we have woven together traditional and contemporary resources and hope that each user of this book will be able to adapt the resources for effective use. Second, we heard the generosity of God's servants. The contributors of materials for this book did so willingly and with the goal of helping their fellow servants. In many cases, names have been changed when referring to participants in a service or other individuals.

ORGANIZATION

These resources appear in three major sections: Weddings, Funerals, and Other Occasions. Within each major section, we include the following resources: sample services, messages and message outlines, and supporting materials. The supporting materials vary in kind and length. Some are brief illustrations whereas others are heart-touching stories. Throughout the volume some sections begin with an "Editors' Note" to suggest ways to use these resources. Some adaptation might be needed to fit your context, but the resources in this book are offered for your use, with full permission to copy and use them as needed, for fruitful ministry to the glory of God.

Acknowledgments

OF COURSE, WE ARE VERY GRATEFUL to the many people who contributed materials for this volume. We also are grateful to two people who helped to type and collate many of the materials: Muriel Rowland and Kristi Wilson. Without their four hands, the handbook would never have come together.

We have sought diligently to locate sources. Nevertheless, a few entries appear with the words *Source Unknown.*

Contributors

Editors' Note: Obviously, this handbook would not have been possible without the following contributors, who have willingly shared their ministries. Each has contributed in a special and generous way, and we are grateful for their liberality.

Jeffrey D. Arthurs teaches communication and preaching at Gordon-Conwell Theological Seminary, South Hamilton, Massachusetts.

Dr. Sidney F. Batts is the Senior Pastor of First Presbyterian Church, Greensboro, North Carolina. He is the author of *The Protestant Wedding Sourcebook* (John Knox Press, 1993).

Tony Beckett, Back to the Bible's Associate Bible Teacher, says that his passion "is to help people understand the Word of God and see how it affects the way they live." He has pastored churches in Iowa, Ohio, and Pennsylvania; worked with camp ministries and church leadership councils; and served as an area representative for Baseball Chapel. Dr. Beckett and his wife, Joan, have three daughters.

Paul D. Borden is the Executive Minister with the American Baptist Churches of the West. He works as a church consultant to large churches across the United States, Australia, and New Zealand. He also is a consultant to the Baptist Union of New Zealand.

Charlie Boyd serves as pastor-teacher of Southside Baptist Church, Simpsonville, South Carolina. He has ministered as a speaker with Family Life Marriage Conferences for ten years and is the author of *Different Children, Different Needs.* Southside Baptist Church is an equipping-focused church. The church emphasizes expository teaching with a more contemporary worship style.

John Breneman directs a counseling center in Grabo, Sweden. John also has an itinerant ministry of teaching, counseling, and marriage and family seminars in churches and schools in the Scandinavian countries as well as other European nations.

Pete Briscoe is senior pastor of Bent Tree Bible Fellowship, Dallas, Texas. Bent Tree is a contemporary ministry in north Dallas. Bent Tree states three value-driven goals: (1) we want to make it hard to go to hell from north Dallas; (2) we want to make it hard to be lonely in north Dallas; and (3) we want to make it hard to be shallow in north Dallas.

Judy Elliott is Development Director at LifeCare Pregnancy Services, Austin, Texas. LifeCare Pregnancy Services works to provide Post-Abortion Counseling and Education (PACE). More information is available from www.austinlifecare.org.

Richard Allen Farmer has, since 1992, served as the president of RAF Ministries in Dallas, Texas, a church renewal ministry using expository preaching and music to stimulate the body of Christ. He spent several years as a senior pastor, and then as dean of the Chapel at Gordon College and at Taylor University. With a Master of Divinity degree from Princeton Theological Seminary, he has also received honorary degrees from Gordon College and Houghton College.

Roland Foreman is Director of Curriculum Development with the Center for Church-Based Training in Richardson, Texas.

Randy Frazee serves as senior pastor of Pantego Bible Church, Arlington, Texas. He is a graduate of Dallas Theological Seminary (M.A./Biblical Studies) and the author of *The Comeback Congregation* and *The Connecting Church: Beyond Small Groups to Authentic Commu-*

nity. Randy frequently serves as a church leadership trainer and consultant with the Willow Creek Association.

Rob Harrell serves as senior pastor of the First Evangelical Free Church, Austin, Texas. The church believes that First Evangelical Free Church can have a vital role in reaching the world for Christ. Strategically located minutes from the heart of the University of Texas, in one of the most densely populated segments of Austin, the church is convinced that God has sovereignly placed it to minister to college students and families.

Howard G. Hendricks is Chairman of the Center for Christian Leadership and Distinguished Professor at Dallas Theological Seminary, where he has taught for more than fifty years.

Dr. Phil Hook currently serves as a Distinguished Professor of Biblical Studies at LeTourneau University, Longview, Texas. He is also the Executive Director of the Education Radio Foundation.

Dale Hummel serves as senior pastor of First Baptist Church, Castro Valley, California. On the bases of the Great Commandment (Matt. 22:37–40) and the Great Commission (28:19–20), First Baptist Church purposes to love God and invite others to follow Jesus. The church's vision is to see unbelievers in the community of Castro Valley become fully devoted followers of Jesus Christ. The church's purpose and vision grow out of a lengthy list of core values and translate into several creative strategies for ministry.

Eddie B. Lane has served on the administrative staff and faculty of Dallas Seminary for more than twenty-five years. Thirty-four years ago, he founded Bibleway Bible Church in Dallas, Texas, and still serves as the church's pastor. A leading researcher and author on urban ministry and the black family, Dr. Lane is also founder and president of the Institute for Black Family Renewal. He maintains an active conference ministry that focuses on the black family in America.

Robertson McQuilkin is a distinguished theological educator, having served as president of Columbia Bible College and Columbia Biblical Seminary, Columbia, South Carolina. Currently, the majority of his time is spent caring for his wife through a lengthy illness in their home.

Andy McQuitty serves as senior pastor of Irving Bible Church, Irving, Texas. Irving Bible Church is a rapidly growing nondenominational church ministering to all ages in the heart of the city of Irving. Dr. McQuitty has served as senior pastor of Irving Bible Church for eighteen years.

James E. Means is Professor of Homiletics and Pastoral Studies at Denver Seminary. He has spent numerous years in pastoral ministry and has led conferences and taught in churches and seminaries in Europe, Africa, China, Russia, and the Philippines.

Ron Moore is senior pastor of South Hills Bible Church, McMurray, Pennsylvania. He earned the Master of Theology degree from Dallas Theological Seminary, where he is also a candidate for the Doctor of Ministry degree. South Hills is a growing, thriving nondenominational church in suburban Pittsburgh.

Bill Oudemolen is senior pastor of Foothills Bible Church in Littleton, Colorado. Foothills is a growing nondenominational church in suburban Denver.

Ditmar and Maura Pauck are missionaries in Brazil.

Ray Pritchard serves as senior pastor of Calvary Memorial Church, Oak Park, Illinois. Dr. Pritchard is a prolific author and a frequent radio guest, and he travels regularly to preach. Calvary Memorial Church is an independent, evangelical congregation located near Chicago in Oak Park, Illinois. Calvary is a community of believers dedicated to fulfilling the Great Commission through worship, discipleship, and evangelism.

John W. Reed serves as Senior Professor of Pastoral Ministries and Director of Doctor of Ministry Studies at Dallas Theological Seminary. He has served thirty-seven years in pastoral ministry in churches in Indiana, Ohio, and Texas. Dr. Reed is also a chaplain (Lt. Col., retired) in the U.S. Air Force Reserves and is a member of the National Guard Association of Texas.

Rick Reed serves as senior pastor of Metropolitan Bible Church, Ottawa, Canada.

Larry Renoe serves as an associate pastor at Centennial Community Church in Littleton, Colorado.

Haddon W. Robinson is the Harold John Ockenga Distinguished Professor of Preaching at Gordon-Conwell Theological Seminary, South Hamilton, Massachusetts. A prolific author and distinguished preacher, Dr. Robinson served as president of Denver Seminary and on the faculty of Dallas Theological Seminary before serving at Gordon-Conwell.

Brent Strawsburg is lead pastor of ShoreLife Church, a contemporary church that meets in the beach community of Huntington Beach, California. The church is nearly eleven years old. A large percentage of the people come from either a Catholic background or a totally unchurched background.

Steve Stroope is senior pastor of Lake Pointe Church in Rockwall, Texas. Lake Pointe's purpose is "to share God's love with the unchurched people of the Lake Ray Hubbard Community and the world in such a way that they have the best opportunity to become fully developing followers of Jesus Christ." Although Lake Pointe has grown in twenty-three years to a weekend attendance of a few thousand people, unquestionably, the focus at Lake Pointe is the medium-sized group, the Adult Bible Fellowship (ABF). Therefore, Pastor Steve regularly reminds the people of Lake Pointe that "we are not a large church; we're a collection of small churches." In the ABF, relationships are built, caregiving takes place, the church gathers for the Lord's Table, and so forth.

John F. Walvoord served as Chancellor Emeritus of Dallas Theological Seminary, until his death in late 2002. An esteemed theologian, Dr. Walvoord served as president of the seminary from 1952 through 1986.

Jeff Watson serves as the Director of Resident Life for Greenspring Village, Springfield, Virginia, and as the Professor of Gerontology at Washington Bible College, Lanham, Maryland. Jeff is an ordained Baptist pastor and a graduate of Capital Seminary (Th.M.), Catholic University (M.A.), Dallas Theological Seminary (D.Min.), and University of Maryland (Doctoral Certificate in Gerontology; M.S.; Ph.D.). For twenty years, Dr. Watson has dedicated himself to working with individuals, families, congregations, and health-care institutions dealing with aging, grieving, and dying.

Denise Willhite is the wife of Dr. Keith Willhite and the mother of David and Katie. She resides with her family in Rowlett, Texas.

part one

WEDDINGS

Introduction

EVERY SEASONED PASTOR KNOWS the joy and challenges of preparing for both a marriage and a wedding. Weddings are symbolic in many ways, but they provide the occasion for a couple to make a covenant before a covenant-making God and His people, the church. Therefore, we view weddings as services of worship. A wedding is a joyous occasion that presents a time of celebration and commitment.

Few occasions in the life of a family present greater potential for good than a wedding. As Dr. W. A. Criswell observed, "The arrangement for the beautiful occasion opens the door for the pastor into the very heart of all the people involved. He is a wise pastor who takes advantage of the providence to counsel the couple in Christian home-making and to encouraging the parties to make Christ and his church the center of their lives."[1]

In this section on weddings, we have attempted to provide resources that will be aesthetic, worshipful, and biblically sound. To that end, each wedding should be a joyous, sanctified, dignified, and enjoyable occasion for everyone involved. As Scott Gibson has explained, "Not all weddings include a sermon. Some consist of only the typical liturgical elements of vows, prayers, and pronouncement. Although rituals for marriage ceremonies in some denominations do not formally include a place for the wedding sermon, there appear to be none that prohibit it."[2] Wedding sermons should have some definite characteristics, including (1) brevity; (2) a theology that clearly represents God's design for marriage; (3) suitability for the occasion, formal or informal; and (4) an appropriate target, on the couple or on the congregation.

Order of Service

EDITORS' NOTE: Some denominations prescribe certain elements and a particular order for the elements in wedding ceremonies, but most of them follow a pattern similar to this traditional outline.

- Prelude
- Musical Solo
- Processional
- Welcome to Guests
- Prayer
- Giving of the Bride
- Scripture Reading
- Message or Meditation
- Declaration of Intent
- Vows
- Presentation of Rings
- Pronouncement
- Prayer of Dedication
- Introduction of the Couple
- Benediction
- Recessional

Sample
Wedding Service
Source Unknown

EDITORS' NOTE: This is a generic sample of a traditional service. Of course, various elements of the service (e.g., vows, declaration, charge, etc.) may be replaced by personalized elements or with other elements presented in this volume.

[The wedding party may enter during either the processional music or the singing of a congregational hymn. As the minister faces the congregation, the bride will stand on the minister's right and the groom on his left, with the other members of the wedding party on either side.]

WELCOME TO GUESTS

Please be seated.

As a community of friends, we are gathered here in God's presence to witness the marriage of (John) and (Mary), and to ask God to bless them.

We are called to rejoice in their happiness, to help them when they have trouble, and to remember them in our prayers. Marriage, like our creation as men and women, owes its existence to God. It is His will and purpose that a husband and wife should love each other throughout their lives and that children born to them should enjoy the security of family and home.

PRAYER

Eternal God, our Creator and Redeemer, as You gladdened the wedding at Cana in Galilee by the presence of Your Son, so by Your pres-

. . . .

ence now bring Your joy to this wedding. In favor, look upon this couple and grant that they, rejoicing in all Your gifts, may at length celebrate with Christ the Bridegroom, the marriage feast that has no end. Amen.

CHARGE TO THE COUPLE

(John) and (Mary), your marriage is intended to join you for life in a relationship so intimate and personal that it will change your whole being. God offers you the hope, and indeed the promise, of a love that is true and mature.

You have made known that you want to be joined in Christian marriage, and no one has shown any valid reason why you may not. If either of you knows of any reason, you are now to declare it.

DECLARATION OF INTENT

(John), do you take (Mary) to be your wife, and do you commit yourself to her, to be responsible in the marriage relationship, to give yourself to her in love and work, to invite her fully into your being so that she can know who you are, to cherish her above all others, and to respect her individuality by encouraging her to be herself and grow in all that God intends?

Groom: Yes, I do [*or,* I do].

(Mary), do you take (John) to be your husband, and do you commit yourself to him, to be responsible in the marriage relationship, to give yourself to him in love and work, to invite him fully into your being so that he can know who you are, to cherish him above all others, and to respect his individuality by encouraging him to be himself and grow in all that God intends?

Bride: Yes, I do [*or,* I do].

. . . .

AFFIRMATION OF PARENTS AND CONGREGATION

[Inviting the parents to stand, the minister shall ask:]

Do you as parents promise to pray for and support your children in the new relationship that they enter as husband and wife? If so, each say, "I do."
Parents: I do.

[Addressing the congregation, the minister will say:]

All of you who witness these vows, will you do everything in your power to support and uphold these two persons in their marriage? If so, then say, "We will!"
Congregation: We will!

[At this point, where space permits, the bride and groom and their two immediate attendants may move into the chancel.]

VOWS

(John) and (Mary), please face each other and join hands.

[The couple, taking each other's hands, shall say their vows.]

Groom: I take you, (Mary), to be my wife. I promise before God and these witnesses to be your faithful husband, to share with you in plenty and in want, in joy and in sorrow, in sickness and in health, to forgive and strengthen you, and to join with you so that together we may serve God and others as long as we both shall live.

Bride: I take you, (John), to be my husband. I promise before God and these witnesses to be your faithful wife, to share with you in plenty and in want, in joy and in sorrow, in sickness and in health, to forgive and strengthen you, and to join with you so that together we may serve God and others as long as we both shall live.

PRESENTATION OF RINGS

[As the minister receives each ring in turn, it is appropriate to pray:]

Bless, Lord, this ring that he [*or,* she] who gives it and she [*or,* he] who wears it may abide in Your peace. Amen.

[Giving the rings in turn, each shall say:]

Groom/Bride: (Mary/John), I love you, and I give you this ring as a sign of my love and faithfulness.

PRONOUNCEMENT

Because (John) and (Mary) have made their vows with each other before God and all of us here, I pronounce them to be husband and wife in the name of God, the Father, the Son, and the Holy Spirit. Amen.

Let no one divide those whom God has united.

BLESSING

The Lord God who created our first parents and established them in marriage, establish and sustain you, that you may find delight in each other and grow in holy love until life's end. Amen.

PRAYERS OF THANKSGIVING AND INTERCESSION

O God, Creator and Father of us all, we thank You for the gift of life—and, in life, for the gift of marriage. We praise and thank You for all the joys that can come to men and women through marriage and for the blessings of home and family.

Today, especially, we think of (John) and (Mary) as they begin their life together as husband and wife. With them, we thank You for the joy they find in each other. Give them strength, Father, to keep the vows they have made and to cherish the love they share, that they may be faithful and devoted. Help them to support each other with patience, understanding, and honesty. (Teach them to be wise and loving parents of any children they may have.) (We pray for their parents, that at this moment of parting, they may rejoice in their children's happiness.)

Look with favor, God, on all of our homes. Defend them from every evil that may threaten them, from outside or within. Let Your Spirit so direct all of us that we may look to the good of others in word and deed and grow in grace as we advance in years, through Jesus Christ our Lord. Amen.

[Here the Lord's Prayer may be included.]

Lord's Prayer

Our Father who art in heaven, Hallowed be thy name. Thy kingdom come. Thy will be done in earth, as it is in heaven. Give us this day our daily bread. And forgive us our debts, as we forgive our debtors. And lead us not into temptation, but deliver us from evil: For thine is the kingdom, and the power, and the glory for ever. Amen. (Matthew 6:9–13 KJV)

INTRODUCTION OF THE COUPLE

Now, it is my privilege to introduce to you (John and Mary Smith).

BENEDICTION

The Lord bless you and keep you; the Lord make His face to shine upon you, and be gracious to you; the Lord lift up His countenance upon you, and give you peace. Amen.

[Recessional]

Suitable for One Another

Brent Strawsburg

WELCOME TO GUESTS

Welcome to this great occasion. On behalf of Dean and Michelle, allow me to express my thanks for your being here this afternoon. We've all looked forward to this moment. Some of you have a shared history with Dean and Michelle. You marvel at the uniqueness of these two friends and how God has brought them together. Some of you, quite frankly, have waited a long time for this day to come. But God is the master of timing.

Dean and Michelle, God brought the two of you together. He planned the circumstances, He molded your lives, and He's been in control of the timing so that both of you would be exactly what He wants you to be—suitable for one another. He didn't want you to be married two years ago or a year ago because it wasn't His time. You weren't ready then, but I believe that you're ready now. I believe that you have the necessary spiritual sensitivity to make your marriage pleasing to God. Because of what is at stake, this ceremony carries tremendous importance and significance. Would you join me as we commit this ceremony to God?

PRAYER

GIVING OF THE BRIDE

When a couple comes together, families also come together. It is important for the families to say, "We believe in this union; we'll always work to support them." Dave and Janine, I want to turn to you first. Speaking as Dean's folks and on behalf of the entire family, are you willing to pledge your support of Dean as he leaves to begin this new family unit and to demonstrate your love to Michelle as your very own daughter? I want to turn to you also, John and Betty. Speaking on behalf of all of Michelle's family, are you willing not only to support this union but also to embrace Dean as your very own son? If so, please say, "We will."

Parents: We will.

[Song]

MESSAGE

It would be safe to say that, over the last one hundred years, people have progressively lost their ability to trust the great institutions of our day. We struggle with the institution of government. Time and time again, our leaders fail to engender genuine support and trust. We sense that the problems of our day are too great for government to solve. In addition, the institution of the church has fallen on hard times. For all of its energy, the church often struggles to make a visible impact in society. It has struggled to help people change the way they actually live.

The institution of marriage has also struggled. A lasting marriage is the exception of our day. Couples today struggle to cope with all of the issues facing them. They struggle with the high levels of commitment. Couples enter marriage still struggling with baggage from their childhood. In our "me-centered" culture, it's becoming increasingly difficult for a couple to focus and live for the good of another person.

It's Dean and Michelle's desire that their marriage model for all of us the importance of commitment to the institution of marriage. They recognize that, far from squelching their happiness in life, the institution of marriage will allow them to experience the deepest levels of intimacy and personal development. They desire that their marriage demonstrate that God's priorities still work in today's age.

. . . .

Let me remind all of us about the design of the institution of marriage. *From the very beginning of humanity, God recognized the need for man to live in relationship.* Listen to God's response as He views Adam in his loneliness in the Garden: "It is not good for the man to be alone" (Gen. 2:18).

As God saw this scene, He responded thus: "I will make a helper suitable for him" (2:18) The actual Hebrew word that God uses means "corresponding to." Here's the idea: Adam looked at Eve and saw the perfect complement to himself. He saw a person who perfectly corresponded to him. You could state it thus: when Adam saw Eve, he saw *a person who helped him to recognize himself.*

It's God's design that a man and a woman be brought together such that they complement each other. The union of two distinctly different people should allow each person to see himself or herself more clearly. They should be able better to recognize their strengths, their weaknesses, and their potential.

Listen to Adam's response after God made Eve. I want you to hear Adam's first expression when he lays eyes on Eve. Listen: "This is now bone of my bones and flesh of my flesh" (2:23). Translated from the Hebrew, it means, "Wow, that's a woman!"

Adam marvels not only at how much Eve's like him but also how beautifully different she is. Adam recognized something right away. For man and woman to live in relationship, they would have to live with and appreciate their differences. God's design in marriage is for two people to understand their differences and learn to love and appreciate those differences.

Dean and Michelle, this is what God intends for you in a Christian marriage. I'm well aware that both of you desire for God to play an integral role in your marriage.

At a distinct point in your past, each of you committed your life to Jesus Christ. You recognized that, apart from what He did on the Cross in dying for your sins, you had no relationship with God. You each had to come to the point where you were not trusting in your good behavior or your relationship with the church but solely on what Christ did on the Cross for you. It was the only way, with nothing else added to it, that guaranteed you that, when you die, you'll go to heaven. When you became a Christian, God became an integral part of your life. As you prepare to embrace the institution of marriage, God wishes to play an active role. I'd like to ask each of you to commit yourselves to the institution of marriage.

DECLARATION OF INTENT

Dean, believing this to be the will of God for your life, and believing that you should live with Michelle the rest of your days, do you this day take Michelle to be your lawfully wedded wife? Will you love her and lead her? Will you keep her in sickness or in health, in plenty or in want? And, forsaking all other women for the rest of your days on earth, will you keep yourself faithfully only unto Michelle so long as both of you shall live?

Dean: I will.

And Michelle, will you take Dean to be your lawfully wedded husband? Will you, in response to his love and leadership, love him and keep him and submit to him in sickness or in health, in plenty or in want? And, forsaking all other men for the rest of your days on earth, will you keep yourself faithfully only unto Dean so long as both of you shall live?

Michelle: I will.

Please ascend the stairs.

[Song]

CHARGE TO THE COUPLE

Within the institution of marriage, God brings two people together. He asks you to commit yourself not only to the institution of marriage but also to each other as distinctly unique people. Your love was meant to thrive and flourish within the boundaries of marriage. It's now your responsibility to learn how better to fan the flames of love for each other. Don't be misled. That's exactly what God wants from the two of you. He desires that you fan the flames of passion, commitment, and love such that fifty years from now you are more in love than ever before.

How can you accomplish this? Let me suggest a couple of things from the greatest love story in the Bible. It's the story of King Solomon and his beautiful young bride.

Build Your Mate's Self-Concept

Song of Solomon gives an interesting portrait of Solomon's bride. Apparently she has struggled with her own self-concept throughout her life. Listen to her self-appraisal. Do you hear the lament of a woman who doesn't feel lovely, who has for too long underappreciated how God had made her? It could also very easily describe a man who struggles with his own self-concept. However, for the first time the woman has met someone who time and time again takes the initiative to build up her self-concept. Listen to how Solomon describes his bride in 1:8–9, 15.

Dean, treat Michelle as the prize possession she is. God has molded her and specially gifted her with talents and personality in a beautiful way. Your privilege is to act and speak in lockstep with God. You must consistently and lovingly and creatively build her self-concept not only in her physical beauty but also in the full range of personality, depth of charm, and spiritual sensitivity.

Michelle, your role is regularly to ignore the rough exterior that Dean as a man might project. You have the tough job of handling the fragile ego of a man. Time after time, you will have the opportunity to bolster the spirit and confidence of Dean. When you build his self-concept, here's what you will find: every day, Dean will become more the man that God intended him to be. When he becomes the man God intended, he will have a greater capacity to love and care for you.

The message of this ultimate love story is to build each other's self-concept. Consistently, patiently, and lovingly build into this person, who will be your mate for the rest of your life. If you build into this person, you will discover a treasure that can never be measured.

Here's the second key to kindling your love and passion:

Communicate Through the Rough Times

Listen to the words of Solomon's bride as she expresses not only her love to Solomon but also her commitment to the process of communication:

> O my dove, in the clefts of the rock,
> In the secret place of the steep pathway,
> Let me see your form,
> Let me hear your voice;
> For your voice is sweet,
> And your form is lovely.
> Catch the foxes for us,
> The little foxes that are ruining the vineyards,
> While our vineyards are in blossom.
> —Song of Songs 2:14–15 (NASB)

What's she saying?

She's asking Solomon to catch the foxes. It's a word picture to describe some potential problems in their relationships. She longingly looks to her husband and says, "You who are so beautiful to me, whose voice I long for, please take care of these issues."

Problems, difficulties, and tensions are a fact of life within marriage. Dean, you will express the highest quality of love if you assume responsibility for dealing with the issues that come into your marriage. Michelle has a right to expect that you won't run away from issues. She has a right to expect that you will lead your household into health and spiritual vitality. Like all of us, you both bring issues to this marriage. You've courageously faced these issues and modeled to me your commitment to emotional and spiritual health in your relationship.

Dean, however hard the process, however difficult it might be, regardless of what has transpired in your life, you must continue to be open and honest with Michelle and share your feelings.

Michelle, your job is to create a safe place for Dean to communicate. This is not done by judging what he says but by listening to what he feels by what he says.

People tend to do the most instinctive thing when things go wrong or the pressure builds too much in a relationship. But it's the wrong thing, the worst thing. They hurl blame at each other. Here's the simple truth: we don't come to marriage perfect. You'll find out areas in each other's lives that you might not appreciate, that you don't like, or that you don't understand.

Let me give both of you a suggestion. Criticism is not the pathway to making positive change in your mate. It doesn't come by shaming or blaming each other into change. All that those actions accomplish is to build up hurt and resentment. True, nonselfish love is the pathway.

The job before both of you is to love each other in a language that each of you can understand. Love one another the way you would like to be loved. Love in a way that your mate wishes to be loved.

Dean, you need to love Michelle in a way that would make her feel special—unique. Make her the kind of priority in your life in which there are no rivals. She needs to know by your language, your time, and even your money that she's loved like no one else. She's not simply number one on your list; in a sense she *is* the list. Other people pale in significance to the place she has in your heart.

Michelle you need to love Dean in a way that makes him know that he's valued for who he is and what he's called to do with his life. He needs to know that, regardless of life situations, you'll always support him, believe in him, and offer him a safe place to be himself. Love each other, and let God use the environment of love in your marriage to make the changes.

Before you express your personal vows to each other, I'd like to read something for you from the files of a famous couple who were married for more than forty-eight years before the wife died of cancer. This was a pledge they made to each other to deal with those inevitable times when they wouldn't be at their best, those times when the pressure was too great, those times when one of them was mad at the other, and those times when one of them was frustrated and took it out on the other.

Pledge to Love the Unlovable

Whenever you are not at your best,
if you will let me,
I will put my arms around you
and hold you close.
Then, while I am holding you, I promise
I will try to keep my cool when you are angry.
I will try to be soft when you are hard.
I will try to act rather than react.
If you will listen, I will promise you:
even when you are down on life,
down on me, and down on yourself,
I will be up on the basic you.
Here, now and forever,
I will do my best to love the unlovable.

As you prepare to read your vows to one another, I need to remind you that the deepest beauty of your vows doesn't come from this moment when no one would doubt for a second that you love each other. Their ultimate beauty comes from the remainder of your lives as you demonstrate that, even when you are down on life, down on good fortune, or down on yourself, your mate will be up on the basic you.

Vows

Michelle, would you read your vows to Dean? *[Bride does so.]*

Dean, would you read your vows to Michelle? *[Groom does so.]*

Presentation of Rings

Would you take your rings from your attendants? Michelle, will you place your ring on Dean's finger? Dean, will you place your ring on Michelle's finger? Would you do me (and yourselves) a great favor? The two of you are embarking upon the weightiest, most important adventure of your life. God expects nothing less than absolute commitment to these vows for the rest of your life.

Regardless of what you have faced as individuals or what you will face as a couple, I believe with all of my heart that God wants you to honor those commitments. I also believe that each of you must throw yourself upon God and give Him again the right to make you into the person He wants you to be. As you do that, you'll have a greater capacity to express genuine selfless love for your mate. I'd like the two of you to begin that process right now. Would you kneel and have some silence before the Lord? Then Dean would you pray on behalf of Michelle and yourself?

[Prayer/Candle Lighting/Song]

Blessing

Today symbolizes a very important juncture in your life. Today you start a new family unit. Although you will continue to consult and look for support from each of your extended families, you will begin the ultimate responsibility of charting a course for your life.

In the Old Testament, we catch a glimpse of a beautiful and powerful experience, the blessing given by the parent, or, in some cases, the spiritual mentor. The blessing was the deepest and most profound statement of the mentor in support and belief of what God wanted to do in a person's life. As they expressed the blessing, it was meant to carry the full weight of God's power in their life. At this crucial juncture, would you give me the liberty to express my blessing upon your marriage?

Dean and Michelle:

As each of you realize your inheritance as a child of God, may you live, not according to the messages from your past but according to what God has already done for you. As each of you faces the issues in life, may you be freed from those things in your past that have kept you from your potential. As you live in a world that often mocks the fidelity of marriage, may you find love only in each other's arms. Amen.

Pronouncement

I know I'm speaking for many friends here today when I say that we love and believe in both of you. I wish that I had the ability to bottle up all of the love and the joy that people in this room feel for the two of you. It is now my privilege, by the authority invested in me as a minister of the Good News concerning Jesus Christ, to pronounce you husband and wife.

You may kiss your bride.

Introduction of the Couple

Ladies and gentlemen, I'm pleased to present to you . . .

Mr. and Mrs. Dean Lewis

[Recessional]

A Covenant Relationship

Wedding with an Evangelistic Appeal

Charlie Boyd

EDITORS' NOTE: This couple requested that the wedding include an evangelistic appeal to friends and family members.

[Seating]

[Song]

[Trumpet—We enter—Processional—Bride enters—All rise]

WELCOME TO GUESTS

We have come together in the presence of God to celebrate the uniting of Daniel Hillman and Lori Barber by the sacred ties of matrimony on this twenty-third day of June *[year]*.

It has been my privilege to meet with Dan and Lori several times over the last few months and to share with them God's plan for marriage from the Scriptures. It is a plan that calls for understanding and appreciating the high value that each of them brings to this new union, a plan in which they assume unique roles and responsibilities for one another, primarily the responsibility to nurture one another spiritually and to meet one another's needs.

As we begin, let us pray to our heavenly Father, the One whose plan it was to bring them together.

· ·

PRAYER

Our Father, we thank You for the gift of marriage, for the beauty of intimate companionship, a companionship in which we can know and be known, in which we can share freely and be accepted completely. Thank You for this taste of Your great unconditional love for us. May the commitment being voiced by Dan and Lori today in this ceremony reflect uniquely to the world this great love and bring glory to Your name. And may it remind each of us of the purpose of our marriages and encourage us to fulfill the vows that we have made to one another. In Jesus name, Amen.

GIVING OF THE BRIDE

Who gives this woman to be married to this man?

Father of the bride: Her mother and I.

[Read letters to parents.]

[Turn, walk up stairs, join hands, bride pass bouquet to maid of honor.]

MESSAGE

The institution of marriage was first set forth by God in the Garden of Eden. God created Adam perfect in every way and placed him in a perfect environment, yet with a need—the need for companionship and fellowship. God Himself said, "It is not good for the man to be alone" (Gen. 2:18 NASB). He then created Eve to meet that need. And she is referred to in Genesis 2 as Adam's helpmate, his complement.

The Scriptures go on to say that God brought Eve to the man. In other words, God took the initiative in meeting Adam's needs, and Adam *received* Eve as a special gift from God.

It's clear from the biblical account that God ordained marriage for the lifelong companionship of a man and a woman. It's a covenant relationship, a legal contract, by which two people pledge themselves to one another, and those two become one. "For this cause a man shall leave his father and his mother, and shall cleave to his wife; and they shall become one flesh" (2:24 NASB).

Dan and Lori, because you both have received Jesus Christ as your personal Savior, the covenant relationship that you are now entering into is not only a covenant that you are making with each other but also a covenant with the Lord Jesus Christ, for He is the One who will sustain and bless your life together.

DECLARATION OF INTENT

Daniel, the Scriptures instruct you to *love* and *lead* your wife unconditionally, just as Christ unconditionally loves and leads His church. The apostle Paul writes:

> Husbands, love your wives, just as Christ also loved the church and gave Himself up for her. . . . Husbands ought also to love their own wives as their own bodies. . . . For no one ever hated his own flesh, but nourishes and cherishes it, just as Christ also does the church. (Ephesians 5:25, 28–29 NASB)

Daniel, will you *receive* Lori to be your wife, to live together with her as your companion for life? Will you *love* her and *lead* her as God has instructed? Will you give yourself for her and to her? Will you *pray* for her, and will you forsake all others, being faithful to her until God shall separate you by death?

Daniel: I will.

Lori, the Scriptures teach that wives are to *honor* and *respect* their husbands, just as the church honors and respects Christ. Again, Paul writes:

. . . .

Wives, be subject to your own husbands, as to the Lord. For the husband is the head of the wife, as Christ also is the head of the church, He Himself being the Savior of the body. But as the church is subject to Christ, so also the wives ought to be to their husbands in everything. (5:22–24 NASB)

Lori, will you *receive* Daniel to be your husband, to live together with him as your companion for life? Will you *honor, respect,* and *love* him as God has instructed? Will you give yourself for him and to him? Will you *pray* for him, and will you forsake all others, being faithful to him until God shall separate you by death?

Lori: I will.

Vows

If you are sitting next to your spouse, Dan and Lori invite you to reaffirm your own vows of commitment by taking hold of the hand of your spouse.

Dan, repeat after me. I, Daniel, take you, Lori, to be my wife, to have and to hold from this day forward, for better, for worse, for richer, for poorer, in sickness and in health, to love and to cherish, until we are parted by death.

Lori, repeat after me. I, Lori, take you, Daniel, to be my husband, to have and to hold from this day forward, for better, for worse, for richer, for poorer, in sickness and in health, to love and to cherish, until we are parted by death.

Presentation of Rings

May I have the rings please?

Every covenant has a sign or a symbol to remind each party of the responsibilities he or she brings to the covenant relationship. These rings are symbols of your love. These rings are visible reminders to you and all others, that what you have promised, you will do. Wear them as a constant reminder that you are pledged together and committed to one another for life.

Daniel, place the ring on the wedding finger of your bride and repeat after me:

> This ring I give to you as a symbol of my love.
> And I pledge to you my loyalty and devotion
> Until we are separated by death.
> In the name of the Father, and of the Son, and
>   of the Holy Spirit.

Lori, place the ring on the wedding finger of your groom and repeat after me:

> This ring I give to you as a reminder of my love.
> And I pledge to you my loyalty and devotion
> Until we are separated by death.
> In the name of the Father, and of the Son, and of
>   the Holy Spirit.

The kind of love and commitment that God desires you to model to the world is described in 1 Corinthians 13.

> Love is patient, love is kind and is not jealous; love does not brag and is not arrogant, does not act unbecomingly; it does not seek its own, is not provoked, does not take into account a wrong suffered, does not rejoice in unrighteousness, but rejoices with the truth; bears all things, believes all things, hopes all things, endures all things. Love never fails. (vv. 4–8 NASB)

PRAYER

Let's unite in prayer.

Father, thank You that the love You demonstrated on the Cross never fails! May that same sacrificial love be demonstrated daily between Dan and Lori. It's in Christ's name that we pray. Amen!

[Song: "Savior like a Shepherd Lead Us"]

EVANGELISTIC APPEAL

It is Dan and Lori's great desire that each of you come to know the God whom they worship, if you haven't already done so. The Savior, who has led them together, also wants very much for you to become a part of His Father's family.

You probably know that Christ died on a cross. You might even know that He also rose from the dead. But it is more than head knowledge that allows us to establish a personal relationship with God.

Just as Dan and Lori have received one another and become a member of each other's family, so we must *receive* Jesus Christ as our personal Savior to become a part of God's family.

It's as if Jesus is the bridegroom and all who hear and believe are the prospective brides. God is saying to each of us, "What will you do with My Son, Jesus?" Will you receive Him, and Him alone, to be your personal Savior? Will you love Him and honor Him? Will you trust Him to forgive your sin and to give you the eternal life that He promised? And everyone who answers, "I will," receives the gift of forgiveness and everlasting life. Everyone who says, "I will," becomes a member of God's forever family.

If you've not made that decision, Dan and Lori want to encourage you to receive Jesus now. It's like a marriage. You simply say "I will" as your personal vow of commitment.

PRONOUNCEMENT

Forasmuch as you, Daniel, and you, Lori have openly pledged yourselves to one another in love and faithfulness, in the presence of God, and before these witnesses, and having confirmed the same by each giving and receiving a ring, and by joining hands, I, as a minister of the gospel of Christ, pronounce you husband and wife.

> What, therefore, God hath joined together,
> let not man put asunder.

You may kiss the bride.

INTRODUCTION OF THE COUPLE

[The couple will turn and face the congregation.]

It is my privilege to be the first to present to you . . .

Mr. and Mrs. Daniel Hillman

[Recessional]

[Escort the mothers and the grandmother out.]

God Is the Creator of Marriage

Charlie Boyd

[Seating of mothers]

[Songs: Solo, "Surely the Presence" and Duet, "So Far, So Good"]

[Men enter—Processional—Bride enters—All rise]

WELCOME

We have come together in the presence of God to celebrate the uniting of Robert Johnson and Christine Alexander by the sacred ties of matrimony on this fifteenth day of May *[year]*.

It has been my privilege to meet with Rob and Christy several times over the last few months and to share with them God's plan for marriage from the Scriptures. It's a plan that calls for understanding and appreciating the high value that each of them brings to this new union, a plan in which they assume unique roles and responsibilities for one another, primarily the responsibility to nurture one another spiritually and to work to meet one another's needs emotionally and physically.

In His original design, God ordained that a man should leave his father and mother, cleave to his wife, and become one with her. From the beginning, a man and a woman have come forward in the midst of their family and friends to begin that new relationship.

So as we begin, let us pray to our heavenly Father, the One whose plan it was to bring them together.

PRAYER

Our Father, we thank You for the gift of marriage, for the beauty of intimate companionship, a companionship in which we can know and be known, in which we can share freely and be accepted completely. Thank You for this taste of Your great unconditional love for us. May the commitment being voiced by Rob and Christy today in this ceremony reflect uniquely to the world this great love and bring glory to Your name. And may it remind each of us of the purpose of our marriages and encourage us to fulfill the vows that we have made to one another. In Jesus name, Amen.

GIVING OF THE BRIDE

Who gives this woman to be married to this man?

Father of the bride: "Her mother and I."

[Turn, walk up the stairs, join hands, and bride pass bouquet to maid of honor.]

MESSAGE

The institution of marriage was first set forth by God in the Garden of Eden. God created Adam perfect in every way and placed him in a perfect environment, yet with a need—the need for companionship and fellowship. God Himself said, "It is not good for the man to be alone" (Gen. 2:18 NASB). God then created Eve to meet that need. And in Genesis 2 He refers to her as Adam's helpmate, his complement.

The Scriptures go on to say that God brought Eve to the man. In other words, God took the initiative in meeting Adam's needs, and Adam *received* Eve as a special gift from God.

It's clear from the biblical account that God ordained marriage for the lifelong companionship of a man and a woman. It's a covenant relationship, a legal contract by which two people pledge themselves to one another. And those two become one. "For this cause a man shall leave his father and his mother, and shall cleave to his wife; and they shall become one flesh" (2:24 NASB).

Rob and Christy, because you both have received Jesus Christ as your personal Savior, the covenant relationship into which you are now entering is not only a covenant that you are making with each other but also a covenant with the Lord Jesus Christ, for He is the One who will sustain and bless your life together.

DECLARATION OF INTENT

Robert, the Scriptures instruct you to *love* and *lead* your wife unconditionally, just as Christ unconditionally loves and leads His church. The apostle Paul writes:

> Husbands, love your wives, just as Christ also loved the church and gave Himself up for her. . . . Husbands ought also to love their own wives even as their own bodies. . . . For no one ever hated his own flesh, but nourishes and cherishes it, just as Christ also does the church. (Ephesians 5:25, 28–29 NASB)

Robert, will you *receive* Christine to be your wife, to live together with her as your companion for life? Will you *love* her and *lead* her as God has instructed? Will you give yourself for her and to her? Will you *pray* with and for her, and will you forsake all others, being faithful to her until God shall separate you by death?

Robert: I will.

Christine, the Scriptures teach that wives are to *honor* and *respect* their husbands, just as the church honors and respects Christ. Again, Paul writes:

> Wives, be subject to your own husbands, as to the Lord. For the husband is the head of the wife, as Christ also is the head

of the church, He Himself being the Savior of the body. But as the church is subject to Christ, so also the wives ought to be to their husbands in everything. (5:22–24 NASB)

Christine, will you *receive* Robert to be your husband, to live together with him as your companion for life? Will you *honor, respect,* and *love* him as God has instructed? Will you give yourself for him and to him? Will you *pray* with and for him, and will you forsake all others, being faithful to him until God shall separate you by death?

Christine: I will.

Vows

Robert, repeat after me: I, Robert, take you, Christine, to be my wife, to have and to hold from this day forward, for better, for worse, for richer, for poorer, in sickness and in health, to love and to cherish, until we are parted by death.

Christine, repeat after me: I, Christine, take you, Robert, to be my husband, to have and to hold from this day forward, for better, for worse, for richer, for poorer, in sickness and in health, to love and to cherish, until we are parted by death.

Presentation of Rings

May I have the rings please?

Every covenant has a sign or a symbol to remind each party of the responsibilities he or she brings to the covenant relationship. These rings are symbols of your love. These rings are visible reminders to you and all others that what you have promised, you will do. Wear them as a constant reminder that you are pledged together and committed to one another for life.

Robert, place the ring on the wedding finger of your bride and repeat after me:

> This ring I give to you as a reminder of my love.
> And I pledge to you my loyalty and devotion,
> Until we are separated by death.
> In the name of the Father, and of the Son, and of
> the Holy Spirit.

Christine, place the ring on the wedding finger of your groom and repeat after me:

> This ring I give to you as a reminder of my love.
> And I pledge to you my loyalty and devotion,
> Until we are separated by death.
> In the name of the Father, and of the Son, and of
> the Holy Spirit.

The kind of love and commitment that God desires you to model to the world is described in 1 Corinthians 13.

> Love is patient, love is kind and is not jealous; love does not brag and is not arrogant, does not act unbecomingly; it does not seek its own, is not provoked, does not take into account a wrong suffered, does not rejoice in unrighteousness, but rejoices with the truth; bears all things, believes all things, hopes all things, endures all things. Love never fails. (vv. 4–8 NASB)

PRAYER

Let's join in prayer.

Father, thank You that the love You demonstrated on the Cross never fails! May that same sacrificial love be demonstrated daily between Rob and Christy. It's in Christ's name that we pray. Amen!

[Solo: "I Take Thee"]

EVANGELISTIC APPEAL

It is Rob and Christy's great desire that each of you come to know the God whom they worship, if you haven't already done so. The Savior who has led them together also wants very much for you to become a part of His Father's family.

You probably know that Christ died on a cross. You might even know that He also rose from the dead. But it is more than head knowledge that allows us to establish a personal relationship with God.

Just as Rob and Christy have received one another and become a member of each other's family, so we must *receive* Jesus Christ as our personal Savior to become a part of God's family.

It's as if Jesus is the bridegroom and all who hear and believe are the prospective brides. God is saying to each of us, "What will you do with My Son, Jesus?" Will you receive Him and Him alone to be your personal Savior? Will you love Him and honor Him? Will you trust Him to forgive your sin and to give you the eternal life that He promised?

And everyone who answers "I will" receives the gift of forgiveness and everlasting life. Everyone who says "I will" becomes a member in God's forever family.

If you've not made that decision, Rob and Christy want to encourage you to receive Him now. It's like a marriage. You simply say, "I will," as your personal vow of commitment.

PRONOUNCEMENT

Forasmuch as you, Robert, and you, Christine, have openly pledged yourselves to one another in love and faithfulness in the presence of God, and before these witnesses, and having confirmed the same by each giving and receiving a ring, and by joining hands, I, as a minister of the gospel of Christ, pronounce you husband and wife.

· ·

What, therefore, God hath joined together,
let not man put asunder.

You may kiss the bride.

[Couple to turn and face the congregation.]

INTRODUCTION OF THE COUPLE

It is my privilege to be the first to present to you . . .

Mr. and Mrs. Robert Johnson

[Recessional]

[Escort out the mothers and grandmother.]

The family invites you to a reception downstairs in the fellowship hall.

Living Life the Way Jesus Intended

A Service Shared by Two Officiates

Brent Strawsburg

EDITORS' NOTE: Humor was added to the ceremony through references to the groom's employment.

WELCOME TO GUESTS

Welcome to this great occasion. On behalf of Tom and Kathleen, allow me to express my thanks for your being here this afternoon. Let me also welcome you to our first annual Ford Convention. Lease agreements and special offers will be available in the lobby following the ceremony. All kidding aside, I hope you sense the excitement as these two come together. It's been my pleasure to spend time with them and be enriched by what God has done in their lives. And as if that's not enough, it's a tremendous honor for me, as Kathleen's cousin, to perform this ceremony.

Today will be a day of tremendous excitement. It will be full of all of the great feelings that you've come to expect at a wedding. Yet, something else will happen today that I hope you'll experience. C. S. Lewis, great Christian author and thinker, captured the point when he said,

> God speaks in our conscience, shouts in our pains but whispers to us in our pleasures.

More than anything else, God wants to speak to each person here today. In the excitement of this moment, I would hope that we might still hear God as He whispers. This afternoon we are going to hear what God says about the essence of marriage. This is a special moment. Don't let it slip by!

PRAYER

You may be seated.

It's a real privilege to have people who've influenced your life to take part in your wedding. Kathleen has asked a very close pastor-friend, Jim Hively, to express some personal thoughts and perspective on their union together.

GIVING OF THE BRIDE

[Song]

MESSAGE

Everything that Jesus Christ did was founded on a very simple fact. He wanted to return to people the capacity to live life as He intended. Listen to this statement from Jesus: "I came that [you] might have life, and might have it abundantly" (John 10:10 NASB). Everything He touches, He desires to elevate to a whole different level. Let me show you what I mean.

God has always desired that a man and a woman experience the ultimate in relationships. From the very beginning of humanity, God recognized the need for man to experience a fulfilling relationship. Listen to Adam's response after God made Eve. Adam saw Eve for the very first time. He'd never even seen a woman before.

"[She] is now bone of my bones and flesh of my flesh" (Gen. 2:23). Translated from the Hebrew, it means, "Wow, that's a woman!" From the very beginning, God wanted Adam to recognize how significant this relationship was going to be.

In addition to this, God makes this statement, "I will make a helper suitable for him" (2:18). Here's what He means. "I'm going to bring someone who ideally corresponds to you, that is, when you see that person, she will tell you more about who you really are. She'll bring out your ultimate potential."

Adam marveled at not only how much Eve was like him (they had some of the same goals, priorities, and aspirations) but also how beautifully different she was (they did things differently and they complemented each other's weaknesses with their strengths). What Adam recognized right away, God wants for the two of you on this day. He uses two words to describe this relationship.

Cleave

Cleave—This word describes the unique kind of bonding that must take place between husband and wife. The Hebrew word for "cleave" has the notion of sticking together. It's kind of a marital version of Super Glue. It tells you that your marriage should be one of the highest forms of closeness and intimacy. It's also a warning that you must avoid situations and people who would draw you away from each other:

- someone who cares more than your spouse,
- someone who listens more than your spouse, and
- someone who seems to understand you better than your spouse.

In a Christian marriage, God intends that you stay attached to each other. You must not allow yourself to become physically or emotionally attached to anyone other than your mate. Don't let that happen to the two of you. God also uses a second term to describe the essence of this marriage.

Become One Flesh

Become one flesh—This describes God's plan for intimacy within marriage. It includes not only meaningful physical intimacy but also the entire realm of emotional and spiritual intimacy. God wants commitment and intimacy to travel together in your life. He doesn't want your intimacy to be shared with another; neither does He want you to be satisfied with a committed relationship that has little or no true intimacy.

Here's the beauty of a marriage as seen from God's perspective. Marriage allows you to reveal the real you within the safety and protection of unconditional commitment. What makes a Christian marriage is not whether a pastor does the ceremony or whether you attend a solid church. What makes a Christian marriage is whether both people have entered a genuine relationship with God and continue to help each other grow in that relationship.

It stands to reason that God should be able to dictate how such a relationship should be formed. That's why He sent Jesus Christ to pay the penalty for our sins. Our response is not to try to be good enough to merit God's approval. Think about it. Can any one of us be good enough to gain a right standing before an utterly perfect God? Our response is to accept the gift that Christ gave to us by dying on the Cross.

What's great about this free gift is that it allows any person, regardless of what they've done in the past, to know that they stand blameless before a perfect God. That's the way God designed it. We no longer have to wonder where we stand with God or wonder if we've done enough of the right things to get to heaven. We accept by faith and faith alone what Christ did for us, and at that moment our relationship to God is changed. In fact, our lives are changed. When two people have done this, they begin to look at each other, their lives, and at God in a totally different way.

Tom, you made this decision about a year and a half ago. Kathleen, you made this decision earlier in life. That decision allows you to see your lives—in fact, this marriage—in a totally different light. You recognize that the vows you take and the promises you make are important because you make them before a God who loves you.

Declaration of Intent

Tom, believing this to be the will of God for your life, and believing that you should live with Kathleen the rest of your days, do you this day take Kathleen to be your lawfully wedded wife? Will you love her, will you lead her, and will you keep her in sickness or in health, in plenty or in want? And, forsaking all other women for the rest of your days on earth, will you keep yourself faithfully only unto Kathleen so long as both of you shall live?

Tom: I will.

And, Kathleen, will you take Tom to be your lawfully wedded husband? Will you, in response to his love and leadership, love him and keep him and submit to him in sickness or in health, in plenty or in want? And, forsaking all other men for the rest of your days on earth, will you keep yourself faithfully only unto Tom so long as both of you shall live?

Kathleen: I will.

Would you ascend the stairs, please?

SCRIPTURE READING

Song of Songs 1:1–17

CHALLENGE TO THE COUPLE

Tom and Kathleen, let me give you some very tangible examples of what your marriage relationship should look like. Today, you are making a commitment not only to the institution of marriage but also to each other. Tom, you're specifically committing to love Kathleen. Kathleen, you're committing to choose Tom over and over again.

The question is how do you do this? Let me illustrate from the marriage of King Solomon and his young bride.

Song of Solomon gives an interesting portrait of Solomon's bride. We see a picture of a woman who has struggled with her own self-concept throughout her life. Listen to her self-appraisal. Do you hear the lament of a woman who doesn't feel lovely and who has for too long underappreciated how God made her? It could very easily describe a man who struggles with his own self-concept. However, for the first time, she has met someone who time and time again takes the initiative to build up her self-concept. Listen to how Solomon describes his bride in 1:8–9 and 15.

[The passage is read.]

Affirm Each Other's Uniqueness

Tom, Kathleen must know that there is uniqueness about her. God has reserved her especially for you. God was kind enough to you to allow her to be here when you came to Bethany. You must never forget those things that attracted you to her. Her infectious personality, her willingness to share her life, her beauty, and her desire to let God do whatever He wants—all of those things must be reminders that she's not merely at the top of the list but that she *is* the list and that she's the only woman. She's the woman that God ideally suited for you.

Kathleen, Tom must sense that you are willing to enter into his world, share his emotions, carry his dreams, buy only Fords, feel his disappointments, and follow his lead in spiritual and emotional health. When a guy feels this kind of affirmation, he can be the man that God intended him to be.

Allow me to give another example of how your marriage should look. In a culture that talks an awful lot about love, I'm amazed at how little we really know about it. We banter the term around. We make it synonymous with a feeling or sexual expression or some romantic moment when the very foundation for the term *love* is action.

Love is a selfless action done for the benefit of another. We find this throughout the pages of the Bible. We find it in God's relationship to humanity. What does the most famous verse in the Bible say? "For [in this way] God so loved the world that he gave his one and only Son" (John 3:16). How did God demonstrate His love for people? Was it by simply feeling something for them? No, He acted. He sent His Son to provide the one and only way to be related to Him.

The Bible says that the same thing should occur between a husband and a wife. Listen to Ephesians 5:28–29.

Public Renewal of Wedding Vows

Keith Willhite

INTRODUCTION

It's a tradition in our church that, on the first Sunday of each year, those of us who are married stand together to renew our wedding vows to our life partners.

So, those of you who are married, please stand together, join hands, and face your spouse. Then, please follow the words on the screen and repeat after me.

VOWS

[The following text should appear on the screen.]

Husbands: I love you and want to continue to enjoy life with you. You are a wonderful gift from God, and I want you to be happy and fulfilled in our relationship. I renew my promise today to be faithful to you and to love you as long as we both shall live.

Wives: I love you and praise God for your leadership in our home. I know that neither of us is perfect, but I want to continue to grow together, to communicate better, to love you more, and to enjoy life together. Today, I renew my promise to love you as long as we both shall live.

Private Renewal of Wedding Vows

Keith Willhite

EDITORS' NOTE: This couple brought their two daughters to witness this renewal.

INTRODUCTION

Greg and Sharon, you come today for a very important and loving renewal of your wedding vows. What a wonderful testimony of your love for one another and your commitment to God and to one another!

VOWS

Please recite your vows as you have written them.

Greg: Sharon, I love you and would never want anyone else as my wife. I love you even more today than fifteen years ago when we married. As God has given to me the wonderful gift of your love and going through life with you, I renew my promise to be faithful to you and to love you as long as we both shall live.

Sharon: Greg, I love you and renew my vows today to be a faithful and loving wife. I want you to be happy and to enjoy life together.

Twenty-Fifth Anniversary Renewal of Vows

Dr. Phil Hook

EDITORS' NOTE: For this very special renewal of vows on their twenty-fifth anniversary, Dr. Phil Hook, who married the Whites, returned to conduct their renewal of vows. Dr. Hook began with a description of his history with the couple.

... When I do a wedding, I require six hours of counseling ahead of time. There is some preparation for the wedding but mostly for the marriage. We who come from the world of tradition often see weddings the way we see salvation. One day you are not a Christian, a decision is made, and you now are a Christian. One day you are single, a wedding occurs, and now you are married. Often, it takes time to become a Christian. For the disciples, it took more than three years. It always takes time to get married; the wedding ceremony is only one of the steps.

When I first began counseling Art and Lillian, as usual, I asked, "What are your goals in life?" If the couple isn't heading in the same direction, the marriage won't last long or it will be a painful journey. Then I ask, "What do you want the audience to hear about your relationship, and what do you want them to take with them when they leave?" Lillian gave me an answer that no one else had ever said: "I want everyone to cry." Because I am not very good at making an audience cry, we put five songs into the ceremony. There are few rules about what needs to be there, so it was easy to fashion a ceremony that fit that purpose.

Then I usually ask, "What drew you to each other?" With Art and Lillian, that question seemed easy to answer. It was like the star quarterback marrying the head cheerleader. That's an easy attraction but a hard relationship to maintain. The wedding was in a beautiful church in Alabama. It was full of beautiful Southern women and handsome Southern gentlemen. The ceremony was a privilege to do, lasting some forty-five minutes, and just about everyone cried.

For me, the process of marriage is traditional and begins when the man and woman leave their fathers and mothers. They shall commit themselves to each other, and "they will become one flesh" (Gen. 2:24) and they were naked and unashamed (v. 25). Jesus adds, "What God has joined together, let man not separate" (Matt. 19:6). A marriage goes together in that order, and if it doesn't work, it comes apart in reverse order. If you skip a step, it makes it harder to go back—and harder to finish.

Because Art and Lillian had lived away from home and were already involved in their work for Christ, the first step was easy. The second step seemed easy—commitment. Statements like this are for real: "She found her soul mate . . . but we are different." But the actuality is much different: I die daily.

I had a professor who taught,

> I am in danger of death daily.
> For poorer—that forces a couple to stay together.
> For better—but not too much better.
> For worse—but not too much worse.
> In sickness—but not too sick.
>
> —Robert McQuilkin

For Lillian, it was a struggle with loss of freedom and independence. For Art, it was, "Which way did she go and how fast?" But time after time they renewed their commitment at each anniversary over the years. They said the vows that they wrote for their wedding, and they kept going.

The two shall become one flesh. This step is symbolized by the loving sexual relationship, but it is far more. It is a oneness of personality.

[The minister continued with remarks about the couple's counseling time.]
The unveiling of body and soul is built upon tremendous trust, and that trust doesn't come with ease or in a few days. All of us as teenagers went on a date, poured out our soul, and heard about it from others the next day or in a few days. This step—following—was hard and painful, revealing that it is never easy. What God has joined together is the umbrella to all of the other steps. Marriage takes three. As we reminisced last night, Art and Lillian told about their Sundays. There were days of rest, spending time in the Scripture and meditation in the afternoon, and their coming together to share a meal and to encourage one another. God is continuing to join them together.

Art and Lillian, talk to each other and to us.

Wife's Vows

Lillian: Art, twenty-five years ago, we stood in a ceremony and made our covenant with one another.

In my vows, I promised "to give to you my life, my love, my all." I prayed "as our lives intertwine, melt together, and become one, that when others see you, they see me and when they see me, they see you and when they see us, they see Jesus."

It is with His grace that I look back and see two people who have examined together many things: our faith, our philosophy of life, our politics. We've struggled with things that are petty.

We've struggled with things that posed a genuine threat to our relationship. We've learned to let God's love wash over us and embrace each other in forgiveness.

And even though your snoring keeps me up at night, and I get irritated when you don't put the CDs back in the cases,

You have absolutely changed my life.
You have never left me or forsaken me in anyway.

If I searched the world over, I would never find a person who loves me as you do.

I love when you tell me I am your greatest gift.
I love for you to make me laugh when I'm down.
I love your new interest in cooking.
I love your unabashed love and devotion to me.
I love calling you my lighthouse because it is so fitting.

I think we may have seen a lighthouse on Nantucket years ago. I remember it was a tall structure firmly planted on rock topped with a powerful light used as a beacon for navigation, showing the way.

Art, you are my Lighthouse.

I read recently that a tango should be danced to the end.
I thought of us.
Like a tango, I plan to dance our marriage to the end.
Art, I love you.

Husband's Vows

Art: Lillian, twenty-five years ago, I told you how I praised God for the joy of committing my life to you in marriage, believing that it was His plan. I didn't know then what I know now, and that is that the commitment we made that day was a step of faith that God has honored in more ways than we can count.

Today, I look back and see how far we've come. We've held hands not only through many storms of life (the deaths of three of our four parents, and my mom with Alzheimer's, just to mention a few) but also through blessings beyond belief. (Probably the greatest blessing of all is being loved by so many of our friends here today!)

Our love has deepened over the years, confirming what we believed so many yeas ago that God was leading us to a life together.

It has been my joy and privilege to know you not only as wife but also as soul mate, best friend, the love of my life, companion, teammate, and the one of whom I am most proud.

Lillian, you have remained true and steadfast, demonstrating to me time and time again that you are my greatest gift from God. I look forward to growing old with you. We might not know what life will bring our way, but I have confidence that, with you by my side, we can face anything! My experience with you has proven that over and over.

One thing I do know: life is short, and we must treasure every day we have together.

Lillian, you are my treasure.

PRAYER

Thank You, Lord, for these two.

For parents who reared them.

Experiences that shaped them.

Friends who encouraged and sometimes hurt them.

And for their marriage and the process they have gone through.

Twenty-five years ago, I prayed—bless them and make their lives fruitful—thank You.

Give them a great trust in You and Your haven.

Bring into their lives struggles to keep driving them together—thank You.

Bring enough failure so that they will not expect perfection of each other but that they would know that You alone are perfect and Your forgiveness would teach them to forgive one another. You have answered.

Now, Lord, we commend them to You and Your work in them— that You will perform it until the Day of Jesus Christ, when we are with You.

In our Savior's name, who loved us and gave Himself for us. Amen.

The Prewedding Service

*For the Couple Having Ceremonies
in Two Locations*

Roland Foreman with Ditmar and Maura Pauck

EDITORS' NOTE: This couple met as students in the United States. Their actual wedding, which took place in Germany, was to follow the ceremony below. This service, for their friends and family in the United States, included their vows but no pronouncement of marriage. The service provided a beautiful ceremony with an emphasis on prayer.

INTRODUCTION

Tonight's service will emphasize prayer in the lives of Ditmar and Maura. Although they will say their vows here, I will not pronounce them husband and wife. That pronouncement will be saved for their actual wedding with Ditmar's parents, in Germany, in a few days.

With that in mind, Ditmar and Maura, I have prepared a few thoughts for you and for your friends gathered here. I hope these thoughts will lead both to your praying these things for one another and to all of us praying them for you.

MESSAGE

These prayers are based on the apostle Paul's prayer to the Ephesians. We find it in Ephesians 3:16–21. Here we find three prayers within Paul's prayer for enlightenment.

I. Pray for strength in the Lord.
   A. Pray this prayer for one another, that you will have your strength in the Lord.
   B. We, your friends, promise to pray this prayer for you.

II. Pray that you will be satisfied with the love of the Lord.
   A. Pray this prayer for one another, that you will always be satisfied with the love for the Lord.
   B. We, your friends, promise to pray this prayer for you.

III. With praise, commit yourselves to the power of God that works within you.
   A. Pray this prayer for one another, that you will keep your hearts committed to God and His power working within you.
   B. We, your friends, promise to pray this prayer for you.

CONCLUSION

[Following this message, the service included a time of worship through singing, followed by three men laying hands on and praying for the couple, and a benediction.]

The Covenant of Marriage

Jeffrey D. Arthurs

WE BEGIN WITH AN APPROPRIATE HYMN, "A Charge to Keep I Have, a God to Glorify." This hymn presents a proper view of marriage because marriage is a covenant.

For some Americans, marriage is a convenience. It is an easier way to manage finances. For others, it is an inconvenience, a worn-out institution, just something to mock.

For God, marriage is a *covenant*. A covenant is a formal agreement made in the presence of God in which both parties vow to carry out their responsibilities.

Soon, you will vow. This is serious business. Your vows will be made *to each other* in the presence of these witnesses. But all Christian vows are also made *to God*.

Marriage is a covenant. Marriage is serious business. Don't break the covenant! "A charge to keep I have! A God to glorify." How can you glorify God in marriage?

MARRIAGE IS FOR ILLUSTRATION

What does marriage illustrate? It illustrates God Himself. Consider the very early account from Genesis:

God . . . put [the *MALE (man)*] in the Garden of Eden (2:15).

It is not good for the *[MALE]* to be alone (2:18).

God caused the *[MALE]* to fall into a deep sleep (2:21).

Man (in the gendered sense) can't illustrate God completely, but "man" in the generic sense can.

Let us make *[HUMANS (man)]* in our image (1:26).

God created *[HUMANS]* in His own image, . . . male and female He created them (1:27).

Marriage is to represent God, reveal Him, and glorify Him. How do a man and a woman united in marriage illustrate God? It's through *love and unity.* Two separate persons who are equal have different functions as they pursue the same goal.

Father, Son, and Holy Spirit are separate persons, yet one and equal. The persons of the Trinity function in perfect harmony seeking the same goals. They are *one in essence, three in function.* They are distinct personalities who form one unit and achieve one goal.

Let your marriage illustrate God. This is part of the reason He wants you to form this covenant: to brag about Him.

But marriage is not only for illustration. There is more.

Marriage Is for Completion

"It is not good for the man to be alone. I will make a helper suitable for him" (Gen. 2:18). This "helper" is someone who matches him, corresponds to him, and completes him.

This term is never used in the Bible to describe an inferior person. It means a person who supplies what you can't. "God is our refuge and strength, an ever-present *help*" (Ps. 46:1, italics added).

What is the husband to do? He is to serve as God's representative, to do His will on earth. To do that, Adam needed help. Most men do. Karen, Curt needs help. Keep hold of him, or he will schedule the Holy Spirit's day for him. Put God's hourly schedule in the computer with little chimes ("you've missed your appointment"). Curt needs your help. Complete each other. Help each other grow in the grace and knowledge of our Lord Jesus Christ.

These lofty goals—illustration and completion—are possible because God has formed a covenant with you. You don't enter marriage equipped with only the latest self-help books, high hopes, and an iron will. You also have the life of God helping you. He has made a covenant with you by the blood of His Son Jesus Christ.

[To audience:]

Curt and Karen are a part of a covenant that Jesus started the night of the Last Supper. Remember? Jesus took the cup and the bread and instituted a new covenant. It was no longer based on law (keeping rules) but on grace. We never could keep the old covenant, so Jesus made a new one. He made it by pouring out life for us to take away our sins and to give us His eternal life. Curt and Karen have entered that new agreement, that new way of connecting with God, that covenant, by trusting in Christ alone for salvation. They have repented and believed in Him.

[To couple:]

So, this is *your covenant:* illustrate God, complete one another. This is your mission, your privilege. I know that you will take the attitude of "A charge to keep I have! A God to glorify." And because you are covenant keepers, I expect the blessings of the covenant of marriage to be yours.

Proverbs
Wedding Message

A Humorous and Realistic Look at Marriage

Larry Renoe

IN THE OLD TESTAMENT BOOK OF Proverbs, Solomon says, "A nagging wife is as annoying as the constant dripping on a rainy day. Trying to stop her complaints is like trying to stop the wind or hold something with greased hands" (27:15–16 NLT).

The Bible is such a tactless book, isn't it? It seems so coarse in places, so unkind and indelicate, and so deeply unromantic. But God calls a spade a spade. He is right to assert that marriage is a tactless affair, full of awkwardness and indelicacy. It is, at least once a day, as unromantic as a sink full of dirty dishes.

It doesn't really matter whether one's spouse is quarrelsome. And I know you're not, Sue, and I know that dripping goes both ways! Marriage creates more or less a "constant dripping" in one's life. I don't know of any marriage that is always smooth sailing on a waveless sea.

Nothing communicates this truth better in our culture than country music. I recently came across some of the more interesting titles of country songs:

Did I Shave My Legs for This? by Deana Carter; *She's Actin' Single (I'm Drinkin' Doubles)* by Gary Stewart; and *You're the Reason Our Kids Are Ugly* by Conway Twitty and Loretta Lynn.

You see, marriage is a crisis, a major crisis, because the concept of two people living together requires constant adjustment. Marriage changes you, and change comes with a cost. That's why the next verse in Proverbs reads, "As iron sharpens iron, a friend sharpens a friend" (v. 17 NLT).

Steve and Sue stand before us today on the threshold of a major crisis we call marriage. And for that we honor them and give thanks to the Lord. But if this is all marriage is—sharpening—it would not be nearly so popular or desirable.

Although marriage takes its hits in our culture these days, with many people thinking that it is an ancient institution whose relevance has succumbed, the fact is that marriage has been around a long time, and I suspect it will continue to be. It will go away only if God goes away. You see, marriage comes from God. He has ordained it. Marriage is the fabric of human existence. When God first spoke in Genesis, He said that it is not good for a man to be alone. Then He took a rib from Adam and fashioned a woman—Eve. And then the Bible says, "This explains why a man leaves his father and mother and is joined to his wife, and the two are united into one" (Gen. 2:24 NLT).

And this is the bottom line for keeping the two of you together in a crisis, in marriage. God has a vested interest in your marriage. He cares about your marriage. He wants you to work to make it good. His honor is at risk in how you persevere in your commitment to each other. This is why it's important to remind you, and us, what you're doing just now. You are making a *covenant* in two ways today, between both of you and between each of you and the Lord.

Covenant is the word. In fact, covenant is the whole message of the Bible. I find it interesting that throughout the Bible, covenant or marriage is employed as the most sublime metaphor for the relationship between God and humans. The great apostle Paul resorted to this picture to describe the loving union between Christ and His church. The Old Testament prophets used marriage as the most transparent example of the type of covenant love the Lord has for His people. Jesus told parables in which a wedding feast became the symbolic setting for the coming of the kingdom. A good Christian marriage, indeed, is more than a religious metaphor. It is a tangible, visible, and most glorious fruit of the kingdom of God.

And so, Steve and Sue, your marriage is much more than an impending crisis. It is a visible sign of the presence of God on this earth. Your enduring relationship will reflect the type of love the Lord has

· ·

for us all. This is why you have every reason to do what it takes to love each other for the rest of your lives.

Despite the caustic marital comments sprinkled throughout Proverbs, notice how the book ends: "Who can find a virtuous and capable wife? She is worth more than precious rubies. Her husband can trust her, and she will greatly enrich his life" (31:10–11 NLT). In other words, Proverbs, as a whole, takes a view of marriage that remains proverbial to this day; namely, that nothing in the world is worse than a bad marriage, and at the same time nothing is better than a good one.

Our prayer is that, over the coming decades, you will collect shared moments of great joy to share with us. Our hope is that you will become witnesses to the unique and priceless satisfaction of two people being totally committed to each other. May you have a good, enduring marriage for God's sake and for your pleasure.

On the basis of Christ's death for our sins and His glorious resurrection, I share these words with you so that you will fulfill these holy vows of marriage. Amen.

How to Keep the Music in Your Marriage

Andy McQuitty

HOW CAN YOU KEEP THE MUSIC in your marriage? In his comic strip, "B.C.," Johnny Hart shows two cavemen chatting about love as they lean on a rock. "What's the difference between a good kiss and a great kiss?" asks the first guy. "It's a good kiss when it makes your toes tingle," answers his friend, "and a great kiss when your shoelaces catch fire."

For all of its "catch fire" idealism, marriage can deteriorate to disappointment over time if a mature love is not nurtured. First Corinthians 13:7 (NASB) tells us how to do that.

> [Love] bears all things, believes all things, hopes all things, endures all things.

Paul here gives us four keys to building a mature love, or to say it another way, to keeping the music in your marriage.

FIGHT THE URGE TO NITPICK

Some married couples invest a great deal of research into the fine art of nitpicking, or paying too much attention to petty details. God describes what nitpicking is like for its target: "A constant dripping on a day of steady rain and a contentious woman are alike" (Prov. 27:15 NASB). As all ladies present would agree, I'm sure, a contentious man is no better! God has a better way for marriage partners than nitpicking. The first phrase in 1 Corinthians 13:7 says that love "bears all things." This is from a Greek word meaning "to cover something." First Peter 4:8 (NASB) says that "love covers a multitude of sins."

Love doesn't nitpick, pointing out every flaw and failing of your

· ·

mate. Rather, love chooses to cut some slack; it doesn't sweat the details. Love knows that nobody's perfect, that not everything can change at once, and that maybe some things never will change. But that's OK, because love never lets the little wrongs tear apart a marriage in which there are big rights. In other words, "if you love someone you will be loyal to him no matter what the cost" (1 Cor. 13:7 TLB).

GIVE YOUR MATE THE BENEFIT OF THE DOUBT

We're sometimes tempted to read the worst into our spouse's motives and interpret the worst in their words. Even our legal system includes the presumption of innocence. Yet, with many of us, our spouses would get a better deal in the courtroom than they get at home.

The second phrase tells us that love "believes all things." That simply means that love believes the best that is possible as long as that can be done. Love, in other words, gives the benefit of the doubt. It takes people at their highest and best, not at their lowest and worst. Paul is not calling for naïve gullibility. Wisdom and love go together. But love does not doubt when there is no reason to doubt and seeks always to encourage, to affirm, and to believe the best.

FOCUS ON THE FUTURE, NOT THE PAST

One of the quickest ways to destroy a marriage is never to let your spouse forget about mistakes he or she has made in the past. But if you carry around a conscious record of your mate's past failures, you're focusing on the past and thereby threatening your future.

The third phrase in verse 7 is "love hopes all things." The *Living Bible* phrases it "always expects the best." Although we don't want to place false expectations on people, people often tend to become what you believe them to be, living up or down to your expectations. Jesus understood that principle perfectly. He said to vacillating Simon, "You are a rock." Jesus said to a prostitute, "Your sins be forgiven." He said to uneducated day laborers, "You shall become fishers of men." Jesus said to a woman caught in adultery, "Go and sin no more."

What a difference it makes when a husband truly believes in his wife, seeing her not only for what she is but also for what she can become. What a difference it makes when a wife says to her husband when his dream is teetering on the brink of destruction, "I believe in you, and no matter what happens, we'll make it through this together."

HANG IN WHEN ALL YOU CAN DO IS HANG ON

For many people, marriage is like boarding a plane for a sunny Florida vacation only to land and find themselves in the Swiss Alps. Instead of beach, sun, and surf, they've got snow, skis, and mountains. They're not prepared for that. They have to learn a new language. It's tough. It takes time. And building a great marriage is just like that.

Paul's final phrase in verse 7 is "love endures all things." This is a military term for standing your ground in the heat of a fierce battle. Love endures while hope is becoming reality. Love hangs on even though the Florida beach turns out to be the Swiss Alps!

But if you hang on, eventually you get prepared. You've got your down coat and your goggles. You've got your mittens and your battery-heated socks. You've even taken ski lessons. One day as you're taking an exhilarating run down the mountain, you realize that the Swiss Alps are every bit as wonderful as you had expected Florida to be, but just in a different way. And the only reason you made it there is because you hung on during the tough time of adjustment.

Fight the urge to nitpick. Give your mate the benefit of the doubt. Focus on the future, not the past. And hang in there when it seems that all you can do is hang on. As you do these four things in a spirit of prayer and obedience to God, I believe that He will pour out His love in your heart and in your spouse's heart, as well. That's how you keep the music in your marriage. That's how to nurture a mature love.

Three Gifts for the Bride and Groom

Tony Beckett

EDITORS' NOTE: The following edited transcript from the *Back to the Bible* radio broadcast, July 6, 2001, shares Associate Bible Teacher Dr. Tony Beckett's thoughts on the day before his daughter's wedding. It gives forthright biblical advice for her marriage and any marriage.

Tony Beckett: I want to share something with you today that is very personal for me and my family. You see, today is the day before my daughter's wedding. Now, I have three girls. God has given my wife, Joan, and me these three ladies to raise; and, well, this is the first wedding in our family.

For a number of years (more than twenty years), I was a pastor. And many times as I stood at the front of the church, I watched that bride come down the aisle. And many times I spent hours with this young couple talking about biblical principles for establishing their marriage. The reason is that one of the principles by which I operated as the pastor is that I would not perform a wedding ceremony without premarital counseling.

There were many opportunities to be the clergyman of record and, as such, to have the couple say their vows and to sign a wedding certificate. But I was not interested in doing weddings. I was interested in helping establish Christian homes.

But you know, this wedding tomorrow is going to be different than all of those others I've done. At this wedding tomorrow, I will not be at the front waiting for the bride to come down the aisle. I will be at the back of the auditorium, some place I've never been at a wedding. And I will be the father of the bride, bringing my daughter down the aisle.

And the current pastor of the church will meet us there at the front. But once we get to that point where we say those words, "Who gives this woman to be married to this man?" I will try to remember what I've always told all of those other fathers of the bride to say, "Her mother and I do."

After I hand her off there at the front to her fiancé, I will then replace the pastor at the front. He'll step aside and probably do what I always did when I would step aside for the father of the bride or the father of the groom. He will probably have the wedding ceremony in his Bible, just in case I can't make it through. But I really am determined to make it through, determined to stand there and to have that opportunity, in a very special way, to share. I think it's going to be the most special wedding sermon that I have ever preached.

Now, let me explain one other thing about wedding sermons. I never thought people came to hear the pastor at a wedding. So my wedding sermons typically were rather brief. And this one will be along that line. I wanted to share it with you today, not in all the details, because there are a few things I want to save for the bride and groom tomorrow.

But would you join me here, in the front of the church, and let me tell you what a father of the bride wants to say to his daughter on her wedding day? The timing is good because this week Dr. Kroll has been talking about the importance of marriage and talking about some very important biblical principles.

And when we deal with the subject of marriage, we do need to start out in Genesis 2:24–25, where we read how a man will leave his father and mother and be united to his wife, and they will become one flesh. The man and his wife were both naked, the Word of God says, and they felt no shame.

Right from the beginning, we keep in mind that when we deal with the subject of marriage—this goes back to a foundational principle, a creation principle from the beginning of the book of Genesis—God is laying out very basic principles, and one of them is marriage. And I always like to remind people that God instituted marriage. Man has instituted the problems; but God instituted marriage itself.

And in those two verses in Genesis 2, which contain very basic principles, there is a principle of *severance*. A man will leave his father and mother. And there is to be a change in the relationship. It's not a breaking of the relationship. But I think about what somebody pointed out (in the days that those words were written), that leaving father and mother meant moving to the other side of the campfire. It's not a geographic thing. But there is a change that takes place when a man and a woman become a husband and wife, a change in relationship with Mom and Dad.

Another principle brought out in those verses is the principle of *permanence*. The two will be united. The man leaves his father and mother and becomes united to his wife. It's not a Post-it Note relationship, you know. That glue on the Post-it Notes is something that is intended to be temporarily permanent. It sounds like an oxymoron. Sometimes people approach marriage that way; you can stick it on and peel it off, and there's no damage left.

Maybe they think it's like a Velcro relationship that is a little bit harder to pull apart. It makes more noise when it pulls apart. But, no, that's not what God intended. God intended permanence. When we bring a young man and a young woman together as husband and wife, it is to be a permanent relationship.

Another principle, after severance and permanence, is *unity*.

The two will become one flesh. And often that's not just in a physical sense. But it's really talking about the two becoming one. And also with that relationship there is to be intimacy. Marriage is where God intended sexual intimacy to take place, not in the other places where the world is saying it can take place. But as God describes it for us, it says that the man and his wife were both naked and they felt no shame. In the marriage relationship, there is to be intimacy.

Now, those are basic principles. But remember this is a different wedding sermon. This is one where Dad is talking to his daughter and future son-in-law, a young man with whom we are thrilled, whom God brought into our family's life. Now, he's going to be a permanent part of our family's life. And I want to give them three reminders. They're like three gifts that I'm bringing for the bride and the groom, gifts that are embodied as reminders of some very important things. The first reminder has to do with *finances*. You start out married life together, and there are some shocking aspects to it; for example, to realize how many things you need to have in the kitchen to cook a meal and how many of them aren't already there because Mom and Dad's house came supplied with salt and pepper and baking soda and all of those other things.

But all that's a shock the first time they go into a grocery store and try to outfit the kitchen. And then there are cleaning supplies and other things. Just the basic outfitting of a first apartment is rather intimidating.

And then everything else starts to add up. The car payments are there, the insurance issues are there, and the leftover college bills might be there. And you keep working on down the line and realize that a major part of what we might encounter in the first days of marriage keep drawing our attention to finances.

That's why it's important for all of us, not just the young bride and young groom, to remember that when it comes to money, we are what the Bible calls stewards. A more contemporary word is *managers*. We are not owners. We go into a store and maybe we will do business with the storeowner, but, more likely, we will intersect with the store manager. And that manager knows that it doesn't belong to him. It belongs to the owner. He only manages it.

And that's how we need to think about our finances; everything we have belongs to God, and He has asked us to return to Him a portion of it. When we build a biblical understanding of how to handle our finances, it will include taking a portion of what God has given to us and returning it to Him.

Now, suppose that I were to meet you on the street one day and hand you ten one-dollar bills and say, "This is my money and I want to give you these ten one-dollar bills. And I want to give you some basic guidelines on what to do with them."

You probably would look at this and think, *This is a little bit odd.* But hang with me here for a moment. Then I would say to you, "Now I want you to give one of them back to me." After I gave you the ten one-dollar bills to hold, it probably wouldn't be very difficult at all to hand one dollar back because you knew that they were my ten one-dollar bills. And I'm giving you directions on how to handle them.

If we just thought that way about everything we have, we would have a biblical understanding, and it would be much easier to be obedient because we understand that it's not ours. It is God's, and He says, "I've given you ten; give Me one back." That would be the beginning point of obedience, I believe—the tithe.

But we give as God prospers us; we build that in right from the beginning of how we handle our finances. Now we keep in mind that one day we will give God an account; a far more significant account than an IRS audit.

And as we read His Word, He instructs us on how to manage His money. I'd encourage you to read Matthew 25:14–30 (the parable of the talents) and see what God is teaching us in story form: we're the managers, and everything we have belongs to Him. We are to handle things as He wants them to be handled. And one day we will give an account to Him.

Do you see the bottom line? That's a good phrase because it's often used in financial discussions, isn't it? The bottom line is that there is a need for money. The bottom line also includes that we will experience pressure to make money. That's when the mailman comes, drops off the bills, and we feel the pressure. And add to it the allure of money. Sadly, some of God's people have gotten sidetracked because of the allure of money.

I appreciated visiting with a friend the other day who was describing some of the things going on in his life, and the selling of their home to build another home, and how they had an acreage set aside, and they thought, *You know, this is going to be great. We're going to move to this acreage.*

But then they realized, *If we go there and build that kind of house, it could really affect how we're able to contribute to the Lord's work.* And they, in a real sense, downsized their plans and expectations because it was more important for them to continue supporting faithfully the work of God than to build an even bigger house.

When we talk to the bride and groom that day, I want to say, "You need to remember that finances are God's, not yours." And then the second reminder I want to give them has to do with *time*. We must also be good managers of time. A lot of times, we don't think about time. That sounds kind of redundant, but isn't that the case?

Yet, when you look at it with a biblical mind-set, you realize that God created time—right from the beginning with sunrise and sunset, kind of a sequencing there—so that you can measure time. And God starts on about the days there and you find that time was created by God.

And with that biblical understanding of time you realize that God creates our timetables. In Ecclesiastes 3, if you read verses 2–8, you will find fourteen pairs of opposites, each referred to as a time. And in verse 1 of Ecclesiastes 3 (NASB) it says, "There is an appointed time for everything. And there is a time for every event under heaven."

When we go to the New Testament Paul says in Ephesians 5, "Therefore be careful how you walk, not as unwise men but as wise, making the most of your time" (vv. 15–16 NASB). The King James Version says, "Redeeming the time, because the days are evil. Wherefore be ye not unwise, but understanding what the will of the Lord is."

The Greek word used here, *kairos,* is not *time* in the sense of measured segments. But *kairos* is "opportunity." So, what God is saying is this: "Be careful how you walk, not as unwise men, but as wise, making the most of your opportunity." Colossians 4:5 says the same thing. I know that we're used to the translation "redeeming the time." But here's what it says, "Conduct yourselves with wisdom toward outsiders, making the most of the opportunity" (NASB).

We just look at time, and we don't worry about or think about it. Well, I think about one friend who, with an excitement in his voice and in his passion for serving Jesus, will say, "We will never live this moment again." He has that consciousness of time. And I want to say to my daughter and future son-in-law, "Redeem the time. Make the most of the opportunity."

But then all of these other things start to crowd in. And I think about a very simple statement that I heard Warren Wiersbe say one day, just one of those simple statements. I wrote it down right after he said it. I don't know that it's in anything that he wrote, but he said this: "There is always time to do the will of God." That's rather simple but very profound. I wrote it down. I'm carrying it in my Bible. There is always time to do the will of God.

Patrick Morley writes, "No test of a man's character is more conclusive than how he spends his time and money." That kind of puts these first two topics—time and money—together, doesn't it? So, as I stand there with this couple, as the father of the bride, I want to remind them about finances; you're the managers, not the owners. I want to remind them about time. They need to be good managers of time as well.

But the third thing of which I want to remind them has to do with *remembering*. I want to borrow a phrase and then I'll explain it. The phrase I want to borrow is this. You need to "mezuzah your universe." Now perhaps you have studied Judaism, or maybe you've traveled to Israel, and you've seen mezuzahs. Or perhaps you have a friend who's Jewish, and you've been to his or her home and have seen the mezuzah. Well the origins of the Christian church lie in Jewish discipleship. Jewish life is just rich and full of home rituals. And on the right side of every Jewish doorpost is nailed a small piece of parchment that's rolled and inserted into a wood, metal, stone, or ceramic case that's called a mezuzah.

And on the front of that little piece of parchment are lettered the twenty-two lines of the Shimal from Deuteronomy 6 and Deuteronomy 11. And the Hebrew word *Shaddai*, which speaks of God, is inscribed on the back of that piece of parchment such that it can be seen from the outside. And typically, on the outside of the mezuzah, you will see the Hebrew letter *shin*. The first letter of *Shaddai* and the mezuzah are visible reminders when a Jewish person puts that mezuzah on the doorpost of their house. It is a visible reminder of who they are and what they are to be.

Now, it's rather interesting for us to go back to Deuteronomy 6 and to read again what Moses said, how these words are to be bound on the doorpost of your house and how Jewish people have literally done that. And that way, as they walk in, sometimes they will touch the mezuzah with their hands and kiss their fingers to show their reverence of and love for the Torah and for the Shimal that is in there.

When we take that practice of mezuzah and then take this phrase that I'm borrowing from another writer, "mezuzah your universe," it's as if we need to tack a mezuzah on everything in life, so that, as we look at our place of work, as we look at the way we drive our cars, as we look at the way we interact with our neighbor, and as we look at the way we go in and out of our home, we are reminded that we are the people of God and reminded of what it is that God wants us to be. And when we "mezuzah our universe," then worship will be a way of life, not just a wayside on Sunday.

It's a challenge sometimes just to trace through the Bible with a group of people about the history of the dwelling place of God; to talk about the tabernacle in the Old Testament and how God's presence was in the tabernacle; then to talk about the temple and the bringing in of the Ark of the Covenant and the representation there, and Solomon praying that God would visibly demonstrate His presence there in the temple; and then to read on as the prophets describe the departure of the presence of God from the temple.

And if you've got some people who are thinking well, and they say, "Where is the temple? Where is the dwelling place of God today?" Then they remember that Paul said our bodies are the temple of God.

And so it's not a matter of the temple being a place that we can go to, but it is a matter of this for the Christ follower: the temple goes with you wherever you go. And it is for us "temple-ing" time. It is living a life of temple "daily-ness." It is building a life infrastructure that's made of biblical material because we are the temple.

G. K. Chesterton writes, "You say grace before meals. All right. But I say grace before the concert and the opera, and grace before the play and pantomime, and grace before I open a book, and grace before sketching, painting, swimming, fencing, boxing, walking, playing, dancing, and grace before I dip the pen in the ink." In other words, he said grace before everything in his life because he understood that he had to "mezuzah his universe." It means that he then lived in a God environment.

As I stand there before that young couple tomorrow, I want to say to them, "Think about your finances. Think about your time. You need to be managers, not owners of what God entrusts to your care, and then your universe."

Don Hawkins: Well, this might not be the typical gift we think of giving to a bride and groom, but God's Word can have a greater effect on a marriage than any other gift. Thank you for sharing this special time with us, Dr. Beckett. I know this will be an important day in your life as well as for your daughter and soon-to-be son-in-law.

Genuine Marital Love

A Charge to the Couple

Keith Willhite

INTRODUCTION

1. In reality, true marital love should be "as Christ loved the church."
2. This means that the purest of marital love is not possible on this side of heaven.
3. Nevertheless, the apostle Paul reminded us of the qualities of love that can strengthen your marriage.

SCRIPTURE READING

1 Corinthians 12:30; 13:1–7

MESSAGE

As marital love is the greatest love expressed in human relationships, your marriage can grow happily by practicing the qualities of this passage.

I. Genuine love is greater than any gift (12:31).
   A. This shows us how important love is.
   B. The spiritual gifts about which Paul had written are vital to the life and function of the church, but love is greater! (OK, so if love is that important, what qualities should your love have?)

II. Love is patient and kind.
   A. Love "hangs in there," not only over the "long haul" but also over the little frustrations and challenges of everyday life.
   B. Be kind to one another.
      1. When the difficulties set in, you will need each other to be kind.
      2. You might be the only source of kindness that your partner has.
      3. More importantly, treat one another with kindness.
         a. Write notes.
         b. Speak kind words.
         c. Represent your spouse well to others.
         d. Help each other with household chores.
         e. Manage "life" together.
         f. Stay on the same team.

(Love is greater than any gift. It is patient and kind, but love sometimes gets more difficult. How can that be?)

III. Genuine love is not jealous, boastful, proud, or rude.
   A. It's not surprising that you wouldn't expect two people who love each other to be rude.
   B. But love is not jealous, boastful, or proud.
      1. Resist the temptation to compete with one another.
         a. Big deal if you know something before she does or if you score higher on the driver's test than he does.
         b. Cheer for each other. If he wins, she wins, and vice versa.
      2. Pull each other up.
         a. If he's down, pull him up.
         b. If she's low, pull her up.
      3. All of us as Christians should be encouragers, but nowhere is this more true than in the home.
         a. Encourage your wife. Learn what things encourage her most.

. . . .

      b. Encourage your husband. Learn the things that encourage him.

4. Although love is not boastful or proud, be thankful for one another.

      a. When she is recognized for an achievement, be her biggest fan!

      b. When he brings home a letter of thanks or recognition, give him a huge kiss and tell him how thankful you are for him.

(We're not finished and the truths do not get any easier.)

IV. Genuine love "gives in."

  A. Paul said that love "does not demand its own way."

    1. Remember, you're on the same team.

      If you get mad and take your ball and go home, guess who's going to be there!

    2. "Give in" to his desires or her wishes.

      a. You'll learn to like that carpet—in time.

      b. You'll learn to eat Brussels sprouts—eventually.

      c. Just decide that you don't always have to get your own way!

(But let's make this love really work. Truth number five about genuine love is that . . .)

V. Genuine love is not irritable, and it keeps no list of wrongs.

  A. We all get tired and a little irritable at times, but try your best not to bring that irritability home to your spouse. And if you do, don't take it out on him or her.

  B. We've talked a lot in our premarital counseling about "forgiveness."

    1. That's because we assume that when two sinners unite in marriage, they are going to need to seek and to grant forgiveness.

    2. Be quick to forgive.

      a. Remember, "forgiveness" does not mean "that's OK."

. . . .

  b. No, it means that something was wrong, but you're not going to hold it against the person or seek justice on your own.

CONCLUSION

1. Love is difficult.
2. The standards of genuine love are high.
3. But strong marriages really do give evidence of these qualities.
4. Be patient with one another. Be kind to each other.
5. Always play on the same team. Do not be jealous, boastful, or rude.
6. You don't always have to get your own way. Give in.
7. And do not be irritable, but do forgive one another.
8. May God bless your marriage with genuine love.

It Takes Three

Keith Willhite

Scripture Reading

Ecclesiastes 4:12

Introduction

It might seem odd in a wedding, the union of two people into one person, to read this verse about the strength of three. But when we understand the proper three, the verse serves a wedding and a marriage very well.

Message

    I.   God recognized at Creation that it was not good for a man to be alone (Gen. 2:18).

   II.   Two are stronger than one (Eccl. 4:12b).

  III.   A marriage is best with three (Eccl. 4:12c).
- A. Typically, we do not think of a marriage triangle as a good thing.
- B. But when Jesus Christ is the unifying cord in a threefold cord, the marriage gains great strength.

CONCLUSION

A wedding of three—the bride, the groom, and Jesus as Lord—is the only strong marriage.

Love Is a Verb

Pete Briscoe

SCRIPTURE READING

Colossians 3:12a: Therefore, as God's chosen people, holy and dearly loved . . .

INTRODUCTION

Not pedigree or coattails but *love*.
Then follow some very exact directions.

MESSAGE

I. Be nice. "Clothe yourselves with compassion, kindness, humility, gentleness and patience" (v. 12b).

II. Be gracious. "Bear with each other and forgive whatever grievances you may have against one another. Forgive as the Lord forgave you" (v. 13).
    A. Do and say things to offer and invite forgiveness.
    B. Cultivate the ability to forgive.

III. Be loving. "And over all these virtues put on love, which binds them all together in perfect unity" (v. 14).
    A. Love is not a feeling. Love is a verb, similar to the word *throw*. There is a "throw" that is a noun, but when we usually use the word *throw*, it is as a verb. Love is a verb.

B. Love in marriage means that you put your spouse first!

IV. Be one. "Let the peace of Christ rule in your hearts, since as members of one body you were called to peace. And be thankful" (v. 15).

Be quick to *adjust*. It's often the little adjustments in a marriage that give evidence of love. Adjust the heat, the toothpaste, the toilet paper, or your snoring.

V. Be learning. "Let the word of Christ dwell in you richly as you teach and admonish one another with all wisdom, and as you sing psalms, hymns and spiritual songs with gratitude in your hearts to God" (v. 16).

Teach each other and learn from each other. Never stop!

VI. Be focused. "And whatever you do, whether in word or deed, do it all in the name of the Lord Jesus, giving thanks to God the Father through him" (v. 17).

Grace

Pete Briscoe

INTRODUCTION

Grace is something we don't deserve, we never repay, and we always need! No place is this truer than in Christian marriages.

MESSAGE

I. God's Grace Has Saved You
   A. "In him [Jesus] we have redemption through his blood, the forgiveness of sins, in accordance with the riches of God's grace" (Eph. 1:7).
   B. "[He] made us alive with Christ even when we were dead in transgressions—it is by grace you have been saved" (Eph. 2:5).
   C. "For God so loved the world that he gave his one and only Son, that whoever believes in him shall not perish but have eternal life" (John 3:16).

II. God's Grace Will Make You
   A. "But by the grace of God I am what I am, and his grace to me was not without effect. No, I worked harder than all of them—yet not I, but the grace of God that was with me" (1 Cor. 15:10).
   B. Good marriage—He made it, glory!

III. God's Grace Will Hold You Up

"But he said to me, 'My grace is sufficient for you, for my power is made perfect in weakness'" (2 Cor. 12:9).

IV. God's Grace Will Mold and Hold Your Marriage

"We have conducted ourselves in the world, and especially in our relations with you, in the holiness and sincerity that are from God. We have done so not according to worldly wisdom [downhill] but according to God's grace" (2 Cor. 1:12).

A God of Second Chances

Pete Briscoe

EDITORS' NOTE: Not every wedding will involve a bride and groom marrying for the first time. Second marriages afford the officiating pastor a chance to affirm the presence of God's redeeming grace.

I. The First Second Chance: Available to All People
    A. "Therefore, if anyone is in Christ, he is a new creation; the old has gone, the new has come!" (2 Cor. 5:17).
    B. "In Christ" faith or reasoned trust

II. The Second Second Chance: All Christians
    Peter: denied Christ three times and was restored.

III. The Third Second Chance: Wounded Christians
    A. "Come to me, all you who are weary and burdened, and I will give you rest. Take my yoke upon you and learn from me, for I am gentle and humble in heart, and you will find rest for your souls" (Matt. 11:28–29).
    B. Weary and burdened
    C. Take My yoke and learn from Me.

Suggested Scripture Readings for Weddings

EDITORS' NOTE: We have culled these passages from numerous weddings and sources. The list is not intended to be exhaustive.

SUGGESTED OLD TESTAMENT READINGS

- Genesis 1:26–28
- Genesis 2:4–9, 15–24
- Ruth 1:16–17
- Psalm 22:25–31
- Psalm 37:3–6
- Psalm 45
- Psalm 127
- Psalm 128
- Song of Songs 2:10–13; 8:6-7
- Isaiah 43:1–7
- Isaiah 55:10–13
- Isaiah 61:1–3, 10–11
- Isaiah 61:10–62:3

SUGGESTED NEW TESTAMENT READINGS

- Matthew 5:1–10, 13–16
- Matthew 7:21, 24–29
- Matthew 19:4–6
- Matthew 22:35–40
- Mark 2:18–22

- Mark 10:6–9, 13–16
- John 2:1–10
- John 15:8–17
- 1 Corinthians 13:1–13
- Ephesians 3:14–21
- Ephesians 5:1–2, 21–33
- Colossians 3:12–17
- 1 Peter 3:1–7
- 1 John 4:7–16
- Revelation 19:4–9

Additional Illustrations

Keith Willhite

LOWER YOUR EXPECTATIONS

We've talked about some of the great joys of marriage. These joys can be found in no other relationship on earth, but one of my favorite pieces of marital advice comes in a little cartoon. The bride and groom are leaving a large, cathedral-like church building, getting into their "getaway" car. The caption reads, "And the prince and the princess lowered their expectations and lived reasonably happily ever after."

PROMISE KEEPING

When a reporter asked Peter Graves how he could keep a marriage going for forty-six years and still have a successful Hollywood career, he responded with only two words: "We promised."

THE VOWS OF COMMITMENT

Guidelines for Wedding Vows

EDITORS' NOTE: These guidelines are a compilation from several seasoned pastors.

I.   Typically, vows take one of two formats.
   A. "Repeat after me," with the pastor giving each party the lines, or,
   B. Personal vows that the two parties say (recite) to one another.
      (The pastor can "prompt" them if they forget, but they should have these memorized.)

II. The pastor has several sample wedding vows, but if the couple prefers to write their own vows, the following criteria must be met.
   A. Each person's vows should be no longer than ninety seconds, spoken audibly and at a ceremonial pace.
   B. The vows must include the permanency of marriage. For example:
      1. "Until by death we do part."
      2. "Until God calls for you or me."
      3. "Until God separates us by death."
   C. The bride's vows must include love, submission, and honesty.
   D. The groom's vows must include love and honesty.

E. The vows must include the idea of covenant or commitment, both with each other and with God.

F. In every way the vows must be consistent with the Bible so as to enhance the worship direction of the wedding celebration.

G. The pastor must give "final approval" of the vows no later than two weeks before the wedding.

H. Couples who will recite their vows must practice them aloud several times before the wedding.

A Sampling of Wedding Vows

EDITORS' NOTE: Wedding vows come in different formats, and contemporary weddings might not follow one of the traditional formats. Often, couples wish to write their own vows (cf. the section titled "Guidelines for Wedding Vows"). In this section, we have included a few of the more traditional vows as well as some more contemporary vows or ones that serve as somewhat of a combination. These may be used as they appear here, or they may serve to assist a couple in writing their own vows.

RECITED OR REPEATED VOWS FACING EACH OTHER

EDITORS' NOTE: With these vows, the couple may memorize them and say them to each other, being prompted by the minister only as needed. Another option is for the minister to use "repeat after me" with a phrase-by-phrase progression.

[The minister may introduce the covenant promises in the following or similar words:]

(John) and (Mary), by your covenant promises, unite yourselves in marriage and be subject to one another out of reverence for Christ.

[Or,]

(John) and (Mary), speak your covenant promises that you have come to offer before God.

[Or,]

(John) and (Mary), you have come to express publicly your desire to be united in the covenant bonds of a Christian marriage. Therefore, I ask you now to join hands, remembering that the closer you keep Christ at the center of your life, the greater can be your closeness to one another.

[Or,]

(John) and (Mary), as it is your desire to join in this covenant of marriage, face one another, join hands, and then, (John), repeat after me.

[The couple then face each other and join hands, the woman first giving her bouquet, if any, to an attendant.]

Groom: I, (John), take you, (Mary), to be my wedded wife, to have and to hold, from this day forward, for better, for worse, for richer, for poorer, in sickness and in health, to love and to cherish, until death us do part according to God's holy ordinance; and thereto I pledge myself truly with all my heart.

Bride: I, (Mary), take you, (John), to be my wedded husband, to have and to hold, from this day forward, for better, for worse, for richer, for poorer, in sickness and in health, to love and to cherish, until death us do part according to God's holy ordinance; and thereto I pledge myself truly with all my heart.

Groom: (Mary), I take you, as a gift from God, to be my lifelong companion through tears and laughter, sickness and health, work and play. I will love you faithfully, constantly, and prayerfully, now and forever. I promise to be faithful to you, open and honest with you. I will respect, trust, help, and care for you. I will share my life with you.

I will forgive you as we have been forgiven. I will lead with you a simple, just, and peaceful life as Christ has called us to live. And, with you, I will work to further simplicity, justice, and peace in our world. I will love you and be thankful for the blessing of your love until death parts us. Amen.

Bride: (John), I, likewise, take you, as a gift from God, to be my lifelong companion through tears and laughter, sickness and health, work and play. I will love you faithfully, constantly, and prayerfully, now and forever. I promise to be faithful to you, open and honest with you. I will respect, trust, help, and care for you. I will share my life with you. I will forgive you as we have been forgiven. I will lead with you a simple, just, and peaceful life as Christ has called us to live. And, with you, I will work to further simplicity, justice, and peace in our world. I will love you and be thankful for the blessing of your love until death parts us. Amen.

Groom: I, (John), take you, (Mary), as my wedded wife, to have and to hold, from this day forward, for better, for worse, for richer, for poorer, in sickness and in health, to love and to cherish, until death us do part, according to God's holy ordinance; and thereto I pledge myself truly with all my heart.

Bride: I, (Mary), take you, (John), as my wedded husband, to have and to hold, from this day forward, for better, for worse, for richer, for poorer, in sickness and in health, to love and to cherish, until death us do part, according to God's holy ordinance; and thereto I pledge myself truly with all my heart.

Groom: I, (John), take you, (Mary), to be my wedded wife; and I do promise and covenant before God and these witnesses; to be your

. . . .

loving and faithful husband; in plenty and in want; in joy and in sorrow; in sickness and in health; as long as we both shall live.

Bride: I, (Mary), take you, (John), to be my wedded husband; and I do promise and covenant before God and these witnesses; to be your loving and faithful wife; in plenty and in want; in joy and in sorrow; in sickness and in health; as long as we both shall live.

Groom: I, (John), take you, (Mary), to be my wife; and I promise, before God and these witnesses, to be your loving and faithful husband; in plenty and in want; in joy and in sorrow; in sickness and in health; as long as we both shall live.

Bride: I, (Mary), take you, (John), to be my husband; and I promise, before God and these witnesses, to be your loving and faithful wife; in plenty and in want; in joy and in sorrow; in sickness and in health; as long as we both shall live.

Groom: I, (John) take you, (Mary), to be my wedded wife, and I pledge you my faithfulness, until death us do part.

Bride: I, (Mary), take you, (John), to be my wedded husband, and I pledge you my faithfulness, until death us do part.

Groom: I, (John), take you, (Mary), to be my wedded wife, to have and to hold, from this day forward, for better, for worse, for richer, for poorer, in sickness and in health, to love and to cherish, until death us do part, according to God's holy ordinance; and to you I pledge my faith.

Bride: I, (Mary), take you, (John), to be my wedded husband, to have and to hold, from this day forward, for better, for worse, for richer, for poorer, in sickness and in health, to love and to cherish, until death us do part, according to God's holy ordinance; and to you I pledge my faith.

[The groom turns and faces the people and says:]

I ask everyone here to witness that I, (John), take (Mary) to be my wife, according to God's holy will.

[He then faces the bride, takes her hands, and says:]

(Mary), all that I am I give to you, and all that I have I share with you. Whatever the future holds, I will love you and stand by you, as long as we both shall live. This is my solemn vow.

[They loose hands.]

[The bride turns and faces the people, and says:]

I ask everyone here to witness that I, (Mary), take (John) to be my husband, according to God's holy will.

[She then faces the groom, takes his hands, and says:]

(John), all that I am I give you, and all that I have I share with you. Whatever the future holds, I will love you and stand by you, as long as we both shall live. This is my solemn vow.

Groom: Before God and these witnesses, and in reliance upon the grace of our Lord Jesus Christ, I, (John), take you, (Mary), to be my wife, to have and to hold, to love and to cherish, to give and to receive, to speak and to listen, to confront and to comfort, to repent and to forgive, to encourage and to respond, to respect and to honor, "for where you go, I will go; your people will be my people; and your God will be my God." I promise to bear with you and to be faithful to you in all circumstances of our life together so that we may join to serve God and others as long as we both shall live.

Bride: Before God and these witnesses, and in reliance upon the grace of our Lord Jesus Christ, I, (Mary), take you, (John), to be my husband, to have and to hold, to love and to cherish, to give and to receive, to speak and to listen, to confront and to comfort, to repent and to forgive, to encourage and to respond, to respect and to honor, "for where you go, I will go; your people will be my people; and your God will be my God." I promise to bear with you and to be faithful to you in all circumstances of our life together so that we may join to serve God and others as long as we both shall live.

Groom: I, (John), take you, (Mary), just as you are, to share the whole of my life as my wife in a Christian marriage. I promise to love you even as Christ loved the church and gave Himself for her. With God's help, I will love and cherish you at all times, in all circumstances. I will value and respect you for the person you are and the wife you will be to me. I promise to provide the necessary leadership to establish our home under the lordship of Christ as we serve Him together to the glory of God.

Bride: I, (Mary), take you, (John), just as you are, to share the whole of my life as my husband in a Christian marriage. I promise to love and respect you, even as the church is subject to Christ, her Lord. With God's help, I will love you at all times and in all circumstances. I will value and respect you for the person you are and the husband you will be to me. I promise to work with you to establish our home under the lordship of Christ as we serve Him together to the glory of God.

Vows Emphasizing *Giving* or *Receiving* Rather than *Taking*

Groom: (Mary), I give myself to you to be your husband. I promise to love and sustain you in the covenant of marriage, from this day forward, in sickness and in health, in plenty and in want, in joy and in sorrow, as long as we both shall live.

Bride: (John), I give myself to you to be your wife. I promise to love and sustain you in the covenant of marriage, from this day forward, in sickness and in health, in plenty and in want, in joy and in sorrow, as long as we both shall live.

Groom: (Mary), I love you as Christ loves us, unconditionally, unselfishly, and eternally. In the presence of God, our family, and friends, I receive you as my wife and helpmate, a gift from the Lord. Using Scripture as my guide, I promise to be the head and spiritual leader of our home, to protect and provide for you. I commit myself to do these things through the power of God's Holy Spirit for as long as we live.

Bride: (John), I love you as Christ loves us, unconditionally, unselfishly, and eternally. In the presence of God, our family, and friends, I receive you as my husband, a gift from God. I will accept your spiritual headship and promise to honor, respect, exhort, trust, and provide a loving home for you. I commit myself to do these things through the power of God's Holy Spirit for as long as we live.

Groom: (Mary), I promise with God's help to be your faithful husband, to love and serve you as Christ commands, as long as we both shall live.

Bride: (John), I promise with God's help to be your faithful wife, to love and serve you as Christ commands, as long as we both shall live.

Vows Requesting the Answer "I Do"

Do you, (John), now take (Mary) to be your wife; and do you promise, in the presence of God and before these witnesses, to be a loving, faithful, and loyal husband to her, until God shall separate you by death?

Groom: I do.

Do you, (Mary), now take (John) to be your husband; and do you promise, in the presence of God and before these witnesses, to be a loving, faithful, and loyal wife to him, until God shall separate you by death?

Bride: I do.

(John), in taking (Mary) to be your lawfully wedded wife, before God and these witnesses, do you promise to love her, to honor and cherish her, and, forsaking all others, to cling only to her as a faithful husband so long as you both shall live? If this expresses your intention and promise, answer "I do, with the Lord's strength and help."

Groom: I do, with the Lord's strength and help.

(Mary), in taking (John) to be your lawfully wedded husband, before God and these witnesses, do you promise to love him, to honor and cherish him, and, forsaking all others, to cling only to him as a

. . . .

faithful husband so long as you both shall live? If this expresses your intention and promise, answer "I do, with the Lord's strength and help."

Bride: I do, with the Lord's strength and help.

Biblical Wedding Vows

Groom

>In the presence of God and these witnesses,
>And by a holy covenant,
>I, James,
>Solemnly pledge
>to respect you as one different in role, equal in Christ;
>to support, protect, and guide you;
>and to encourage your walk in the Spirit.
>I will love you with all my strength;
>Always seeking the best for you;
>Putting your good before my own;
>Remaining faithful to you, forsaking all others,
>Even unto death.

Bride

>In the presence of God and these witnesses,
>And by a holy covenant,
>I, Rebecca,
>Solemnly pledge
>To submit to your leadership under Christ;
>To honor, encourage, and uphold you;
>And to be your partner in the ministry of the Word.
>I will love you with all my strength;
>Always seeking the best for you;
>Putting your good before my own;
>Remaining faithful to you, forsaking all others,
>Even unto death.

Vows as a Visual Reminder

Randy Frazee

EDITORS' NOTE: The church prints the wedding vows on a very nice parchment of 3 x 5 inches, frames them, and gives them to the couple to display in their new home. The frame is a beautiful, hinged, polished brass frame with the husband's vows on one side of the frame and the wife's vows on the other. What a wonderful visual reminder of commitment! For example, here are one couple's vows.

David to Gayle

> I, David, take you, Gayle,
> To be my wedded wife,
> To have and to hold from this day forward
> For better and for worse,
> For richer and for poorer,
> In sickness and in health,
> To love and to cherish
> Until death do we part,
> According to God's holy ordinance.
> With this ring, I thee wed
> In the name of the Father,
> And the Son, and the Holy Spirit.

Gayle to David

> I, Gayle, take you, David,
> To be my wedded husband,

To have and to hold from this day forward
For better and for worse,
For richer and for poorer,
In sickness and in health,
To love and to cherish
Until death do we part,
According to God's holy ordinance.
With this ring, I thee wed
In the name of the Father,
And the Son, and the Holy Spirit.

Marriage Laws

EVERY PASTOR MUST LEARN THE marriage laws for the state and country in which the wedding is to take place. Although a wedding is a service of worship of the church, it is also a civil ceremony and must meet the laws of the state.

In some states, the wedding official (pastor or minister) is required to register credentials. Other states require no such registration. Laws differ by state for marriage licenses too. To learn the requirements in your state, contact the county clerk's office or the office of the secretary of state.

The primary questions to ask include the following:

1. Do any credentials, such as ordination papers, need to be registered?
2. Legally, what is required in the ceremony (a pronouncement of marriage, etc.)?
3. What is the procedure and time line for marriage licenses?

Wedding Planner

Ron Moore

EDITORS' NOTE: While several "wedding planners" are available, South Hills Bible Chapel clearly leads the pack in excellence. Their planner is a personalized, three-ring notebook that includes the following items and information sheets:

- Personalized letter to the bride from the wedding coordinator
- Forms to complete to reserve the auditorium or other rooms in the church building
- Directions for selecting the officiate
- Twelve-week plan for premarital counseling
- Wedding setups (arrangements of platform furnishings, auditorium, etc.)
- Chapel wedding fees, with due dates
- Chapel wedding accessories
- Musicians and soloists
- Rehearsal planning and the wedding party
- Time considerations
- Florist and caterer guidelines
- Wedding planner/organizer/vendor schedule
- Explanation of who pays for what
- Marriage license information

Wedding Rehearsal Planning Guide

Keith Willhite

_____ WEDDING REHEARSAL

Date: _____ Time: _____

EDITORS' NOTE: Prior to coming into the auditorium, have every member of the wedding party please put on a nametag.

I.   Welcome (5 min.)

"We're headin' for a weddin'."

"A wedding usually means showers for the bride and curtains for the groom."

But we want to spend these minutes together tonight to try to ensure a beautiful and memorable wedding tomorrow.
A. Prayer
B. Introductions
    1. Pastor(s)
    2. Bride and groom introduce parents and wedding party members, respectively.
C. While it's important to stay on schedule tonight, if at any time during the rehearsal any of you have questions, please don't hesitate to ask. Now is the time!

II. Verbal Explanation of the Wedding (5 min.)
    A. Refer to outline (printed for everyone).
    B. Questions?

III. Walk-Through of the Wedding
    Special Notes:
    A. Begin with everyone where they will be just before the recessional. ("Let's start at the very end.")
        1. This is where you will eventually stand. Mark this in your mind somehow.
        2. (From my last words), go through the recessional to escorting out of mothers.
    B. Discuss and walk through the processional (from the seating of the mothers).
        1. Giving of bride.
        2. "Usually after you pay for the wedding, all you have left to give away is the bride!"
    C. Discuss and walk through "moves" (transitions) by the wedding party within the ceremony.
        1. Bride and groom
            a. Lighting the unity candle
                "Does everyone understand the significance of blowing out the two candles? No more old flames!"
            b. Kneeling for prayer
            c. Other
        2. Everyone else (musicians—when)
    D. Go through processional, moves, and recessional.

IV. Instructions
    A. Duties have been spelled out to each of you by the bride and groom or the host and hostess.
    B. Introduce the host and hostess and make clear that they are in charge on the wedding day!
    C. Time for everyone to be at church: _____

. . . .

    D. Special Instructions

        1. What if someone makes a mistake? (It will probably be me. If I make one, I'll keep going. You do the same.)

        2. Pictures/video (When and where)

        3. _____

        4. _____

        5. _____

        6. _____

        7. _____

        8. _____

    E. Close in Prayer

    F. Obtain marriage license from the couple and complete, except for signatures.

Pianist: _____

Organist: _____

Best Man: _____

Matron of Honor: _____

Singer(s): _____

_____

_____

_____

_____

_____

Instrumentalist(s): _____

_____

_____

_____

Pastor Keith's Guidelines for Smoother Weddings

Keith Willhite

1. Children in weddings are usually adorable, but it might be wise to have them sit down in the front rows with parents of the bride and groom after they have walked down the aisle. (Their attention span for the ceremony is much shorter than that of the adults.)

   A little boy was in a relative's wedding. As he was coming down the aisle, he would take two steps, stop, and turn to the crowd. While facing the crowd, he would put his hands up like claws and roar. So it went, step, step, ROAR, step, step, ROAR, all the way down the aisle. As you can imagine, the crowd was near tears from laughing so hard by the time he reached the pulpit. The little boy, however, was getting more and more distressed from all the laughing and was also near tears by the time he reached the pulpit. When asked what he was doing, the child sniffed and said, "I was being the Ring Bear."

2. Tell the bride and groom that it is *their responsibility* to have everyone at the *rehearsal* and the *wedding* on time. (Simple principle: the smoother the rehearsal, the smoother the wedding.)

3. Have the person who will run sound equipment at the rehearsal. (He or she has to know the cues.)

4. If the pastor is wearing a lapel microphone, do not raise the volume on the microphone until the bride is in place, having walked down the aisle. (This may permit the pastor to whisper to the wedding party so as to center them in the room.)

5. Even if you're accustomed to preaching without notes, carry a

full manuscript for the wedding. (This will help with names and help to avoid bloopers. Use a small [4 x 6] black loose-leaf binder, the kind that looks much like a Bible.)

6. Depending on the church's tradition, keep the length of the entire ceremony to twenty-five minutes and the "pastor's charge" to a maximum of ten minutes.

7. At the rehearsal, ensure that everyone in the wedding party knows how and when to exit.

8. Warn members of the wedding party not to lock their knees.

9. Carry a handkerchief in case you start perspiring.

10. Just before the wedding march, give a breath mint to the bride, groom, and yourself.

11. No weddings or rehearsals will be conducted if any member of the wedding party is under the influence of alcohol. (Of course, some traditions might not practice this.)

12. Despite the tradition of the bride and the groom not seeing each other before the ceremony, taking pictures before the ceremony has several advantages: (1) it avoids a long delay between the wedding and the reception; (2) everyone looks their best, including hairdos; and (3) the photographer can work within a time frame not governed by the waiting crowd. Of course, taking pictures before the ceremony necessitates that the entire wedding party is at the church building and dressed at least ninety minutes before the wedding. Also, ushers will be needed to keep guests from disturbing the photo session.

13. Any wedding fees (building, custodial, etc.) should be paid in full one week before the wedding. Honoraria for musicians or other participants should be given on the day of the wedding.

14. For the couple to plan lighting for the wedding, they should visit the auditorium at the same time of day that the wedding will be held. They should include their photographer for a similar visit.

Instructions for Ushers

Keith Willhite

SIMPLE PRINCIPLE

Probably no one is more responsible to see that the wedding begins on time than the ushers.

PRECEREMONY RESPONSIBILITIES

1. Be at the church building no less than ninety minutes before the wedding.
2. Begin seating guests as they arrive, usually about one hour before the wedding. (Most guests will arrive only a few minutes before the wedding, so it is important to seat people as they arrive so that seating of guests will not delay the start of the wedding.)
3. Ask guests if they are guests of the bride or of the groom, or if they have a seating preference.
    a. Facing the platform, seat guests of the bride on the left side of the room, beginning from the fourth row following to the back of the room. (Leave the first three rows empty.)
    b. Facing the platform, seat guests of the groom on the right side of the room, beginning from the fourth row following to the back of the room. (Leave the first three rows empty.)
    c. Seat people as they arrive; do not allow them to delay the seating. (Be firm but courteous.)
    d. If guests do not have a seating preference, fill the room by trying to balance the number of guests on each side.
    e. *Escorting:* As you seat a couple, offer the woman the arm for the side of the room on which she will sit. Ask the man

to follow you. When you arrive at their seats, simply step aside so that the man can follow the woman into the seats.

4. At the designated time (to be covered in the rehearsal), usually five minutes before the wedding, seat the grandparents and parents of the groom on the second row of the right side of the room. (Leave the first and third rows empty.)

5. Immediately following the seating of the groom's grandparents and parents, seat the grandparents and parents of the bride on the second row of the left side of the room. (Leave the first and third rows empty.)

6. If the wedding includes an aisle runner, the two designated ushers should now pull the aisle runner to its full length.

7. If you are a groomsman as well as an usher, come to the designated location for the wedding party (groomsmen).

CEREMONY RESPONSIBILITIES

1. Act as a groomsman, as covered in the wedding rehearsal.

2. Walk out in the recessional, as practiced in the wedding rehearsal.

3. Those groomsmen who are so designated return to escort out the grandparents and parents of the bride. (The mother of the bride enters last and leaves first.)

4. Those groomsmen who are so designated return to escort out the grandparents and parents of the groom.

POSTCEREMONY RESPONSIBILITIES

1. *Dismissal of guests:* Two ushers come down the center aisle to the fourth row (first row of guests) and stand in front of them. Nod for them to exit. As soon as this row is empty on *both* sides of the room, move to the next aisle and nod for the guests to exit. Continue in this procedure.

2. If you are not dismissing guests, follow the instructions of the

wedding host or hostess, especially if you are to assist in setting up for the reception or forming a receiving line.

3. If the bride and the groom wish to form a receiving line, direct guests to the line.

Prayers of Dedication

EDITORS' NOTE: This sample of prayers is a compilation from several sources.

Our Father, You have heard and we have witnessed the covenant made in these spoken vows. Seal this covenant with Your good pleasure and blessing for a happy, fruitful, fulfilling, and lifelong relationship. We ask this for Your honor and glory in the name of Your Son, Jesus, Amen.

Our Father, thank You for (John) and (Mary) and the commitment that they have made today to one another and to You. Bless their new life together with Your grace and goodness. May they live to please and honor You. For we ask this in Jesus' name. Amen.

Our great God, we have enjoyed this celebration of a beautiful wedding. Now, we commit (John) and (Mary) to You and ask that You will make their new union a beautiful marriage. By the grace of God, may they please You and rejoice in their relationship with You and with one another. Amen.

Pronouncements of Marriage

EDITORS' NOTE: In most states, a pronouncement (or "declaration") of marriage is a civil requirement for the ceremony. Some couples even note the exact minute of the pastor's pronouncement so that they can say that they became husband and wife at (for example) 11:42 A.M. The pronouncement comes near the end of the ceremony, definitely after the vows.

PRONOUNCEMENTS TO THE COUPLE

(John) and (Mary), in that you have shared your marriage vows today before God and these witnesses, and because you desire to live your lives together in accord with God's holy ordinance and God's Holy Word, by the authority invested in me by this church and this state, *I now pronounce you husband and wife.*

(John) and (Mary), you have committed yourselves to each other in this joyous and sacred covenant.

Become one. Fulfill your promises.

Love and serve God, honor Christ and each other, and rejoice in the power of the Holy Spirit.

For now, and from this day forward, *you are husband and wife.*

Pronouncements to the Witnesses

Forasmuch as (John) and (Mary) have consented together in holy wedlock, and have witnessed the same before God and this company, and thereto have pledged their faith each to the other, and have declared the same by joining hands and by giving and receiving rings, *I pronounce that they are husband and wife together,* in the name of the Father, and of the Son, and of the Holy Spirit. Those whom God hath joined together, let no one put asunder. Amen.

By their promises, made before us this day, *(John)* and *(Mary)* have united themselves as husband and wife in sacred covenant.

Those whom God has joined together let no one separate.

Wedding Benedictions

EDITORS' NOTE: This sample of benedictions is a compilation from numerous sources.

Our loving Father, thank You for (John) and (Mary) and their commitment to You and to one another spoken here this day. Protect the solemn vows that they have uttered. Help them to be good to one another. Remind them to be concerned more about understanding than being understood. And thank You, Father, that You understand them even when they fail to understand one another. Please make their marriage truly an image of Your love for Your church. May Your Spirit inhabit their marriage and fill it with Your joy. Amen.

May God the Father, God the Son, and God the Holy Spirit, bless, preserve, and keep you. May the Lord look upon you mercifully with His favor and fill you with all spiritual benediction and grace that you may so live together in this life that in the world to come you may have life everlasting. Amen.

And now may the God of all grace seal this covenant with His blessing and joy for His praise and honor, forever. Amen.

Cyber Wedding Invitation

Ditmar and Maura Pauck

EDITORS' NOTE: This couple developed a Web site to serve as their wedding invitation. They sent e-mails to their guest list with a hyperlink to get to the Web site. This had some interesting advantages over traditional paper invitations: (1) a beautiful color picture of the couple, (2) almost instant RSVP via e-mail, (3) the opportunity to personalize the invitation, and so forth. Moreover, this couple was going to have a second ceremony in the groom's home in Germany, so the Web site facilitated international invitations. The first part of the invitation was in English for the wedding in America, and the second part was in German for the ceremony to be held in Germany. Here, we have used only the English version (see next page).

. . . .

God has brought us together!

Maura Negrao & Ditmar Pauck

Therefore, as God's chosen people, holy and dearly loved, clothe yourselves with compassion, kindness, humility, gentleness and patience. Bear with each other and forgive whatever grievances you may have against one another. Forgive as the Lord forgave you. And over all these virtues put on love, which binds them all together in perfect unity.

Colossians 3:12–14

We are glad to announce that our Lord is in the process of making us one flesh, uniting our hearts and our ministries. Our vision is to become missionaries to Brazil, functioning in the local church context to develop Christian leaders. We love you and would like to request your presence at a brief commitment ceremony and prayer service on Saturday evening, August 11th at 7:00 P.M. A cake and punch reception will follow. Ceremony and Reception location: Fellowship Bible Church North (Fellowship Center), 850 Lexington Drive; Plano, Texas

RSVP by return e-mail

Please include your name and the number attending. Children are welcome.

Remembering Our Future

Keith Willhite

EDITORS' NOTE: After the couple had repeated their vows and the minister pronounced them "husband and wife," they stepped up on the platform to light the unity candle. Two large screens had been placed in the front of the auditorium, one on the bride's side of the room and the other on the groom's side. While the organ played and the couple lit the unity candle, the following pictures (slides) appeared on the two screens. (Others have seen this as distracting during the ceremony, so they have shown the slides during the reception.)

Timing	Bride's Screen	Groom's Screen
As they take their first steps toward the unity candle	One of her earliest baby pictures	One of his earliest baby pictures
As they walk toward the unity candle	A picture of her playing the violin at an elementary school recital	A picture from his Little League baseball years
As they both take their respective candles to move toward the unity candle	A picture of her as a young adult	A picture of him as a young adult

. . . .

Timing	Bride's Screen	Groom's Screen
As they light the unity candle and blow out their respective candles	A picture of the couple from their courtship or engagement	The same picture of the couple from their courtship or engagement
As they return to their position in front of the guests and minister	The words appear on the screen: "Mr. and Mrs. Samuel Williams. No longer two but one!"	The words appear on the screen: "Mr. and Mrs. Samuel Williams. No longer two but one!"
	"Only What God Wills"	"Only What God Wills"

EDITORS' NOTE: The "adult" pictures can be posed, but candid shots usually capture their lives better.

"Father of the Bride" Cards

EDITORS' NOTE: One man left the following business cards on the tables at the reception following his daughter's wedding.

I AM THE FATHER OF THE BRIDE

No one will pay much attention to me today, but I can assure you that I am getting my share of attention because the banks and several business places are watching me very closely.

Additional Resources for Weddings

Sidney F. Batts

Christensen, James L. *The Minister's Marriage Handbook.* Old Tappan, N.J.: Revell, 1974.

Criswell, W. A. *Criswell's Guidebook for Pastors.* Nashville: Broadman, 1980.

Engle, Paul E. *Baker's Wedding Handbook.* Grand Rapids: Baker, 1994.

Gibson, Scott M. *Preaching for Special Services.* Grand Rapids: Baker, 2001.

Henry, Jim. *The Pastor's Wedding Manual.* Nashville: Broadman, 1985.

Kirschenbaum, Howard, and Rockwell Stensrud. *The Wedding Book: Alternative Ways to Celebrate Marriage.* New York: Seabury, 1974.

Langford, Andy. *Christian Weddings: Resources to Make Your Ceremony Unique.* Nashville: Abingdon, 1995.

Monckton, Shirley. *Complete Book of Wedding Flowers: Stunning Flower Arranging Inspiration for Everyone and Every Location.* New York: Cassell Sterling, 1995.

Muzzy, Ruth, and R. Kent Hughes. *The Christian Wedding Planner.* Wheaton: Tyndale House, 1991.

The Protestant Wedding Sourcebook: A Complete Guide for Developing Your Own Service. Louisville: Westminster/John Knox, 1992.

Vincent, Arthur M., ed. *Join Your Right Hands: Addresses and Worship Aids for Church Weddings.* St. Louis: Concordia, 1965.

Warner, D. *Complete Book of Wedding Vows.* Franklin Lakes, N.J.: Career Press, 1996.

Wiersbe, Warren W. *Be Quoted from A to Z with Warren W. Wiersbe.* Ed. James R. Adair. Grand Rapids: Baker, 2000.

. . . .

Wilkinson, Mary, ed. *Planning a Beautiful Wedding.* Sydney: Gregory's, 1968.

EDITORS' NOTE: Denominations often publish or print wedding guidelines or resources. Several Web sites also address wedding planning.

part two

FUNERALS

Introduction

Keith Willhite

AS THE SON OF A FUNERAL DIRECTOR, my ministry in funerals began at a very early age. During my years of pastoral ministry, I found few circumstances more challenging or rewarding than memorial services. I have conducted funerals for children, suicide victims, accident victims, people who have never darkened the door of a church, and devout believers. These are different occasions, and they require different messages to some extent. Hence, we have arranged most of the funeral messages by occasion.

Death comes so quickly, even for the terminally ill patient, the one we all knew for months was going to die. Death is so final, except for the Christian. Death is not painless for the Christian, but it can be overshadowed through the hope of the Cross and the Resurrection. Often, it's up to the pastor to speak a word of that hope or to remind God's people not to grieve as those who have no hope.

In this section of funeral resources, we have sought to include items that will be helpful in various circumstances. Along the way, we have found these observations helpful:

1. No matter what the circumstances of the death, the focus of the service should be on the Lord Jesus and His redemptive work. This does not mean that we should try to turn every memorial into an evangelistic event. But it does mean that we can point to the hope that is in Christ Jesus.
2. Every funeral should "find the good" in the life of the deceased without "deifying" him or her.
3. Funeral traditions vary significantly from region to region or church to church. For example, in some areas, every memorial service must include a eulogy. In other contexts, a eulogy seems

out of place. The traditions should be upheld to the extent that the church feels that the traditions are appropriate and the family of the deceased desires the traditions.

4. The newer pastor can seek guidance from the church leadership and the funeral director as to the traditions and local expectations.

In this *Handbook,* we have distinguished a funeral message from a eulogy in the following way.

- *Funeral Message:* A message based on at least one biblical passage that intends to comfort the bereaved and exalt the finished work of Christ.

- *Eulogy:* A brief reading by the pastor or a family member, telling the "story" of the person's life in a way that gives tribute to the person.

This distinction does not hold true everywhere. Some people use the terms interchangeably. Our focus in this book is more on the funeral message.

Funeral Service Outline

General Guidelines

1. It is important to follow local and denominational customs.
2. Most funerals should not exceed twenty minutes.
3. Often, families will have special requests (a song, a testimony, etc.)
4. Give an order of service to the funeral director and all other participants (musicians, readers, sound technician, etc.)

Planning the Service

With these guidelines in mind, the following outline can be used or adapted.

I. Instrumental music
   A. Often, the music is selected per requests of the family.
   B. Common selections include:
      1. "Great Is Thy Faithfulness"
      2. "Safe in the Arms of Jesus"
      3. "How Great Thou Art"
      4. "Fairest Lord Jesus"
      5. "Jesus Paid It All"

II. Opening Scripture sentences
   Common selections include:
      1. 1 Corinthians 15:20–25, 50–58
      2. Psalm 23
      3. Psalm 100

III. Prayer—a general prayer to thank God for who He is, His plan, and His grace

IV. Solo (optional musical selection)

V. Message (10–15 minutes)

VI. Closing prayer
More specific with thanks for the person and prayer for comfort for the family and needs.

VII. Dismissal: funeral director

Typically, the funeral director will dismiss the audience, but ensure that this is the plan before the service. Typically, the pastor stays with the casket, either leading it out of the auditorium or standing with it as guests leave. (Check these details with the funeral director. He or she is there to help you.)

Order of Service

Keith Willhite

EDITORS' NOTE: It is beneficial for a smooth flow of the service for the pastor to prepare an "Order of Service" for each participant to have (including musicians, pallbearers, and funeral directors). This can usually be given to each person on a half sheet of paper. For example:

- Prelude: Rev. David Luce (seating of the family)
- Scripture reading: Pastor Willhite (Psalm 46:1–7)
- Solo: Susan English
- Message: Pastor Willhite
- Congregational singing: Rev. Luce ("Christ the Lord Is Risen Today")
- Closing prayer: Pastor Willhite
- Dismissal of guests (family remaining): Mr. Piell, funeral director

Eulogy Outline

EDITORS' NOTE: Typically, a eulogy is read by the pastor or a family member and is no longer than three to four minutes. The elements of a eulogy usually include:

I. Background
   A. Where the deceased was born and raised
   B. Major "benchmarks" or "turning points" in the person's life (e.g., when and where they graduated from high school or college, who and when they married, when children were born, etc.)

II. Significant contributions in life
   A. Noteworthy accomplishments
   B. Employment
   C. Service in the church
   D. Family

Committal Service

Graveside Comments

SCRIPTURE READING

Revelation 22:16–17, 20

COMMENTS TO THE FAMILY

We who are gathered with you in these treasured yet trying moments do desire to help you, to serve you, to love you, and to share your burden. Allow us that privilege. Call on us that we may help or comfort you. Most of all, call upon Him who is the God of Comfort.

PRAYER

Our precious Lord, You are the deliverer of affliction. In this day, when we remember the One who is the forgiveness of sins and the resurrection to life, we ask that He might remember these who come in sorrow. Watch over these in this hallowed place, in holy remembrance, until the trumpet shall sound, and the dead shall be raised in glory. Return to us then these we have lost for a while. Until that day, abide with this dear family as their strength. In Your strong name we pray. Amen.

Eyes of Faith

Mark 5:21–24, 35–43

Andy McQuitty

INTRODUCTION

It's a scary thing to walk where you can't see. When the power's off and the lights are out and you're feeling your way through the darkness, it's uncomfortable not knowing if your next step might be into a doorjamb or onto your child's skateboard. It's just no fun to move around in darkness. It's like taking a sudden turn into a dark cave, where grief and questions form thick darkness but where there are no light switches. In such a time and place, one can see only with eyes of faith.

A father was standing outside his burning home, shouting up to his five-year old son, who was trapped in a second story window. "Jump, son! Jump! I'll catch you."

The boy, choking on smoke, replied, "But, Daddy, I can't see you."

"I know," his father called, "but I can see you." When the lad jumped into his daddy's arms, he did so not because he saw but because he trusted. That's faith.

> What is faith? It is the confident assurance that something we want is going to happen. It is the certainty that what we hope for is waiting for us, even though we cannot see it up ahead. (Hebrews 11:1 TLB)

One of the hardest tests of faith in a time like this is to believe that death is not the end, that one day *[our loved one]* will live again and that we'll be back with them again. It's hard to have faith when you're surrounded by black limousines and funeral flowers and caskets. But we can, and God calls us to do so. He calls us to the confident assurance that what we hope for in the face of death is waiting for us, although we cannot see it up ahead. How can we have such eyes of faith? A story about Jesus in Mark 5 gives us two answers.

CHOOSE TO FOCUS ON THE HEALER, NOT THE HURT

> When Jesus had again crossed over by boat to the other side of the lake, a large crowd gathered around him while he was by the lake. Then one of the synagogue rulers, named Jairus, came there. Seeing Jesus, he fell at his feet and pleaded earnestly with him, "My little daughter is dying. Please come and put your hands on her so that she will be healed and live." So Jesus went with him. A large crowd followed and pressed around him. . . . While Jesus was still speaking, some men came from the house of Jairus, the synagogue ruler. "Your daughter is dead," they said. "Why bother the teacher any more?" Ignoring what they said, Jesus told the synagogue ruler, "Don't be afraid; just believe." He did not let anyone follow him except Peter, James and John the brother of James. (Mark 5:21–24, 35–37)

"Ignoring what they said." I love that line. The people around Jairus were consumed entirely by the dark circumstances surrounding the little girl's death. They were in the cave. All they could talk about was the tragedy of her untimely passing. They were focused on only the hurt.

But Jesus wanted Jairus to focus, not on the hurt but on the Healer. So he ignored what they said and thereby invited Jairus to do the same. Sometimes faith begins by stuffing your ears with cotton to the despair of those with no faith.

Instead, Jesus told Jairus, "Just believe." He didn't want Jairus to listen to only the audible and see only the visible. He wanted Jairus to have eyes of faith. He wanted Jairus to believe that there is more to life and death than meets the eye.

On the wall of a concentration camp a condemned prisoner wrote,

> I believe in the sun, even though it doesn't shine. I believe in love, even when it isn't shown. I believe in God, even when He doesn't speak.

There was a man who believed that there is more to life than meets the eye. There was a man who lit a candle of faith. There was a man who focused not on the hurt but on the Healer. That's also what Jesus wants for you today. Ignore the inner voices of despair that pull your eyes exclusively to the hurt. Don't be afraid; just believe. Focus on the Healer, not the hurt. When we focus on the Healer, we're ready for the second part of the answer.

Look at Death from the Healer's Perspective, Not a Human Perspective

> When they came to the home of the synagogue ruler, Jesus saw a commotion, with people crying and wailing loudly. He went in and said to them, "Why all this commotion and wailing? *The child is not dead but asleep.*" But they laughed at him. After *he put them all out,* he took the child's father and mother and the disciples who were with him, and went in where the child was. (Mark 5:38–40, italics added)

From Jesus' perspective, the girl was not dead, just asleep. Sleep is not a permanent condition, and to God, neither is death. It's just a necessary step in passing from this world to the next. It's not an end but a beginning. That's what the Bible says:

> I declare to you, brothers, that flesh and blood cannot inherit the kingdom of God, nor does the perishable inherit the imperishable. . . . For the perishable must clothe itself with the imperishable, and the mortal with immortality. (1 Corinthians 15:50, 53)

When we see death, we see disaster. When Jesus sees death, He sees deliverance. However, instead of waking the little girl up in heaven, Jesus chose on this particular occasion to wake her up again back in this world. He did so that we might learn to see with eyes of faith:

> He took her by the hand and said to her, *"Talitha koum!"* (which means, "Little girl, I say to you, get up!"). Immediately the girl stood up and walked around (she was twelve years old). At this they were completely astonished. He gave strict orders not to let anyone know about this, and told them to give her something to eat. (Mark 5:41–43)

If, from God's perspective, death is deliverance and not disaster, why did He raise this little girl from the dead? Certainly not for her sake, for she was better off in heaven. He raised her for *our* sake. God knows that you and I must often walk in darkness and that faith doesn't come easily or naturally. In the face of death, God knows that we need the assurance that death is not the last act.

I believe that Jesus raised this little girl, not as a promise that He *will* do the same in this world for every loved one who dies but as a sign that He *can* do so for every loved one who dies. That brings us great comfort, for what we now know Jesus *can* do—that is, raise the dead—He has promised that He *will* do at the end of time. That's the Healer's perspective: death is temporary, resurrection is coming, life is forever. If you look at death from God's perspective, you, too, can see with eyes of faith. As the apostle Paul wrote,

> So we fix our eyes not on what is seen, but on what is unseen. For what is seen is temporary, but what is unseen is eternal. (2 Corinthians 4:18)

EVANGELISTIC CONCLUSION

Like Jairus, put your trust in the Lord Jesus Christ!
How can we see with eyes of faith? How can we have the certainty

. . . .

that what we hope for is waiting for us, although we cannot see it up ahead? By focusing in this hour on the Healer, not the hurt. By looking at death from the Healer's perspective, not man's. Did you notice that both steps involve the Healer, Jesus Christ? In the dark face of death, without Him, nothing is important, and with Him nothing is impossible. This much is obvious to those who see with eyes of faith.

May I ask you a question? Are you seeing with eyes of faith at this moment, or are you groping in the dark cave without even a candle to light? If you are doing the latter, please take to heart these words of Jesus:

> No one has ever gone into heaven except the one who came from heaven—the Son of Man. Just as Moses lifted up the snake in the desert, so the Son of Man must be lifted up, that everyone who believes in him may have eternal life. For God so loved the world that he gave his one and only Son, that whoever believes in him shall not perish but have eternal life. (John 3:13–16)

I have news for you. *[Our loved one]* believed in Jesus Christ, the same Jesus Christ who took a little dead girl by the hand and called her back into time. Because of [our loved one's] belief in Jesus, Jesus will one day take her by the hand and call her to eternal life. We know that He can do it! And we believe His promise that He will.

What about you? Do you see with eyes of faith? Like Jairus, is your trust in the Lord Jesus Christ? Like *[our loved one],* is your trust in Jesus Christ? If not, I invite you to put it there. Don't be afraid. Just believe. For whoever believes in Him shall not perish but have eternal life. Amen.

A Suffering Grace

Memorial Service Following an Extended Illness

Larry Renoe

INTRODUCTION

And shouldst thou offer us the bitter cup, resembling sorrow,
Filled to the brim and overflowing,
We will receive it thankfully, without trembling,
From thy hand, so good and ever-loving.

These words come from a prayer written in a Gestapo jail cell by German Christian Dietrich Bonhoeffer several months before his death at the hands of the Nazi regime. Pastor Bonhoeffer called on a biblical metaphor—the cup—to describe the frequent and most defining event of his life—suffering.

Philip Andersen drank from the "bitter cup, resembling sorrow, filled to the brim and overflowing."

THE BITTER CUP

Psalm 88:15 says, "I have been sickly and close to death since my youth. I stand helpless and desperate before your terrors" (NLT). Philip could voice these words. Almost every day of his life, he experienced physical pain, the likes of which most of us will never know.

From childhood, in the daily stick of needles and testing of blood for the diabetes, to the thirteen major surgeries in the last four years that laid open nearly every cavity and limb, Philip endured a depth and constancy of pain that would bring from us the response of numbed silence and the shaking of our heads in disbelief.

161

. . . .

The physical pain was accompanied by other losses. In the last years of his life, Philip was not able to work to support the family, and he lost the ability to be physically active. Those losses strike at the core of what it is to be a man. It seems that Philip's calling in this life was to suffer; if he was to live, he was to live in pain.

To be sure, Philip did live. There were days when the bitter cup could not deplete his vigor. His childhood and teen years were active in spite of diabetes. Philip excelled as a shortstop on baseball teams, and he played basketball too. They say that he was fast. The apple didn't fall far from the tree where Philip's boys are concerned. Philip went on to earn a business degree and an MBA. Philip obeyed the Lord's command to work by forging a career in commercial sales, selling everything from dental supplies to forklifts. Philip was good with people and good for them. His parents were so proud of how Philip lived, encouraged by the choices he made. They were even more confident in Philip's character as both husband and father. George, our hearts break for you. You've lost your wife and now both of your sons. May God have mercy and bring comfort to boundary your sorrow.

Then the real education for Philip came, however, when he met and married Linda. We've gleaned their good times. We've glimpsed their hard times. Linda told me that in their marriage, Philip was the depth of the relationship while Linda was the width. It takes both to make the beautiful and dangerous ocean we call marriage.

Many have sat with Linda through hours of waiting in hospitals, and we've heard her say again and again the same words she said the day after Philip died: "He was a big man. Name any man of wealth or prestige or influence in our land, and he does not compare to Philip."

Linda, you shared the bitter cup with Philip. You know about "for better for worse, for richer for poorer, in sickness and in health until death do you part." You and Philip knew them all. May God, in the years ahead of you, bring greenness to your life out of this long winter.

None of us who knew Philip will forget him as a father. Philip's ability and worth as a father is summarized in the tender, approachable name that his sons bestowed on him—"Papa." These sweet young men adored their father. There is no doubt that the boys will carry on not only their family name but also their father's heart.

None of us who knew Philip as a Christian brother will forget him as being exactly what the heavenly Father desires—a worshiper in spirit and in truth. There is the lasting image of Philip's dragging himself here to this room to give himself to the Lord. I can see him sitting in a wheelchair, hands raised straight up, eyes closed and head back, as if he was waiting for the Father to reach down and lift him right up. Philip loved the Lord in worship. He also loved the Lord in the church. He was deeply embedded in our lives. He resisted turning inward to self-pity, and he resisted the locked-on-self tunnel vision that pain so often produces. He dragged himself to ball games, to small groups, to breakfast appointments with pastors to keep the church lined up, and to welcoming visitors in his home. He was a big man.

But why Philip? Death is such a cruel thief when it strikes down our loved ones with suffering and death before they are old.

Why did Philip have to drink the bitter cup? Why did all of this suffering come upon him?

I could stand here and float you the textbook answers about God's working all things for good or that God will not give anyone more than they can handle. But you know what? Although I might agree with those statements in my mind, they are empty right now, as hollow and as dark as a tunnel.

What we need to hear right now, with Philip's suffering and death locked on to our minds, is that God knows Philip suffered, and He cares!

I cannot explain this loss. I cannot defend God in this situation, nor should I. It's not my role or place. What I do know is that only He who permits the wounds is able to heal them. No one else can. Illusions about death cannot do this; neither can hushed silence about the subject. Philip's life was God's possession, as is my life and yours. God alone can heal the wound, because only He fully knows the wounds.

How does He know Philip's wounds? It's because Jesus drank the bitter cup. Here is the moment in the history of world that speaks to Philip's suffering and your suffering and mine: Jesus praying in the Garden of Gethsemane, "My Father, if it is possible, may this cup be taken from me. Yet not as I will, but as you will" (Matt. 26:39).

And Jesus got up from there and began to drink the bitter cup down to the dregs—betrayal and beatings, torture and taunting, a crooked trial, nailed to a cross, and hung up to die by the world for the entire world to see.

But why did He, the Son of God, drink the bitter cup? It's because God the Father wanted to offer Philip, you, me, and the entire world a different cup, a new cup—the cup of salvation!

The Cup of Salvation

After Jesus ate the Last Supper with His disciples, He lifted up a cup of wine and said to them, "This cup is the new covenant in my blood; do this, whenever you drink it, in remembrance of me" (1 Cor. 11:25).

Through the suffering and death of Jesus Christ for our sins, God extends to us the cup of salvation. Anyone who drinks from this cup will live, even though he or she dies. Anyone who receives Jesus into his or her life now, here, will live forever with Him. And there is no louder, stronger, clearer way for us to hear this: God knows, and God cares!

Philip drank from the cup of salvation. He lived and died inviting people to drink from the cup of salvation. Philip was a "grace man." He knew God's favor was on him, not because of the good things he did, not because he went to church, and not because he worked at being a good husband and father. God's grace was drenched upon his entire being—unmerited and undeserved, regardless of any sins committed—only because of Jesus Christ and what He has done.

This cup of grace is the greatest power ever unleashed in this world. Grace gives us life. Grace helps us walk. Grace binds our wounds. Grace gives meaning to our sufferings. Grace deepens our joys. Grace puts boundaries on the past. Grace brings the promise of a future. Grace

. . . .

plants the seeds of purpose in our lives. This grace is greater than our sins and greater than our sufferings.

Philip drank deeply from the cup of grace, and so the most important word for us to hear right now is this: Philip is alive! By the grace of God, he has never been more alive. Philip now knows fully the power of the death and resurrection of Jesus Christ.

CONCLUSION

[The minister spoke briefly about the day of Philip's death.]

And shouldst thou offer us the bitter cup, resembling sorrow,
Filled to the brim and overflowing,
We will receive it thankfully, without trembling,
From thy hand, so good and ever-loving.

Bonhoeffer's prayer went on:

But if it be thy will again to give
Joy of this world and bright sunshine,
Then in our minds we will past times relive
And all our days be wholly thine.

PRAYER

Almighty God, Lord of life and Conqueror over death, our help in every time of trouble, breathe Your peace into our hearts, and remove from us all fear of death. Help us to share in that joy that You have in the death of Your saints, who have completed their pilgrimage through a world that was not their home and have entered into a more intimate fellowship with You.

Strengthen us in our sorrow, and enable us so to hear Your Holy Word, that through patience and the comfort of the Scriptures our hope may be firmly anchored. And grant us the consolation of Your Holy Spirit, that we may be lifted above the shadows of mortality into the light of Your countenance and the joy of Your presence; through Him who died and rose again and lives forever with You, even Jesus Christ. Amen.

[Congregational Singing: "Great Is Thy Faithfulness"]

Scriptural Metaphors for Death

Memorial Service for a Godly Woman

Howard G. Hendricks

INTRODUCTION

A delightful personal friend, now in heaven, was flying to Chicago and to the city of Los Angeles. He engaged the woman sitting next to him in conversation. She was a little more than forty, well dressed, and quite articulate. He asked, "Where are you from?"

She said, "From Palm Springs."

Knowing Palm Springs to be a city of the rich and the famous, he asked, "What's Palm Springs like?"

Very perceptive, she answered, "Palm Springs is a beautiful, beautiful place, filled with unhappy people."

Taking advantage of the occasion, he pressed the question, "And are you unhappy?"

She said, "Yes, I certainly am."

"Why?" he asked.

She said, "I can answer in one word, and that word is *mortality*. Until I was forty," she said, "I had perfect eyesight. But shortly after, I went to the doctor because I couldn't see as well as I could before. Ever since that time, these corrective glasses have been a sign to me that not only are my eyes wearing out, but I'm wearing out. Some day I'm going to die, and I really haven't been happy since that time."

Ladies and gentlemen, these words summarize the feelings of millions of Americans today. We don't want to lose what we have here. We don't want to be reminded that death is going to come to us, as for everyone else in the human race. As someone has said, "The only certainty in life is death." There are only three things you can do about death. You can accept it, and therefore prepare for it by receiving Jesus Christ as your only Savior. You can fear it, and therefore spend all of your money, and all of your time, and all of your resources running to escape it. Or you can ignore it, and subscribe to the words of H. L. Menken, who said that death is a universal conspiracy not to be mentioned.

This forces a question: How do the Scriptures view death, particularly for the believer? What does a spiritual, eternal perspective look like? In Psalm 116:15 (NASB), the psalmist says, "Precious in the sight of the LORD is the death of His godly ones." Why? What is it about death for the Christian that constitutes it precious to God, and therefore, to the believer? The Scriptures use three graphic, compelling pictures, or metaphors for the death of a believer.

GOING TO SLEEP

First, it's "going to sleep." Let me read some familiar words to most of you. I want you to underscore in your mind the repeated statement "falling asleep." It's mentioned three times in I Thessalonians 4, for emphasis.

> Brothers, we do not want you to be ignorant about those who *fall asleep,* or to grieve like the rest of men, who have no hope. We believe that Jesus died and rose again and so we believe that God will bring with Jesus those who have *fallen asleep* in him. According to the Lord's own word, we tell you that we who are still alive, who are left till the coming of the Lord, will certainly not precede those who have *fallen asleep.* For the Lord himself will come down from heaven, with a loud command, with the voice of the archangel and with the trumpet call of God, and the dead in Christ [those who have fallen asleep] will rise first. After that, we who are still alive and are left will be caught up together with them in the clouds to meet the

Lord in the air. And so we will be with the Lord forever. (vv. 13–17, italics added)

Dr. Luke, penning his account of the martyrdom of Stephen, informs us that his last words were, "Do not hold this sin against them." This is a reflection of his Savior's words. And then he adds, "When he had said this, he fell asleep" (Acts 7:60). The apostle Paul in 1 Corinthians 15 on two occasions refers to the death of the believer as "falling asleep."

But where did these New Testament writers get that concept? I would like to submit that they got it from the mouth of Jesus Christ. In Mark, chapter 5, you have a page out of the life of our Lord: "Jairus, a ruler of the Synagogue was a desperate man. He ran into the presence of the Savior, prostrated himself on the ground before Him and pleaded earnestly that He would come and put His hand upon his little girl, who was at the point of death." And Jesus responded, but en route they encountered a woman with an illness of thirty-eight years duration. You can almost identify with Jairus as the Lord stops to heal her: "And Lord, we're running out of time." And while the Lord is speaking, the men come and say, "She's dead. Why bother the teacher any more?"

That's a human reaction. As long as there's life there's hope. On more than one occasion I have been in a very desperate situation. A man who had drowned was just pulled from a lake. A woman who, in O'Hare field in Chicago, dropped to the floor of a massive heart attack. The paramedics were called. They worked feverishly in both cases to revive the individual, only to have a physician come and say, "He's gone." "She's dead." You see, Jesus is in this kind of a situation, and He says in the midst of that kind of a crisis, "Don't be afraid; just believe."

And when they arrived at the home, the professional mourners had gathered and were doing their thing. They were ripping their garments, tearing their hair, and crying with loud shrieks. Jesus comes in and says, "What's all the commotion about? She's not dead; she is asleep."

And they roared at the funeral. After all, we are the professionals. We know what death is. She's not asleep. She's dead. Who has the right view of death? Jesus or man? You see, to most people death is permanent and sleep is temporary. Death is the end of life, whereas sleep is the continuation of life. It's the recouping of one's strength and energies so that you might go on in life.

Jesus said, "She's asleep." And so is Elizabeth. You see, death is going to sleep, and we are forced to ask, "Who's afraid to go to sleep?" Oh, some of us were when we were small children. I remember begging my father, "Daddy, leave the light on." Jesus understands. That's why He said, "He that walks with me does not walk in darkness, but shall have the light of life." Elizabeth fell asleep on Friday, June 21, only to awaken to see the face of her Savior.

Going on a Journey

But death is not only going to sleep. The Scriptures use a second metaphor: death is going on a journey. In 2 Timothy 4:6, we read about Paul at the end of his life: "I am already being poured out like a drink offering, and the time has come for my departure." He uses two graphic figures, one to express the end of his life. He has spent the bulk of his life pouring it out like a drink offering for others. Now the time of his departure has arrived. That's the beginning of another life.

The word *departure* is fascinating. It's used of the striking of a tent. We're planning to move our location, and so we loosen the ropes and take the tent down. We use the untying of a boat from its moorings, the anchor is weighed, the ropes are loosened, we put out to sea, and we head for a distant shore.

Before the great adventure of his new voyage, Paul looked back over his ministry of thirty years and said, "I have fought the good fight, I have finished the race, I have kept the faith" (v. 7).

The Christian life is viewed realistically. It's a battle, and the opposition is relentless. The bullets are real, and the casualties are high. It's not a piece of cake. It wasn't for Elizabeth, and it isn't for us. He finished the race.

In Acts 20, with the Ephesian elders, he said, "That's the goal of my life, to finish the race and complete the work that God has given me to do." And may I remind you that the race is won only at the end. I have a new appreciation for older men and women who have been walking with Jesus Christ for many years and who finish well.

Finally, he said, "Who have kept the faith." They guarded the treasure even though it meant pain and suffering. And in each there's labor, there's sacrifice, and there's danger. But now Paul said that nothing remained but the prize, the crown.

I cannot think of a better epitaph for Elizabeth than those three expressions. She fought the good fight, she finished the race, and she kept the faith.

Tributes

I hold in my hand a little card that I know must have meant worlds to Elizabeth, knowing her heart. "P.S. Thank you very much for being my Sunday school teacher and teaching me how to accept Jesus Christ into my life. You are a great example of a godly woman."

Isn't that neat?

Here's one beautiful tribute, beautiful to me because it's my daughter's tribute. She was very close to the woman she called affectionately "Aunt." She wrote this card: "I think of you often, mostly in the continuation of the contribution that you have made to my own life, especially as a child. You were always one of my favorite mothers, mostly because of your bright and cheerful disposition. I got to see you in a lot of different situations: church, Sunday school, Vacation Bible School, and then just the times our families got together, and you were always so kind and had a thoughtful word for everyone. You really are a great example to me. Maybe that is what Paul had in mind in Titus, when he called the older women to be examples in their lives to train the younger women. You certainly have been that to me, and I do appreciate that input in my own life."

Elizabeth's gone on a journey, only to have arrived at the Celestial City because death is going on a journey. Who's afraid of going on a journey, especially that one?

GOING HOME

Finally, there is a third metaphor in the Bible for death. The Scriptures teach us that death is "going home." In John 14, our Lord was involved with the disciples. He had informed them repeatedly that He was soon to die. He was going to leave them, and that prospect threw them into a panic. That's why Jesus said, "Do not let your hearts be troubled. Trust in God; trust also in me. In my Father's house are many rooms; if it were not so, I would have told you. I am going there to prepare a place for you. And if I go and prepare a place for you, I will come back and take you to be with me that you also may be where I am."

Jesus said to the disciples and to us, "I want you to know that the destination has been determined, and it involves two things. It involves, first of all, a place." What kind of a place? One that Jesus is preparing for us, completely ready, completely perfect, and completely mine. I think that if I were to interview Elizabeth, she would say in her characteristically precise manner, "Howie, you wouldn't believe it." And she is right. It fascinates me that invariably in the New Testament, when the writers of Scripture wanted to describe heaven, they used the negative. They said that it's not like it is here. For instance, in Peter it's the inheritance. What kind? Incorruptible, undefiled, and that fades not away.

My friends, how do you describe an infinite place to a finite person? Students at the seminary will always walk up and ask me questions. I'll do my best and try to answer them, and then often they will say, "Is that the best you can do?"

"That's the best I can do."

"Well, how come you're teaching in a seminary?"

And I respond, "I don't know. Maybe that's why they don't pay me more." Then I jog them by asking, "Does it really bother you that I, as a finite person, cannot fully comprehend an infinite God? Does that really bother you?"

Men and women, the only way we will ever be able to explain heaven is seeing it firsthand and experiencing it in reality.

But I want you not to miss the second thing that heaven involves. Heaven is much more than a place. This text informs me that heaven is a person. Jesus will be there, and, men and women, the thing that makes heaven *heaven* is the presence of the Savior, and the thing that makes hell *hell* is the absence of the Savior. You see, it's the presence of Christ that makes the place glorious. And that's why Paul said in Philippians 1:21, "For to me, to live is Christ and to die is gain." How so? More Christ. That's why Paul in a number of places in the New Testament said, "I'm struggling. It's far better to go home, but it's necessary for me to remain."

Do we want Elizabeth back? Well, for our sakes, of course. But for her sake, never. How selfish we would be to want that! Death is going home, and who's afraid to go home? No matter how exciting the trip, I can assure you from more experience than I would care to have, there's nothing more exciting as going home.

What is death for the believer? It's going to sleep in the arms of Jesus. It's going on a journey to the Celestial City. It's going home to a place specifically prepared for you.

When I saw Elizabeth shortly after she had passed away, her body was wasted, discolored, drawn, and, as I felt it, cold. Standing by that body, I understood in a new way that never was Elizabeth more alive than she was at that moment.

EVANGELISTIC CONCLUSION

May I ask you a question? What's the most exciting experience of your life? If the only answer you can give to that question is in the past, then you are either a hopelessly uninformed Christian or a lost person, and you need to understand that all of us have sinned. There's none righteous, not one. The wages of sin are death, but the gift of God is eternal life. Life begins not at death but at the new birth, and it reaches its culmination in glory with the Savior. It's the greatest experience of every Christian, of every Christian yet ahead, and Elizabeth has experienced it. Wherefore, comfort one another with these words.

Past, Present, and Future

A Eulogy for a Late-Life Convert

Jeff Watson

INTRODUCTION

We have gathered here today to say farewell to Henry Jackson and to draw comfort from the Word of God. As the psalmist says, "Precious in the sight of the LORD is the death of his saints" (Ps. 116:15 KJV). Although some speakers have already described the attractiveness of Henry's life *at work* and *at home,* it is my privilege to describe how Henry's life became attractive *to God.*

THE PAST: WHAT HAD HE BEEN THROUGH?

The Little Word *Now*

Over the past several weeks, as we sensed that Henry's body was shutting down, a phrase has kept running through my mind: "I am *now* ready" (2 Tim. 4:6a KJV, italics added). The words of the apostle Paul, recorded from his prison cell, could have been spoken by Henry: "For I am *now* ready to be offered, and the time of my departure is at hand. I have fought a good fight, I have finished my course, I have kept the faith: Henceforth there is laid up for me a crown of righteousness, which the Lord, the righteous judge, shall give me at that day: and not to me only, but unto all them also that love his appearing" (vv. 6–8 KJV, italics added). In these words, spoken on the doorstep to eternity, the apostle says honestly, "I am *now* ready." He wasn't *always* ready and wasn't *born* ready. He *became* ready. How? *Christ made him ready!* That's also Henry's story, and I'm honored to tell it.

174

This passage of Scripture pushes us to think about the past, the present, and the future. We might ask, "What had Paul been through in the past?" In verse 7, Paul described his past like a heavyweight boxer: "I have fought a good fight" (v. 7a KJV). He was like a Boston marathoner: "I have finished my [long] course" (v. 7b KJV). He also spoke like an Olympic gymnast: "I have kept [a firm grip on] the faith" (v. 7c KJV).

The Good Life Then

What had Henry been through? In love with Marian since seventh grade, this New Englander had never had eyes for anyone else. By the time those sweethearts attended the freshman prom on September 14, 1933—Henry a sophomore and Marian a freshman—they knew that this was a love for a lifetime. Henry's love for Marian made him gladly leave his religious roots for hers. When they married and moved to Washington, D.C., God blessed them with four fantastic children and a well-ordered home.

We can only imagine the pain that Henry felt ten years ago when he thought that he was losing Marian. After a lifetime of smoking, Marian's body had begun to thin with the ravages of emphysema, heart disease, and impending strokes. After one long night at Washington Hospital Center, as Marian hung between life and death, Henry's seventy-something sweetheart opened her eyes and said, "Thought I was going to leave you last night. I saw my parents and grandparents, traveling down a long tunnel. They looked at me and nodded: 'No, it's not your time.'" They were right. Marian recovered, and God gave her three more years.

Eternal Life Forever

What did Henry and Marian do with their gift of renewed life? As a couple in their seventies, they began searching for a church. Years before, they had grown disillusioned with their house of faith, a place that had degenerated from sermons against the Vietnam War to the ordination of a lesbian. Although this senior couple had quit going, they hadn't quit caring.

With Marian's rebound to life, they asked a deacon-friend to tell them more about his church. Based on his humble integrity and warm hospitality, they tried out his Bible-centered congregation. With welcoming arms, this awkward-sized assembly drew them in, gave them a Bible, and began sincerely building them in the faith.

As you can imagine, it wasn't long before they wanted to join officially. The outreach pastor visited, shared the gospel, and came to a mixed conclusion. "Marian knows the Lord," he reported, "but Henry is really an agnostic." The senior pastor followed suit and offered the same verdict: "Henry, in my estimation, you are a *christian*—small *c*. It's your heritage, your culture. Marian would be what I would call a *Christian*—capital *C*. She has asked Christ to save her from her sins based on nothing more than the death and resurrection of Jesus."

Like many married couples, they didn't want to join halfway. They didn't want Marian to be welcomed up front with Henry sitting in the pew. So they both remained nonmembers officially. But, to their credit, they stayed in the mainstream of the church.

Seven years ago, Marian died, and it was as though Henry's heart had been pulled out. As we laid her petite, little body in the landscaped lawn of Fort Lincoln Cemetery, Henry pointed out a phrase in their joint headstone: "Together Forever." "That'll be true, won't it?" he asked me.

"Only if you trust Christ alone for your salvation," I whispered privately.

With a tearful grimace, he countered, "Keep that up and you'll make a Christian of me yet!"

THE PRESENT: WHAT WAS HE GOING THROUGH?

The Tent Analogy

From Paul's prison cell again, we learn not just about his past—what he had been through—but also about the present—what he was going through. In verse 6, Paul said, "I am now ready to be offered, and the time of my departure is at hand" (2 Tim. 4:6 KJV).

For a tentmaker, Paul's words were picturesque. No doubt a craftsman who had frequently sewn tents for the Roman army, Paul used a military term of the trade: "The time of my departure [Gr., *analyseos;* "my breaking camp"] is at hand" (v. 6 KJV). Paul sensed that the Commander in Chief was about to give the order to "Break camp!" This body in which he had lived, this human address, this shell of a tent was about to become empty, quiet, still, and dead.

The one who had lived in that tent—the real Paul, the one who laughed, and loved, and cried, and played—was about to travel. The outer Paul, the part that people saw—the skin, the hair, the eyes—was about to be lovingly packed away and buried. The true Paul—the soul or spirit—was about to take its final marching orders from the General of the Universe.

This body before us today is really not Henry; it's Henry's tent. Last Wednesday, God said, "Pack it up, Henry, and come home. Join Me in a land where there is no sorrow, tears, darkness, or death (Rev. 21:4; 22:5). Come and rejoin Marian; I know you've missed her."

The Tombstone Wish

I know that he missed her desperately. As the first anniversary of her death drew near, Henry became progressively depressed. Yes, he missed her, and that was awful; but, even more than that, he dreaded the idea that she might be in heaven forever—alone. It's like that tombstone in Indiana that reads, "Pause, stranger, when you pass me by. As you are now, so once was I. As I am now, so you will be. So prepare for death and follow me." Henry's thoughts were like the unknown passerby who later handwrote on that tombstone, "To follow you, I'm not content until I know which way you went." For himself, Henry had to have that question answered.

The Real Question

One February day, this seventy-four-year-old man put himself on my calendar, ten o'clock until noon. It was a morning of laughter,

. . . .

memories, and tears. It was a morning when Henry wrestled as deeply as I've ever seen anyone wrestle with a religious question: "Will God receive me when I die?" He meant, "Have I lived good enough to be welcomed in His presence?"

As much as I wanted to affirm Henry, God led me to indict him. "Not by works of righteousness which we have done" (Titus 3:5 KJV). For "all our righteousnesses are as filthy rags" (Isa. 64:6 KJV). "There is none good but . . . God" (Matt. 19:17 KJV). "There is none righteous, no, not one" (Rom. 3:10 KJV). "For whosoever shall keep the whole law, and yet offend in one point, he is guilty of all" (James 2:10 KJV). "For all have sinned, and come short of the glory of God" (Rom. 3:23 KJV). "For the wages of sin is death; but the gift of God is eternal life through Jesus Christ our Lord" (Rom. 6:23 KJV). "For whosoever shall call upon the name of the Lord shall be saved" (Rom. 10:13 KJV).

"Henry," I said, "the question is not whether He will receive *you;* the question is whether *you* will receive *Him.* It says, 'But as many as received him, to them gave he power to become the sons of God' (John 1:12 KJV). The rich young ruler had asked, 'What shall I do to inherit eternal life?' (Luke 18:18 KJV). Jesus answered clearly that there are only two ways to please God: perfect obedience—of which none of us is capable—or perfect surrender to His grace."

Henry thought for a minute. "That's what Stuart always said, that he was 'not good enough.' I had heard a lot of people talk about religion, but I had lived better than all of them, except Stuart. When I complimented him on being the best Christian man I knew, he told me he was 'not good enough,' that 'only Jesus was good enough.' In the end, that's why I accepted his invitation to come to this church."

"Stuart was right," I said. "It's not what we do for God—that's religion—it's what God has done for us in Christ—that's relationship."

Henry got it. He prayed with me to receive Christ that day. He believed the A, B, Cs of the gospel—that "*all* have sinned, and come short of the glory of God" (Rom. 3:23 KJV, italics added); that if we would "*believe* on the Lord Jesus Christ," we would be saved (Acts 16:31 KJV, italics added); and that whoever would "*call* upon the name of the Lord shall be saved" (Rom. 10:13 KJV, italics added).

With our four hands piled on top of one another, Henry bathed our hands in tears. He was like that geriatric Supreme Court justice of Israel, Nicodemus (John 3:4). That beloved unbeliever (vv. 9–10) became a sincere seeker (7:50–51) and, eventually—after three years—a true believer (19:38–42). His faith was secret at first but public at last.

Until that day in my office, the eighteenth-century hymn writer, Joseph Hart, might well have been speaking to Henry when he wrote, "Let not conscience make you linger, nor of fitness fondly dream. All the fitness He requireth is to feel your need of Him. Come, ye weary, heavy laden, lost and ruined by the fall. If you tarry until you're better, you will never come at all" ("Come, Ye Sinners, Poor and Needy").

THE FUTURE: WHAT DID HE HAVE TO LOOK FORWARD TO?

A Crown

The past, the present, and the future: what had Henry been through? What was he going through? And what did he have to look forward to?

In verse 8, Paul lifted his eyes toward the horizon: "Henceforth there is laid up for me a crown of righteousness, which the Lord, the righteous judge, shall give me at that day: and not to me only, but unto all them also that love his appearing" (2 Tim. 4:8 KJV). Amazingly, Paul—the one who called himself the chief of sinners (see 1 Tim. 1:15)—looked forward to a crown, not a metal crown but an aurora of righteousness. He looked forward to wearing a wardrobe of righteousness—not of his own doing—but a righteousness *given* to him by Christ.

Christ, the King of Righteousness, had donated a deposit of innocent goodness to Paul on the Cross: the potential for full forgiveness through faith in the substitutionary death of Christ. According to verse 8 of 2 Timothy 4, Christ would soon donate in final measure the full investment of His righteousness on the day of His appearing. Hadn't Paul already told us, "he [Jesus] . . . who knew no sin" became the sin bearer for us, "that we might be made the righteousness of God in him" (2 Cor. 5:21 KJV)? And did you notice? This crown is not just for apostles and missionaries. It is for "all them . . . that love his appearing" (2 Tim. 4:8 KJV). Do you love His appearing today? Are you looking forward to, living toward, that day when the Lord will return or will call you home?

This story, Henry's story, pushes each of us to decide what we truly believe. Is there a God? Life after death? A heaven and hell? Salvation by grace through faith?

A Cave

For me, our life on earth can be pictured in a story. As a kid, I had been aware of a cave down in the woods for a long time. It was a scary cave and none of my buddies had ever dared to go very far in. But one summer day, two of us were daring enough to go in. We went in a few steps, then a few farther. As we turned a corner, it became darker, moist smelling, and uneven underfoot. We panicked and backpedaled all of the way out of the cave.

Relieved to be out, we leaned against the little hill, breathing hard and trying to calm ourselves. Before long, an older kid came along. "You want to go through that cave?" he asked.

"No, not really," we both said in unison.

"I've done it before. No problem," he boasted.

"Really? And you came out OK?" I doubted.

"Yeah, I'll take you, if you want," he offered.

"OK," I shook my head, "but only if you hold my hand. I don't want to lose you in there."

Grabbing my sweaty palm, this older kid took my right hand and pulled me into the darkness. It was like I was descending into the grave, stumbling into the valley of the shadow of death, entering that final tunnel of transition. As I walked deeper and deeper, the light disappeared behind me. I seemed to have been swallowed up in total blackness, but I continued to walk by faith, trusting in my guide who had gone this way before.

Eventually, I spotted a dim light in front of me, growing brighter with each faltering step. Before I knew it, we stepped out into the bright sunlight on the far side of the hill. Immediately, my heart began to calm. Never did the sunlight seem as bright or the daylight as warm as it did on that day. And that's how I believe it was for Marian, seven years ago. And that's how I believe it was for Henry this past Wednesday. Jesus, who entered death for us and emerged in the sunlight of resurrection, said, "I will never leave thee, nor forsake thee" (Heb. 13:5 KJV). "I am Alpha and Omega, the beginning and the ending. . . . I am he that liveth and was dead; and, behold, I am alive for evermore, Amen; and have the keys of hell and of death" (Rev. 1:8a, 18 KJV).

EVANGELISTIC CONCLUSION

Today, I challenge you to put *your* hand in *His* hand by faith. Learn to walk not by sight but by faith. For "without faith it is impossible to please [God]" (Heb. 11:6 KJV). But with faith comes the greatest of gifts: "For God so loved the world, that he gave his only begotten Son, that whosoever believeth in him should not perish, but have everlasting life" (John 3:16 KJV).

Prepared to Meet God

Eulogy with an Evangelistic Appeal for a Godly Man

Brent Strawsburg

EDITORS' NOTE: This service might be useful for someone whom the pastor does not know.

I would like to welcome you here this afternoon to the funeral of Adam Connor. This is a sacred moment. It is sacred because we honor the life of a wonderful man. It's also sacred because we come face-to-face with the temporary nature of life here on earth. All of us need to recognize this sacredness and honor his memory by reflecting quietly on his life and the existence of life after death.

No service could possibly do justice to the entire life of Adam Connor. Every person who interacted with him carries with him or her memories, or an imprint, of what he was like. He did too many things and had too many acts of kindness and too much love for his family to encapsulate all of that in one service.

I never had the opportunity to meet Adam. Yet, through my friendship with those close to him, I've begun to see the person whom they loved intensely. As I've spoken to his grandchildren *[insert names]*, I've been touched by their affection for him. I can tell you that his family will never forget Grandpa. They'll never forget Pa!

Adam Connor was dedicated to his family and to his friends. He was family oriented. He was always helping with some construction project—a room addition or pouring concrete.

Adam had an aptitude as a mechanic, something that his sons *[insert names]* tell me they didn't inherit. But guess who would be over to help when one of the cars wasn't working?

He was always available to watch the grandkids.

There's something to be said for the things that marked Adam—integrity and honor. Adam worked for Mobil for thirty-three years until he retired in 1989.

He valued his friends. After he retired, it was Adam who initiated the Thursday Lunch Club with a close cluster of his friends. When he'd travel back to his hometown, he would get together with his close friends there, a group called the Breakfast Club.

He was the consummate father. Because of his shift work at Mobil, he always had time to be with the boys as they participated in sports. He was the one who made minivacations possible and memorable. No task was too small and nothing was too insignificant that he couldn't help his kids. He was never so busy that he couldn't attend a soccer event. Adam Connor was the consummate family man.

To the family, I can barely express my sense of hurt and loss for each of you. You have lost your dad, your grandpa. No words can remove its reality or lessen its awful sting. In the weeks and months and even years to come, you will face situations that will remind you of his love, memories that will make you smile or memories that will make you cry.

Today and for weeks and months to come, that smile will be mixed with tears. But months from now, when you think of Adam making a plate of fudge for Christmas, you'll smile. Months and years from now, as the pain of your loss lessens, you'll think about certain things and the smile will break across your face. When you think about the Thursday Lunch Club, you'll smile. When you think about Adam and the aquarium, you'll smile. When you think about the devoted pa, the loving grandpa, you'll smile. You'll smile because you'll recognize how blessed you were to have been touched by his life.

As a family, you'll need each other more in the future than ever before. You'll need to listen to each other. You'll need to love the grandkids more than ever because the relationship between a grandparent and grandchild is special. The loss they feel must be handled carefully. You must all give each other the freedom to "lose it" from time to time. It's OK to cry for no reason at all, to all of a sudden feel sad. It's OK because he meant everything to you.

. . . .

I've asked Brian to express some thoughts about his dad. Several members of the family wanted me to express their comments.
[Family comments were made here.]

This service is sacred not simply because we honor the life of a godly man. It is sacred because we pause to recognize the temporary nature of life here on earth.

This week has been a painful reminder that life here on earth will not always go on. Life here on earth must eventually come to a close. This reminder comes far too quickly for those whom we love. Although Adam's battle in the ICU for the last nine weeks prepared the family for the unthinkable, none of us is fully prepared to say "good-bye." But I need to remind every person here that you can be prepared for eternity.

Over the years, society has become increasingly uncomfortable with the subject of death. It has been ignored or its implication carefully avoided. For many people, death is seen as just the final chapter. Nothing happens after death. It's just over. For others, heaven is seen as a catchall for just about everyone who is a good person.

Frankly, the reality of life after death must be considered very carefully. People are more than just a complex arrangement of physical systems. We are not simply the by-products of the physical mechanisms of evolution. People have souls, something above and beyond this body. That soul was created by God and designed to have a relationship with Him.

Jesus, facing one of the more difficult situations in His life, came to the funeral of His good friend Lazarus. As He came to console the family, Mary, Lazarus's sister, came to Jesus, saying, "Lord, if You had been here, my brother would not have died" (John 11:21 NASB).

Jesus responded, "Your brother shall rise again" (v. 23 NASB). It was then that Jesus distinguished Himself from all people at all times when He said, "I am the resurrection and the life; he who believes in Me will live even if he dies, and everyone who lives and believes in Me will never die" (vv. 25–26 NASB).

What was He saying? He promised people the opportunity to live, even if they die physically. If we don't have souls, that sentence doesn't make sense at all. How can you live if you die? What Jesus said makes sense only if you and I have souls that last beyond this life in our bodies.

My belief in the God of the Bible tells me that every person is ultimately accountable to God for his or her life. People don't just die and that's it. Our souls live. When you and I die, we must eventually give account of ourselves before a perfect and holy God.

Listen once more to Jesus' response. Jesus came upon another of Lazarus's sisters, who immediately fell at His feet and said, "Lord, if You had been here, my brother would not have died" (v. 32 NASB). And when Jesus saw all of the people weeping and heard Mary's comment, the Bible tells us that Jesus Himself wept. Why do I mention that? First, Jesus understands the human pain of loss. There's not been a moment this week that He has not felt deeply your pain as a family.

But I believe the even bigger reason why He wept is that, for a brief moment, Mary had seen things from a purely physical level—"Jesus, You could have prevented my brother from dying"—instead of seeing that ultimately the far more pressing question is that belief in Christ could guarantee an eternal relationship with the God of this whole world.

In these painful moments, life actually affords each of us a unique opportunity to understand and evaluate our relationship with God. Quite simply, there's a world beyond this one. After a person dies, their soul lives on either with God or apart from God.

For all of the advances of science and technology, people still wonder why we haven't solved our deepest problems. With all of the information and education, our society is struggling more than ever. We have more material possessions than ever, but we have less true happiness than ever.

Here's how C. S. Lewis put it:

> If I have a desire that nothing in this world can satisfy, then I was made for another world.

If there is a life after this one, you must ask one simple question: Are you good enough to meet God's standard? The Bible says that none of us can meet God's perfect standard. Our sin blots our record with God. The Bible says that we've all sinned and we've all fallen short of God's perfect standard. God can't simply wink at our sins. Although He loves us, His justice demands that He do something about our sin. Jesus Christ came and died in your place to provide you the solution. As God, Jesus Christ could offer the one sacrifice able to meet God's perfect standard. As man, Jesus Christ could stand in your place and my place and make restitution for our lives.

You must ask yourself, "What will it take to prepare me for my eternity?" It's a simple matter of refusing to trust in your own goodness and to trust solely in what Christ did on the Cross. You must tell God that you will trust only in Christ's dying for your sins to get you to heaven. You can't trust in your attendance in church, or your better-than-average morality, or the good deeds done in your life. None of those things could ever be good enough to meet the perfect standard of a holy God.

Jesus wanted His good friends to know that it all came down to whether they placed their faith in Him. Jesus, in the most definitive statement about the key to getting to heaven, said, "I am the way, and the truth, and the life; no one comes to the Father but through Me" (John 14:6 NASB).

Many of you have heard this truth before. However, it does you no good unless the truth is united with faith.

Others of you have tried to ignore the reality of death, or you've tried to raise obstacle after obstacle to convince yourself that there are just too many problems with this Christianity stuff. Pascal, the brilliant French mathematician and physicist in the 1600s, put it thus:

> God has given evidence sufficiently clear for those with an open heart, but sufficiently vague so as not to compel those whose hearts are closed.

Folks, if your heart is open, if you wonder what will happen when you die, you must not miss this moment.

I hold out this hope, the only hope that makes sense out of life. It's the hope that, at any time in this life, we can place our trust in what Jesus Christ did on the Cross. It's only by trusting in what He did that we can prepare our souls for the finality of death.

In this sacred moment, please don't let the memory of Adam Connor dim before you. Ensure that you can measure up to the perfect standard of God. The only way to meet that standard is to trust in Christ's death on the Cross. The moment you do that, you will be prepared to meet God.

Would you join me as I pray?

Celebration of a Godly Servant

Eulogy for a Lifelong Friend

Eddie B. Lane

EDITORS' NOTE: As you will notice, the eulogy was delivered by a close personal friend. Although many of the personal narratives and associations have been removed, the body of the message remains here.

I want you to turn with me to 2 Timothy 4. You might have brought with you a text. If you didn't, make a note somewhere in your program, and I want to read from the New American Standard Version, verses 6–8: "For I am already being poured out as a drink offering, and the time of my departure has come. I have fought the good fight. I have finished the course, I have kept the faith; in the future there is laid up for me the crown of righteousness, which the Lord, the righteous Judge, will award to me on that day; and not only to me, but also to all who have loved His appearing."

I want to talk about a death worth dying. A life lived well results in a death worth dying. Second Timothy 4:6–8. Time will not permit, nor is this the appropriate time and place for me to share with you in depth the friendship that Harvey and Maggie had, and what that friendship has meant to my wife and me for close to forty years. We have been friends that long.

In the text before us today, the apostle Paul sets before us the idea that it is possible to live life in this present world in such a manner that it will result in a death worth dying. Now I fully realize that most of us are quite familiar with the phrase "a life worth living." We know that phrase, we hear it, and perhaps use it frequently ourselves. But we're not as familiar with the phrase "a death worth dying." And in this home-going service for my friend, Margaret, I want to suggest to you that a life lived well in this present world results in a death worth dying.

I'm tempted to use this time, this occasion, to talk to you about the life of Margaret. I could do that, and should I yield to this strong impulse, and strong it is, I would focus on the particulars in the life of Margaret that place her life into the unique category of a life lived well in this present world. In this context, I would mention the fact that Maggie bore five children and raised them well. I could spend more than a little bit of time talking to you about how Margaret served the Lord in church planting, singing, teaching, praying, and doing whatever necessary to further the cause of Christ. But then most of you know all of that because you knew Margaret. And I've sat here and listened to folk talk about Margaret.

She gave me specific instructions about what she wanted me to do on this occasion. You see, I knew Margaret, and she knew me as well as I knew her, and because she knew me so well, she did not leave this occasion as to what I would talk about to my own discretion. So she said, "This is what I want you to do." In obedience to Margaret, whom I love dearly, I turn my attention to this biblical text that's before us today.

A LIFE LIVED WELL

As you look at this text, you will notice first of all that the apostle Paul takes the time to give us a description of what it means to live life well. In doing so, he does not focus on the social, the economic, or the political involvement. He does not focus on these things as markers for the life lived well. The focus of this text is on a person whose whole life is lived in such a way that it is, in its totality, an act of praise and worship to the risen Christ.

Notice the words of this text: "As for me," Paul wrote, "my life has already been poured out as an offering to God" (2 Tim. 4:6 NLT) He recognized that the imagery here is of a bottle of wine that is brought before the holy altar in the temple of the living God and then poured out as an act of worship. I take it that the apostle Paul is saying here that his life, in its totality, is an act of worship, poured out in its totality in worship and praise to the living God.

So it was with the life of Margaret. She didn't live her life as long and short spurts of spirituality and service to the Lord. No, her life was one continuous act of worship and service to the Lord. I daresay that Maggie didn't know how to serve the Lord in any other way but by giving Him her best every day. She gave all she had.

For Maggie, her life belonged to the Lord, and no matter how she felt, she served. No matter what she had, or did not have, she served. No matter what the circumstances in her human situation were at the moment, she served. She knew service. She knew how to serve.

We country people always have a way of thinking things. But Maggie knew that the time of her departure was at hand. She knew that. In this text, Paul says, "the time of my departure has come" (2 Tim. 4:6 NASB). Brothers and sisters, there's something good about knowing that the time of your departure is near. When you know that the departure time is near, it motivates you to put things in order so that when the departure date arrives, you are prepared to travel well. In many years of pastoring, you bury a lot of people, not a lot of whom are ready to go. It takes you ten years to find all of the pieces of their lives. When you know the departure date is coming, it helps you get your stuff together. Maggie knew that.

Some of you are tempted to think that Maggie is at rest now, and so she is. However, I suggest to you that Maggie is not at rest because she got tired and decided to rest. No, Maggie entered her time of rest Monday evening, March 26, because she had finished her mission. Her brother said—and I'd never thought of it—he said, "You know, the seventh day Jesus rested, but not because He was tired, He rested because He was through."

And then this pastor said, "It's hard to rest when your job isn't done."

That's true. I want you to know that Maggie is at rest today because she finished her job, her mission—all done. That's a good thing.

Look again at the text: "I've fought the good fight." I take it that the

. . . .

text is saying that those who live well and die a death worth dying are those who choose to fight the good fight. I take it that fighting the good fight means keeping the faith. We country people sing an old hymn in the church that says, "A charge to keep I have." None of you young people know this; you just don't know it: "A God to glorify." Maggie knew it, "and ever thine soul to save, I will answer, by and by." I want you to know today that she fought the good fight, she kept the faith, and a few days ago, God called and she answered. She kept her charge.

Now I have said that a life lived well in this present world results in a death worth dying. When we speak of a life worth living in this world, we most often have reference to the rich and famous of this world. Living well in this world is most often defined even in the church as a life filled with prosperity. We tend, you see, to associate living well with having a lot of stuff. I want you to know that Maggie lived well in the world. I daresay that she had most, if not all, the things she ever wanted. Were we to measure the life of Margaret by the standards of this present world, we would have to conclude that she lived well.

Sunday evening, Harvey and I sat, as friends do, and he said, "Lane, the thing that hurts the most is I can't do anything to stop the pain." For those of you who don't know, and those of you who are just married or planning to marry, I want you to know that you ought to live life in such a way that, when you have the opportunity, you do the best you can for your mate. And you do it as frequently as you can because the day might come when you can't reach where they are to stop, or reverse, or change what's happening. And I said, "But, you gave Maggie the best you had." And that, my friend, is good enough.

It's no accident that Maggie loved Harvey. No, she couldn't help it; he loved her. What was she supposed to do? All of the stuff that he was throwing at her because he loved her, she had to love him back. She had to. A life lived well in this present world. And what I'm speaking of today is not about how much stuff you have. It is not about how many famous folk you know or who knows your name. A life lived well in this present world is all about the level of commitment and depth of service one renders to his or her Lord. That person who lives well in this present world is one who has taken his or her life to the

Lord—Romans 12:1–2 speaks of the risen Christ—and surrendered that life to the Lord so that He could do with it whatever He wanted.

Maggie gave her life to the Lord, and He honored it. Remember the text that says that a person who saves his or her life shall lose it. She didn't keep hers. A life lived well is a life lived out as an expression of worship and praise to the risen Christ.

A DEATH WORTH DYING

What, then, is a death worth dying? A death worth dying is transition from this world to the next. But listen to me. It is not the transition from this world or this life to the next that is, in and of itself, the death worth dying. Listen to me now. The thing that makes death worth dying is that, as the text says, "There is laid up for me [not *a* crown] *the* crown of righteousness," (2 Tim. 4:8 NASB, italics added). Not *an angel* will give it to me, "Which *the Lord*, the righteous Judge, will award to me on that day" (2 Tim. 4:8 NASB, italics added).

It's not the trip that's important; it's where you're going and when you get there. Listen to me now. It is this crown of righteousness that every believer will receive when they see Jesus that makes death worth dying. Now hear what I'm saying. Listen, listen. If you listen, if you just hush for a moment in the sanctuary of this church, just listen for a moment, and you will hear within the content of your mind the voice of Margaret. Listen to me now. Just listen, and you will hear her singing, "We shall be behold Him." You can hear what was distinguished and distinct from all other voices. You will hear her say, "We will behold Him."

Now you listen to me. You see face-to-face in all of His glory. When Maggie got to heaven Monday evening, some of you think that she went looking for her Ma'dear. Others of you think that she went looking for her daddy, and well she might. But this friend believes that when Maggie stepped off into glory, Margaret had something like this on her mind. I think she said, "Oh, I want to see Him. I want to look upon His face. I want to walk up and down the streets of glory. I want to sing about His saving grace." And she got to see Him.

Oh, what a good thing that is! Oh, I know you think sometimes this stuff we do ain't worth nothing. I know some of you preachers' wives and preachers think that this thing is all about a lot of hot air. I know that you think sometimes that the journey and the sacrifices are not worth putting up with. I know all of that. But I want you to know something, my friend. It's a good thing that heaven is real. Oh yes, it is now. You might have eight bathrooms in your house, sixteen bedrooms, and carpet that you don't know when you are stepping on. You may have maids and stewards, and all of that stuff, but I want to tell you heaven is better than that. You may have in your possession a checkbook that you don't have to worry about checks bouncing, but I want you to know heaven is better than a balance in your checkbook, and when you get to heaven, I want you to know something.

Now when you get to heaven it's good to know that the streets are made of gold. Oh yes, it is. It's good to wander around there and count angels and listen to them sing, but nothing you could ever imagine compares to looking into the face of Jesus, and seeing Him for yourself, and then hearing Him say, "You did a good job. You served Me well. I saw those years you sang in that half-empty church with no music backing you up, but you sang anyway. I remember the time when your husband got paid too little and the groceries were short, but you served Me anyway. I remember when you didn't feel like going, but you went. You didn't feel like singing, but you sang. You didn't feel like teaching, but you taught. Well done," Jesus will say. "Well done," Jesus will say. "Well done," Jesus will say. It makes the trip worth making; it makes death worth dying.

Yes, we'll miss her. If Maggie would call me today, she'd say, "Eddie, you know all that stuff you and Harvey used to talk about all night long? You remember that? You remember the stuff you all thought you had answers to and didn't? You remember? You remember how you all used to disagree on stuff?" She'd say, "Listen, Eddie. Heaven is real."

She'd say, "Eddie, my death was worth dying, 'cause my life was lived well.'"

Some of you got mess in your life. Yes, you do. You got mess in your

. . . .

life. You celebrate it as whole. Then you walk out of here and you say Margaret was a good lady, but you can die and go to hell. Did you know that? I hope, by God's grace, you don't die. Because if Maggie is in heaven, there's the other side, and it's hell. You don't want to go there. Brothers and sisters, we have had a rare privilege. We have had the privilege of watching one of God's choice servants live before us and die before us with amazing grace. From her, we learn that a life worth living results in a death worth dying.

Let's sing together Maggie's favorite hymn, "Great Is Thy Faithfulness."

Memorial Service for a Believer

Ephesians 1:3–14

Keith Willhite

EDITORS' NOTE: This service might be useful for someone whom the pastor does not know well.

INTRODUCTION

We've gathered today for "the reading of the will." You might have thought that this was only a memorial service, but Faith wanted the emphasis of this service to be not on her life but on her inheritance. So, I will begin with "the reading of the will" and then conclude with some observations. Thus, the will reads as follows:

SCRIPTURE READING

Praise be to the God and Father of our Lord Jesus Christ, who has blessed us in the heavenly realms with every spiritual blessing in Christ. For he chose us in him before the creation of the world to be holy and blameless in his sight. In love he predestined us to be adopted as his sons through Jesus Christ, in accordance with his pleasure and will—to the praise of his glorious grace, which he has freely given us in the One he loves. In him we have redemption through his blood, the forgiveness of sins, in accordance with the riches of God's grace that he lavished on us with all wisdom and understanding. And he made known to us the mystery of his will according to his good pleasure, which he purposed in Christ, to be put into effect when the times will have reached their fulfillment—to bring all things in heaven and on earth together under one head, even Christ. In him we were also chosen, having been predestined according to the plan of him who works out everything in conformity with the purpose of his *will*, in order that we, who were the first to hope in Christ, might be for the praise of his glory. And you also were included in Christ when you heard the word of truth, the gospel of your salvation. Having believed, you were marked in him with a seal, the promised Holy Spirit, who is a deposit guaranteeing our *inheritance* until the redemption of those who are God's possession—to the praise of his glory. (Ephesians 1:3–14, italics added)

MESSAGE

I. Obviously, this is the reading of *God's* will.

II. The focus of God's will is *inheritance.*

III. Of course, as with the reading of any will, we must ask two questions.
   A. Who was named in the will?
   B. What was the inheritance?

IV. As I look back at the text of the will, I find these named:
   A. In the first few lines of the will, those named are referred to as "us."
   B. Later, this same group gains a bit more specificity, when they are described as
   "chosen"
   "predestined"
   "those who put their hope in Christ"
   "adopted as sons"

C. So, those named in this will are the adopted children of God.

D. How did they become the adopted children of God?

   1. As the will explains, "And you also were included in Christ when you heard the word of truth, the gospel of your salvation. Having believed, you were marked in him with a seal, the promised Holy Spirit, who is a deposit guaranteeing our *inheritance* until the redemption of those who are God's possession—to the praise of his glory" (vv. 13–14, italics added).

   2. To say it more in our own words, the people to receive this inheritance are those who put their faith in Jesus Christ as their Savior and Lord. He is the sole object of their hope. He saves them from the penalty of sins, which the Bible tells us is eternal separation from God and damnation.

E. This inheritance begins with a sealed relationship with God. The basis of this relationship is justification or salvation, provided only through the Lord Jesus Christ.

F. That's how we know that Faith is named in this will. She put her hope in Christ and was sealed for an inheritance. Today, she is enjoying her first taste of that inheritance.

G. The truth of the matter is that I read only a brief portion of this will. This entire book *[hold up the Bible]* is the will of God. (Now, relax. I'm not going to read the entire will.)

H. What, then, does it tell us about the inheritance to be received by these adopted children of God?

   1. Those who have placed their faith in Jesus' atoning sacrifice for their sins have become "adopted sons." They are God's children. Galatians 4:4–5 summarizes this succinctly: "When the fulness of the time was come, God sent forth his Son, made of a woman, made under the law, to redeem them that were under the law, that we might receive the adoption of sons" (KJV).

   2. Thus, "the inheritance" that God wills to His adopted children is nothing short of eternal life with God.

. . . .

3. Before the inheritance is realized fully, God nurtures His children through a process during this earthly life.

   a. As Romans and Galatians tell us, God sends His Spirit into the hearts of His children to witness with their spirit to the authenticity of their adoptive status.

   b. The evidence of this sonship is the fruit of the Spirit in the child's life. Paul delineated the fruit of the Spirit in his epistle to the Galatians: "The fruit of the Spirit is love, joy, peace, patience, kindness, goodness, faithfulness, gentleness and self-control. Against such things there is no law" (Gal. 5:22).

   c. It is God's Spirit who teaches the child of God to live in a relationship to God.

   d. He is also the one who maintains a living communion with God.

CONCLUSION

All of these things are part of this great inheritance.

Today, Faith is just beginning to realize the fullness of her inheritance. But she has all of eternity to experience it.

Now, that's a will worth reading and worth being named in.

A Brief Funeral Message for a Believer

John W. Reed

SCRIPTURE READING

1 Thessalonians 4:13f.

MESSAGE

People usually fit into one of the following three categories.

I.   Some people are ready.

II.   Some people need to get ready.

III. Some people are keeping ready.

In the Father's House

John W. Reed

INTRODUCTION

The memory of our departed loved one is rich in our minds. He is remembered as a faithful father, an honest citizen, a good friend, and a neighbor. *[A brief eulogy of the deceased could be included here.]* May God rest his soul and through His Holy Spirit bring comfort to our hearts. Were he able to speak to us, I believe he would say, "Speak little of me and much of God."

SCRIPTURE READING

I direct your attention to John 14:1–6.

These are the words of our Lord Jesus Christ spoken at the Passover Feast we commonly call the Last Supper. Jesus encouraged His disciples with His last words before His death. He spoke about His departure and sought to bring comfort to the disciples to help them deal with His leaving. Christ's words may bring comfort to all believers today.

MESSAGE

I. Be comforted by the realization that Christ is truly God (John 14:1).
    A. Trust in God the Father.
    B. Trust in Jesus, who is as fully God as is the Father.

II. Let your troubled heart rest in the hope of Christ's return (John 14:2–3).
    A. Be aware that Christ went to His eternal home from which He had come.

B. Rejoice that Christ has gone to prepare a place for His own.
1. It is a place prepared for our departed loved one.
2. It is a place prepared for you, if you have trusted in Jesus for your salvation.
3. It is a place prepared for me.
I take great comfort in the reality that the Architect of the Universe cares enough to prepare a place designed especially for me.

C. Expect Christ to return and take us to that special home.

III. Accept Jesus Christ as the way to the Father's house (John 14:4–6).
A. The way to the Father's house can be known.
B. Trusting Jesus Christ as Savior is the only path to eternal life.
1. Jesus Christ is the way or door to the Father's house.
2. Jesus Christ is the truth about God and how to know Him.
3. Jesus Christ is the source and essence of true life.

CONCLUSION

In the Father's house, both God the Father and God the Son are present. The Bible makes very clear that the only way to the Father's house is through Jesus Christ, the Way, the Truth, and the Life. Our only way to the Father's house is through faith alone in Christ alone. Our departed loved one had that hope and is in the presence of Christ. If you do not know Jesus Christ, will you trust Him now?

The Ultimate Death

Being Made Alive

Keith Willhite

INTRODUCTION

1. As Christians, we need to think about death in light of the ultimate death, the death of Jesus Christ.
2. To do that, we need to think about what His death accomplished.
3. That's possible only as we think about our human condition on this earth and then how Jesus' death gained victory over our condition and our death.
4. Yet, when we come to this gathering today, we do not feel like winners. So, what is this victory and what did Jesus' death have to do with it?

MESSAGE

I. All of us are not necessarily as bad as we could be, but we're as bad *off* as we could be (Eph. 2:1–3; Rom. 3:23).
    A. We are fallen—sinners, each of us.
    B. In this temporal life on earth, we are in a fallen condition.
    C. Thankfully, God is a God of redemption, so He made a plan of redemption for us, a plan that was very costly to God.

II. But God planned an eternal solution for our temporary fallen condition (Eph. 2:4–6; Rom. 6:23).

    Perhaps the most important words in all of biblical theology appear in verse 4: "But God" (NASB).

III. For eternity, God wants to show the riches of His grace (Eph. 2:7–10; 1 Cor. 15:17).
   A. The blood of Jesus purchased us!
   B. Even in this temporal, earthly life, God keeps giving us the victory through the death and resurrection of Jesus.

CONCLUSION

1. As we think about death in light of the ultimate death, the death of Jesus Christ, we see that His death brings life!
2. Our redemption comes through His resurrection.
3. Therefore, we can be sad at the absence we feel today, but as the apostle Paul told the Thessalonian Christians, we should not sorrow as those "who have no hope."
4. In the death and resurrection of Christ, we have the ultimate hope—eternal life!

Funeral of a Believer

God's Promises

Source Unknown

SCRIPTURE READING

John 14:1–6

INTRODUCTION

1. At a time like this, the Word of God becomes very precious and comforting
    *   for only words spoken from the very heart of God can meet our deep needs
    *   and comfort our aching hearts.
2. It was to the Word of God where *[name]* so often went to find strength and help.

    Similarly, we, too, must listen to the Lord as He speaks to us in His Word, the Bible.
3. A passage of Scripture that speaks to us in this hour is found in John 14:1–6.
4. The disciples, like we do today, found themselves in deep distress.

    His words to them remain to give everlasting comfort and revelation to those in distress.

MESSAGE

To those in distress, the Lord promises:

. . . .

I. Peace at Heart (John 14:1)
   A. Read verse 1.
   B. The disciples' whole world seemed to be crumbling around them.

   > The Savior had just told them that Peter, their leader, was going to deny that he ever knew the Lord.

   C. Earlier, Jesus Himself had announced that He was leaving them.
   D. Everything seemed to be happening at once, and everything seemed to be at the verge of collapse.
   E. Jesus noticed their stunned gaze and with a compassionate voice told them,
      1. "Let not your heart be troubled" (v. 1a KJV).
      2. "Ye believe in God, believe also in me" (v. 1b KJV).
   F. Don't be troubled; trust Him; lay hold of Him in your hour of trial.
      1. Our Savior experienced every emotion that we experience. He wept with those who grieved, and He experienced the sorrow that death brings.
      2. He understands and wants us not to be troubled but to trust Him and to lean upon Him.
   G. "Let not your heart be troubled: ye believe in God, believe also in me."

   > (But our Savior not only asks us to trust Him in trials but also instructs us about the future.)

      1. Not only can we have peace of heart as we trust Him but also
      2. He reveals to us that there is . . .

II. A Prepared Place for Us (John 14:2–3)
   A. Yes, the Lord was leaving them, but He had not forgotten them.
   B. He was preparing them a place among His Father's mansions, and someday He would come and take them unto Himself.
   C. That we may be with Him forever.

D. Other portions of Scripture give us more detail of this revelation of the Savior.

E. We are told:
1. In Philippians 1 that when a Christian passes from this life he is with the Lord.
2. In 2 Corinthians 5 that when we are absent from the body we are present (at home) with the Lord.
3. In 1 Corinthians 15 and 1 Thessalonians 4 that one day these bodies that now sleep will be resurrected and united with the spirits, and in this new and incorruptible form, we will ever be with the Lord.
4. In Revelation 21–22 that not only are there mansions in glory (heaven), but also there will be no more sorrow, no more pain, no more sin, no more night, and no more death.

F. So we sorrow today but we do not sorrow as others who have no hope, for we know that *[name]* is with the Lord.
The Savior whom he loved so dearly has prepared a place for him.

G. Do not be troubled; trust in the Lord.
1. You can have peace in your hearts
2. For the Savior loved *[name]* so much that He has prepared a place for him.
(But the Savior, in response to a question by Thomas, makes clear that for anyone to enjoy the prepared place in heaven, he needs to be a prepared person.)

III. A Prepared Person (John 14:4–6)
A. Read verse 6.
B. This verse makes clear that there is only one way to God, and that is through Jesus Christ.
C. Man's sin is what separates him from God.
D. Jesus (God's Son) provided *the* way back to God
1. By Himself bearing our sin in His own body on the tree (1 Peter 2:24).

    2. By becoming our substitute and paying the penalty for our sin (2 Cor. 5:21).

    3. By His death, burial, and resurrection.

E. But these facts of the gospel demand a response.

    1. We can either accept them or

    2. We can reject and ignore them.

F. The Lord asks each of us to believe on Him.

    1. That is, by an act of our will to trust Jesus Christ to be our personal Savior from sin.

    2. To entrust to Him our soul's destiny (on the basis of His work on Calvary) and invite Him into our lives.

G. I invite you right now where you are seated to trust Jesus Christ to be your personal Savior from sin.

H. On the basis of God's Word, if you will do this, your sins are forgiven, you have eternal life, and you stand before God justified (John 3:18, 36; Rev. 3:23–24; 8:1).

I. One did not have to talk long with *[name]* to realize that he had trusted Jesus Christ as his personal Savior.

    1. In the months of his illness, he shared with many people the claims of Jesus Christ and saw several respond in faith to the claims of the gospel.

    2. He had a peace in his heart that the Bible describes as "passeth all understanding" (Phil. 4:7 KJV).

J. It was a peace that came from knowing his Savior.
A Savior who loved him deeply and had a purpose and plan for everything He allowed to come into his life.

K. *[Name]* truly experienced the reality of these verses.

    1. He had a peace in his heart
For he trusted his loving, all-wise Savior.

    2. He had a vital awareness that this life was not all there was to life.

       a. That there is a heaven to which to look forward.

       b. That there is a prepared place for God's children.

    3. And he was himself a prepared person.
He was ready to meet his Savior.

CONCLUSION

1. These truths give us much comfort in this time of sorrow.
2. Two verses in the first chapter of Philippians summarize his life:

According to my earnest expectation and my hope, that in nothing I shall be ashamed, but that with all boldness, as always, so now also *Christ shall be magnified* in my body, *whether it be by life,* or by *death. For me to live* is Christ, and *to die is gain.* (vv. 20–21 KJV, italics added)

How Do You Put Your Hope in God?

Psalm 131

Keith Willhite

INTRODUCTION

1. When we face the death of a loved one, it's difficult to find hope.
2. Hope is really an *objective* concept. The *object* of your hope is really what matters.
3. Repeatedly, the Bible tells us to put our hope in God.
4. But how? How, in sorrow and pain, can you do that?
5. In a very brief psalm, God's Word tells us how to put our hope in God. Let's look together at Psalm 131.

MESSAGE

I. Put your hope in God rather than in your pride.

II. Put your hope in God with a still soul and a childlike faith.

III. Avoid demanding the answers to life's toughest questions.
   A. Again, some humility is necessary.
   B. We don't hope in God through mere intellectual ascent.
   C. Our theology has to explain life (and this psalm does).

. . . .

Conclusion

1. How do you put your hope in God?
2. With genuine humility.
3. When we face the death of a loved one, we probably need humility to hope in God.
4. If you are too proud to hope in God, you probably have not accepted that God is sovereign and has allowed this death.
5. Put your hope in God with humility.

Guidelines for Difficult Funerals

Haddon W. Robinson, James E. Means, and Paul D. Borden

EDITORS' NOTE: During Haddon Robinson's tenure as president of Denver Seminary, the seminary produced a series of audiotapes titled *Expositapes* on various subjects related to preaching. One of the tapes, titled "How to Prepare a Funeral Sermon," included the following excellent guidelines for preparing the difficult funeral, such as a death of a child or the death of an unbeliever. The following guidelines are excerpts from this presentation.[1]

1. Many times in these difficult situations, family members have very difficult questions. We cannot answer all of those questions, especially when non-Christians are asking them.

2. We need to avoid "blaming God" for a seeming tragedy but at the same time not try to "excuse God." God is sovereign and good, and we should not represent Him otherwise. We cannot get into a lengthy explanation of the "problem of evil" in a funeral message. Theologians have debated this for centuries and still do. The single funeral message is not the place to answer these difficult questions. Later, in our work with the family, perhaps some of these questions should and can be addressed. A pastor would probably serve the congregation well to preach on some of these issues in the regular preaching of the church, apart from a specific instance.

3. An implicit assumption here, especially when most of those attending the funeral are not Christians, is that the preacher is

not speaking primarily to the immediate family. Their current grief probably causes them not to hear what the preacher has to say at this moment. That does not mean that we should not try to speak a few words of comfort, but primarily I'm going to speak to the extended friends and family who are there.

4. Suicides present a very difficult situation, regardless of whether the person is a believer. If you're going to touch on the fact that the person is a believer, you probably need to touch on the fact that all of us as believers do things wrong. Moreover, those who attend the funeral of a suicide victim are usually guilt stricken. We do not want to pile onto their guilt. It seems wise to avoid trying to explain a suicide.

5. It is completely inappropriate to suggest that the deceased has gone to a place of eternal damnation. This might be a true statement, but the preacher is not God and cannot know the heart of the person. Much better is the approach that all of us are mortal and need to deal with the questions of eternity.

The Strange Mix of Grief and Worship

A Funeral for a Young Wife and Mother

Charlie Boyd

Introduction

It might seem strange to some people to talk about praise and worship at a time like this, especially because, to some people, our prayers for Sarah in her suffering did not remove her cancer or prevent her death. And when we hear the testimonies and the many good things about Sarah, it only makes the matter of her death more painful to us.

How is it that we should worship God at a time of tragedy?

We need to understand that . . .

Grief Is Not Inconsistent with Worship

We know from the first chapter of the book of Job that Job was a righteous man, a man who was blameless and who feared God and turned away from evil (vv. 1, 8). We also know that he was a man blessed by God. He was blessed with abundant material goods (v. 3) and he was blessed with a family of ten children (v. 2).

We also know something that Job did not know: that God had chosen to use Job as an example of a faithful man. I don't want to focus on the discussion of what went on in heaven between God and Satan, but I do want to highlight how Job responded in a time of family tragedy.

The Bible tells us that wave upon wave of announcements of tragedy were thrust quickly upon this godly man. One messenger reported that all of Job's oxen and donkeys had been stolen and the servants who kept them were slaughtered (vv. 14–15). Then another messenger came to convey the news that lightning had destroyed all of his sheep and those who tended them (v. 16). Then another messenger came to report that a raiding band had stolen his camels and killed his servants who cared for them (v. 17). The most devastating report came last. A wind had struck and collapsed the home of his eldest son, where he and all of the other children were gathered, and all ten children died (vv. 18–19).

Satan was certain that Job's faith would collapse, like the roof of the house of his eldest son, crushing his devotion to God. And there was good reason in Satan's mind to expect Job to turn away from God. After all, Job was a righteous man, a good man. Why *should* God allow tragedy to strike not only his possessions but also his children? The text tells us that Job's habit was to pray for his children, asking God's special care for them. Well, God didn't answer his prayer. So it seemed logical that Job would conclude that God is not good and loving, because, if God was good, He certainly would have answered this prayer and spared the lives of his children.

How did Job respond? He tore his clothes and shaved his head—all signs of mourning and grief. But what he did after this is the key to our comfort in the face of grief. Job fell to the ground and worshiped God, and these are his words:

> "Naked I came from my mother's womb, and naked I shall return there. The LORD gave and the LORD has taken away. Blessed be the name of the LORD." Through all this Job did not sin nor did he blame God. (vv. 21–22 NASB)

The first point I want to make is this. Grief is not inconsistent with worship and worship is not inconsistent with grief.

Job worshiped God with a torn robe, a shaved head, and a tear-stained face—all genuine tokens of his grief. But in his grief, he did not lose sight of his God. In fact, it was in his grief that God became even more real.

I do not want you to think that grief is inappropriate tonight. It is right, it is normal, and it is expected. But in our grief, we will find consolation only as we are able to worship God in the face of tragedy. We will find comfort only when we do not blame God, when we do not see God as being in any way "at fault," as doing wrong in Sarah's death. We find comfort when we trust that God's ways are right, although at times His ways and His timing don't make sense to us.

Grief is not inconsistent with worship, and second . . .

Grief Is Not Inconsistent with Faith

We grieve because godly parents lost a precious daughter. We grieve because a godly young man lost his wife. We grieve because a little baby boy lost his mother. We grieve because brothers and sisters lost their sister. We grieve because we all have lost a faithful friend, an enthusiastic teacher, and an inspiring musician. That grief is not selfish. God made us to live in relationships with each other. He created us with a need that only human companionship could fill, and when that relationship is severed—even temporarily—we feel the pain, the sadness, and the hurt.

And grieving is right and appropriate, but we do not grieve as those "who have no hope." That's how the apostle Paul puts it in 1 Thessalonians 4:13.

Because we take comfort and we comfort one another with these truths—that Sarah is with the Lord, and, as Pastor Mark reminded us at the graveside, to die and be with the Lord is gain for her—we are comforted by the fact that we will be reunited one day.

Conclusion

British literary critic and Christian apologist C. S. Lewis noted that the first thing we will say when we enter heaven is, "Of course. Of course." What didn't make sense will make sense. What we *didn't* understand—*couldn't* understand from our limited perspective—we *will* understand because we will see it from an eternal perspective.

I submit to you that, in the face of Sarah's home going, there is

· ·

more than enough reason to worship God. But you will be able to do that only when you have placed your faith in Christ as your personal hope for heaven, just as Sarah did. He died on the Cross and rose from the dead that we all could have what Sarah has today: eternal life.

PRAYER

Father, I thank You for the life of Sarah O'Donnell. I pray that through faith in Jesus Christ each of us may worship You through her death, that we would grow in faith through her death. May we rejoice in Your goodness and power and in Your plans that are beyond our ability to understand on this side of heaven.

May each of us here, through faith in the person and work of Jesus Christ, experience the peace that passes all understanding, the peace that assures us that as You are present with us, Sarah is present with You. Amen.

The Untimely Death of a Young Man

An Evangelistic Message

Charlie Boyd

INTRODUCTION

Several days ago, a terrible thing happened. To make it worse, there is no adequate explanation as to why it happened. We want to believe that it didn't happen. We wish we could "wake up" and realize that this was all a bad dream. We long for life to be the way it was. But then we realize this is for real, and life has changed.

You are here today because you love Paul; you love this family, and you want to support them; and you want them to know that you care. Really, we are here because we need each other at a time like this. The temptation is to want to go off and hide and to try to handle this alone. But everyone here needs a supportive community to make it through intact; all of us are hurting, and we need each other.

We are also here because we need God; we need to hear a word from God. We know that nothing *we* say will "make things better," and that nothing *we* say can undo what has happened. But comfort comes when we open our hearts to hear God speak. And believe me, He is speaking through all of this. We need to allow God to speak to the hurt and even the anger that we might feel. We need a word of hope and ultimately that word can come only from Him.

Because I've only been here a short time, I did not have the privilege of knowing Paul the way many of you did.

Each of you has your own memories and moments that you will carry with you the rest of your life.

. . . .

MESSAGE

We have come today shocked, numbed, confused, hurt, and angry.

- We don't know *what* to think.
- We don't know *how* to think.

We've got questions. We don't understand. When something bad happens, we tend to look for someone to blame. Often, God gets the blame. After all, He is the most likely candidate. I mean, *if* there is a God and *if* He could have prevented Paul's death, why didn't He? *If* God is all-powerful and *if* God is really good, then why didn't He use some of that power and goodness to save him? The first question boils down to this one.

Why Did God Let This Happen?

I cannot tell you specifically why God allowed Paul to die, but I can tell you something about the way life generally happens in this world. I can tell you why horrible things like this happen *in general* and how God figures into the whole thing.

The Bible tells us that we live in a "fallen" world, a world that has gone wrong. Things are not the way they are supposed to be, not the way they should be. Sin, sickness, suffering, and death were not a part of God's original plan. He wanted things to be different, but He would not force us to live His way. As a result, our first grandparents and everyone in every generation after them chose to live life without much thought of God. In fact, if there is one way to sum up what the world is like today, it would be that the vast majority of people on planet Earth go about their daily lives with little or no thought of God.

And what we see in our world today—all of the wrongs that need righting, all of the disease that needs healing, all of the pain and hurt and suffering and death, and all of the garbage—has come because generation after generation our world has refused, for the most part, to let God be God. That's what the Bible calls sin.

Mark it down. If people paid attention to God's original design for life, the world would be a very different place.

But things are not the way they should be. And, as a result, God is not at peace with the world that we have messed up. When people blame God for all of the bad in the world, I can almost hear Him thunder, "That's not Me; that's not anything like Me!" God is the enemy of sin and sickness and death. He didn't bring these evils into the world. They came as a result of humanity's indifference and rebellion against God.

Although God's perfect love was betrayed, God did not abandon us. God instead gave the promise of life. He promised to send One who would remove our sentence of death and show us the way back to life as God meant it to be.

And the Promised One did come. God appeared among us, and His name was Jesus. Peter characterized Jesus as one who "went about doing good and healing all that were oppressed by the Devil." Jesus' life was one long protest against the pain and suffering that sin brought into this world.

Jesus understands the sting of death that we feel. He Himself wept at the untimely death of His friend Lazarus, which tells me that He is weeping with us today. He hurts because we hurt. Jesus' tears tell me how grieved God is when He sees the hurt that is so common in our fallen world.

Jesus not only understands the sting of death but also experienced that sting firsthand. Jesus was despised and rejected and finally crucified at the hands of His own people. By dying for us, Jesus paid the penalty for our sin and removed the offense that separated us from God.

But there's more. Three days later, Jesus rose from the dead. Hundreds of eyewitnesses saw Him, spoke with Him, and touched Him. By conquering death, He proved that He was the Promised One who is able to give life to those who will trust Him for it.

You see, Jesus shows us the way back to God—the way back to a life that brings freedom and forgiveness and peace and the promise of a future life with no disease or death.

So my "general" answer to why horrible things like this happen is that things are not the way they're supposed to be—not now, not here. Every time a tragedy like this happens, it's a reminder that something is terribly wrong.

But it also reminds us that God has taken the initiative, by sending Jesus, to make things right again.

This leads to my next question.

What About Paul? Where Is He Right Now?

Paul is in heaven, not because he was a good son, a good brother, a good husband, a good friend, or a good church member. He was all of those things and more. No, Paul is in heaven for one reason: Paul had trusted Jesus as his Savior. He knew what it meant to be forgiven. He knew what real life was all about. The Bible makes clear that the one thing—the only thing—that matters is what you do with Jesus. And Paul believed with all of his heart that Jesus was God's answer to his own sin and death problem.

God never forces anyone to believe in Him. God is not going to force you to live His way. He gives us the choice to love and follow Him or continue to go our own way. Going our way is another way to define sin. The Bible tells us that this life lasts only a little while, and then we will have to answer for how we have lived and what we've done with Jesus. Those who choose to live their lives independent of God will be sentenced to endless anguish, separated from God. But those who have trusted Christ for forgiveness and life will live life in its fullness and enjoy God for all eternity.

You see, where God is, there is peace and life. There is no pain, no tears, no sin, no suffering, no disease, and no death. There is only life the way God intended it to be from the beginning. And that's where Paul is because Paul took Jesus and His promises seriously.

Let me read a few of those promises to you.

> Yet to all who received him, to those who believed in his name,
> he gave the right to become children of God. (John 1:12)

For God so loved the world that he gave his one and only Son, that whoever believes in him shall not perish but have eternal life. (John 3:16)

I tell you the truth, he who believes has everlasting life. (John 6:47)

Jesus said to her, "I am the resurrection and the life. He who believes in me will live, even though he dies; and whoever lives and believes in me will never die. Do you believe this?" (John 11:25–26)

Those are just a few examples of the promises upon which Paul hung his hope. There are many more promises just like that. God promises forgiveness and life to anyone who trusts Jesus Christ as their hope for heaven. And as a child of God, Paul is now enjoying life and peace in the presence of God.

Here's the final question. It's the question that Jesus asked.

Do You Believe This?

What about you? What are you going to do with the sadness, the hurt, and the anger that you feel? What are you going to do with all of that?

You see, at a time like this, people can either lower their faith or lean on their faith. Some people reject God altogether, whereas others find faith in Jesus to be the one thing that is capable of carrying them through.

What about it? Will you believe that Jesus is the way back to God? Will you believe that when He died on the Cross, He died so that *your* sins could be forgiven? Will you believe that, as a result of His resurrection, you can have the kind of life that lasts forever? It's not about simply being a good person. It's certainly not about having your name on a church roll. It's about Jesus and what you do with Him.

Here are two final thoughts.

- *Don't let your questions drive you away from God.* Don't let your questions become a barrier between you and God. *"Why?"* is a question that no one can really answer. No one knows why. Maybe faith is not knowing the answer to why. Maybe faith is being willing to wait for the answer. The answer to the why question might not come in our lifetime. The Bible says that looking at things from an eternal perspective now is hard. It's like looking through a dark glass. It's all so dim. But one day, we will see face-to-face, the way Paul sees right now.
- *Don't just hold on to your feelings.* Tell God how you feel. Talk to Him just as you would talk to another person. He can handle your hurt. He's not put off by your tears. (He gave us tear ducts and He expects us to use them.) Tears are not inconsistent with faith. We sorrow, but not as those who have no hope. Grief is not an enemy; it is a friend. It is a natural process of walking through hurt and sorrow, and it is not a denial of faith.

This might surprise you, but God is not upset with you because you might be upset with Him. He knows that you are wounded. Just tell Him about it. The Psalms are a good place to learn how to pour out your heart to God when you don't understand what's happening to you, but at the same time, you are trying to hold on to Him with all you've got.

What God offers us at a time like this is not answers to all of our questions. Instead, He offers us Himself. He says, "Trust Me. Keep trusting Me." He tells us that He's the enemy of death and that He has sent Jesus to remove the sting of death.

The Bible asks, "Where, O death, is your victory?" (1 Cor. 15:55). It then gives the answer: "Thanks be to God! He gives *us* the victory through our Lord Jesus Christ" (v. 57, italics added).

A little girl was sitting with her mother in a field of wild flowers when a bee landed on her mother's arm. Instinctively, the mother slapped the bee, which stung her in the process. The bee fell on the little girl's thigh and she began to scream and cry. The mother calmly said, "Don't be afraid. The bee cannot hurt you now. He left his stinger in me."

Folks, Friday morning, Jesus said to Paul, "It's time to come home. Don't be afraid. Death left its stinger in me."

CONCLUSION

God invites you to turn away from the life you've been living on your own and turn to Him. He invites you to choose the life that Jesus offers, and His invitation is open to all who hear and turn to Him, trusting Jesus to forgive their sin and to give them the abundant life that He made possible through His death and resurrection.

Would you do that if you've not done it before? Trust Jesus as your hope for heaven. He died and rose again to prove that He can conquer death and give you life. I guarantee that nothing would make Paul happier than to know that one day he will see you in heaven. How do you do it? Turning to Jesus and trusting Him as your personal Savior means telling God that you are sorry for living life your way and leaving Him out. It means asking God to forgive you of your sin and asking Him to give you eternal life just as He promised He would.

You can do that now.

Does Death Really Sting?

Service for a Faithful Believer, Spoken to Believers

Keith Willhite

DURING MY YEARS IN SEMINARY, I worked a part-time job servicing (mostly cleaning) swimming pools. I was "the pool man." It did not take me long in this position to discover that red wasps like pool equipment. They especially like the wooden fences used to "hide" the pool equipment in the backyard. Those fences are perfect for building nests. It also did not take me long to discover that I do not like red wasps. Without any provocation, they sting pool men! After a few stings, I decided, "That hurts!"

Stings hurt. The good thing is that they don't hurt for very long. When I got stung, I usually jumped into the pool. It was the closest thing I had to ice. Then I put some Benadryl or something similar on the sting and went on to finish my route. In a few minutes, usually, the sting was gone. Then came the hard part: five days of itching. But soon that, too, was gone.

In the New Testament, the apostle Paul refers to death as a sting. More accurately, he refers to "the sting of death." Like the sting of the red wasp, death sometimes comes suddenly and with little warning. It can be soothed initially with a few hugs and comforting "medicine." Then comes the hard part: several days, even weeks sometimes, of irritation and ache. But that's where the comparison stops. In fact, when Paul mentioned the sting of death, he talked about it almost in a tone of mockery. Listen to his words:

> "Where, O death, is your victory? Where, O death, is your sting?" The sting of death is sin, and the power of sin is the law. But thanks be to God! He gives us the victory through our Lord Jesus Christ. (1 Corinthians 15:55–57)

In this passage, Paul is telling the Christians in Corinth—and you and me—that Satan seemed to be victorious in the Garden of Eden and at the Cross of Jesus. But in reality, God turned Satan's victory into defeat when Jesus rose from the dead. Thus, death should no longer be a source of dread or fear.

Of course, death still has a short-lived sting. It comes suddenly and painfully; none of us would deny that. But it can be a short-lived sting because we do not grieve as those who have no hope (1 Thess. 4).

The sting of death struck us this past weekend. We cannot explain, or even begin to try to understand, why such a faithful Christian man was struck by a drunk driver and his life immediately taken away. We'd like to think that God's people would be sheltered from such tragedies, but we all know differently. The good news is that the sting of Stephen's death can be a short-lived sting. Yes, there are long-term implications for you, Rachael, and your family. There are implications for our church family. And I hope that all of us will serve you and help you as only the family of God can. But because of what Jesus did, the sting of death has no victory here today.

You might think, *Well, how do you* know *that?* Because I knew Stephen and the life he led. He was so obviously Spirit filled. His life manifested the fruit of the Spirit. If anyone abided in Christ, it was Stephen. So, today, Stephen is with his Savior, Jesus. And although we feel the sting of his loss, we do not have to feel the sting of defeat. Jesus is the victor, even in this.

I like the way Dr. Bryan Chapell described this reality in his book *The Wonder of It All.* He wrote,

> But are the treasures of our resurrection just for another day? Does heaven only offer "pie in the sky by and by"? Not for the apostle Paul. Though the full realities of our resurrection remain future, he rejoices that the benefits begin now. Heaven not only grants us joy in the tomorrow; it grants us strength for today.[2]

That is why those of us who are Christians can face life, not with

. . . .

naivete but with genuine hope—assurance of our salvation and eternal destiny with God. We must remind ourselves of that truth today. That's not just some "pie-in-the-sky" theology. Those are the facts!

"Where, O death, is your victory? Where, O death, is your sting?" The sting of death is sin, and the power of sin is the law. But thanks be to God! He gives us the victory through our Lord Jesus Christ. (1 Corinthians 15:55–57)

Today, Stephen is enjoying his new home and the victory celebration. Only Jesus can claim victory. He defeated the sting of death to win for us. Of course, your loss stings today, but may it be short-lived for Stephen is a victor, thanks to the Lord Jesus. As Paul wrote, "Thanks be to God!"

The Funeral Service of an Adult Suicide

Unlucky Thirteen?

Jeff Watson

EDITORS' NOTE: This message also speaks about the issue of cremation.

INTRODUCTION

We are gathered here today to say farewell to Brent Douglas, born as the last of thirteen children. This past Wednesday, our worlds stopped as we all caught our collective breath in shock. Here, at the age of forty-one, Brent had taken his own life, purposely inhaling the fumes from his car to put an end to his downward spiral of emotional pain.

But we are gathered here today not only to say farewell to Brent but also to comfort one another, to gather strength for tomorrow, and to renew our understanding of the Word of God. As both testaments confirm, "The grass withereth, the flower fadeth: but the word of our God shall stand for ever" (Isa. 40:8 KJV; see also 1 Peter 1:24b).

MESSAGE

About Brent

I am told that Brent sometimes considered himself "The Unlucky Thirteen." As the thirteenth child in this good family, Brent probably did suffer more than most of you; after all, he was only seven when your father died and ten when your mother's cancer left him an orphan. With the hopeful lament of the psalmist, Brent could have written, "When my father and my mother forsake me, then the LORD will take me up" (Ps. 27:10 KJV).

And in those years when he lived with you older brothers and sisters, even later when he came to live on the Boys Farm, and finally when he joined the U.S. Army, we are certain that the Lord was whispering in his ear, "Come unto me, [Brent,] all ye that labour and are heavy laden [emotionally and spiritually] and I will give you rest" (Matt. 11:28 KJV). During those years, we understand that he did hear and respond positively to the gospel.

About the Survivors

To you today—big brothers and sisters, little nieces and nephews—Jesus says in all compassion, "Don't drown in guilt." In circumstances like these, you could torture yourself with regret, dreaming day and night, "If only, if only." A devilish skeleton could hang in your closet as you replay the ninth inning over and over again. But no "I told you so" ever brought someone back. Even emergency room physicians have a hard time knowing how hopeless a person feels.

The Apostle of Love says to you,

> If [you] confess [y]our sins [any shortcomings you remember], [God] is faithful and just to forgive [you] [y]our sins, and to cleanse [you] from all unrighteousness.... For if [y]our heart condemns [you] [tempting you to feel guiltier than you really are], God is greater than [y]our heart, and knoweth all things.... If [y]our heart condemn [you] not, then have ... confidence toward God. (1 John 1:9; 3:20–21 KJV)

About Responsibility

Listen, Jesus was perfect, never selfish, never impatient; but His own disciple, His student-friend Judas, hung himself with a noose of unbearable guilt (Matt. 27:3–10; Acts 1:16–20). You aren't perfect; none of us is. But Jesus—as perfect as He was—still lost one. So remember, Judas made a choice. Last Wednesday, Brent made a choice. And today, you can make a choice to say yes to God and no to the Devil (James 4:7–8a).

Don't let the Adversary destroy you with his ancient weapon, the blame game (1 Peter 5:8); don't let the Accuser of the brethren flood your heart with condemnation or spit the venom of hurtful criticism through your lips (Rev. 12:10). If you blame yourself or blame another person, you only keep the destruction going and threaten to lose more lives in the after quake of depression. No one can take full responsibility for another person's choices. For each one "shall bear his own burden" (Gal. 6:5 KJV; see 1 Cor. 3:12–15).

About Spiritual Warfare

In John 10:10–18, Jesus, the ultimate Coach, lays out the playing field. On one side of the field is the Thief, the Devil. He has one escalating agenda—"to steal, and to kill, and to destroy" (v. 10a KJV). He wants to steal your innocence, rob your trust, kill your joy, and push you off the cliff of life, destroying all hope that you will ever get victory over this wicked loss. This week, Brent caught a hand grenade from hell. Maybe he had thrown it back at the Tempter a thousand times (1 Thess. 3:5). But on Wednesday, he caught it and held on. Four out of five Americans have held that grenade in their hand, at least for a moment. Brent wasn't unlucky, jinxed, cursed, or destined to live a bad-luck life. He was the object of sulfuric hatred, and he got tired of fighting, maybe even lazy in fighting.

About Redemption

But let us not forget that Brent was also the object of divine love. Jesus, the Good Shepherd, called to Brent from the other sideline of choice. "I don't come to steal," Jesus said. "I come to give. I don't come to kill; I come to give life. I don't come to destroy; I come to give life abundantly" (see John 10:10). Jesus understood temptation; He had been tempted "in all points . . . like as we are" (Heb. 4:15 KJV), even tempted to throw Himself off the temple (Matt. 4:6) in what would have been a satanically sure, suicidal plunge. But instead of killing Himself, Jesus gave Himself (John 10:11).

As the Good Shepherd, Jesus knew Brent by name (v. 14) and lovingly laid down His life for Brent on the Cross to pay for his sins, all of them: past, present, and future (vv. 15, 17–18). We don't believe that Brent's death this week was "the unpardonable sin"; there's only one sin that seems to last forever—permanently rejecting the Good Shepherd (John 3:36; Rev. 20:15). The only unpardonable sin is the sin of utter unbelief.

About Hope

A day like today could tempt even the strongest among us to doubt God. But God says, "There hath no temptation [no trial or test] taken you [or Brent], but such as is common to man: but God is faithful, who will not permit you to be tempted [or Brent to be tempted] above that ye are able [he was able]; but will with the temptation also make a way of escape, that ye may be able to bear it" (1 Cor. 10:13 KJV). No matter how we feel, most problems are temporary and solvable. Felt hopelessness is not true hopelessness.

About Life

Moses, who had seen hundreds of thousands of his peers die in the wilderness, reminds us that God is eternally strong (Ps. 90:1–2). Thus, this time-wisened psalmist could pray, "LORD, thou hast been our dwellingplace in all generations" (v. 1 KJV); their dwelling place was not Egypt, not Midian, not the Wilderness, not Canaan, and not even in their parents or their brothers and sisters. Even Jesus said, "Abide in me, and I in you" (John 15:4 KJV); let Me be your dwelling place.

Although God is eternally strong, humanity is sinfully weak (Ps. 90:3–11). Thus, we are warned against trying desperately to climb some ladder of success only to find when we get to the top that it's been leaning against the wrong wall. Because God is eternally strong and man is sinfully weak, grace is desperately needed (vv. 12–17).

About Suicide

Although suicide is not the unpardonable sin, it is an awful sin; it is the sin of self-murder. But if God forgave Saul of Tarsus, the one we know as the apostle Paul, we know that God can forgive even the sin of murder (Acts 7:54–8:3; 1 Tim. 1:12–17). Somehow, being in the image of God is a double-edged sword (Gen. 1:26–27). Higher than the animals, we suffer with the blessed melancholy of conscience, creativity, and language; with these God-shaped gifts, we can feel piercing guilt. We can invent tools that destroy. And we can rationalize our folly until it "makes sense."

When others killed themselves—seven in the Bible: Abimelech, Samson, Saul, his armor bearer, Ahithophel, Zimri, and Judas—suicide was never the major issue. Just like a Polaroid can capture any of us with a weird grimace, in an awkward pose, or wearing a confused expression, the central issue is not how his life ended in that moment. The central issue is the long-play video of life. How did Brent live over the years? How did he walk with God from then till now? Indeed, how would God write his biography, or yours, if today were the last day?

About Cremation

Some of you might be upset today about Brent's request in his final note that he be cremated. You might be bothered that in the Bible the bodies of notorious criminals were sometimes consumed with fire (Gen. 38:24; Lev. 20:14; 21:9; Amos 2:1). But we also read in the Scriptures how the Green Beret of Saul's day retrieved his body after it had been desecrated by pagan enemies; this special force of brave men lovingly rescued their king's body from its place of public humiliation and burned it before burial (1 Sam. 31:1–6, 12–13; 1 Chron. 10:12). And so I am at peace with the decision to honor Brent's request and for us to carry his ashes and to inter them between the headstones of his parents.

Conclusion

Don't bury Brent's life in silence, in secrecy, or in shame. Let's learn again how to feel, how to talk, and how to trust. As we go forward from today, let's accept the challenge to love each other "not . . . in word, neither in tongue; but in deed and in truth" (1 John 3:18 KJV). May you find the grace to forgive yourselves for not stopping this, to forgive each other for not being perfect, to forgive Brent for sinning in this way, and to "forgive" God for allowing all of this to happen.

The Interment of a SIDS Baby

Tears in Heaven

Jeff Watson

INTRODUCTION

We've gathered together today to say farewell to a loving little lad, Andrew David Kessler. I know most of you had met him and all of you had loved him during his seven brief weeks on earth. But today, we lay his little body in this resurrection ground. Today, we confront an awful reality: that death does not come merely to some; it comes most certainly to all. We confront the news that death does not always politely wait its turn after a long, happy life. All too frequently, death smashes down the door, charging brutally into our lives for no apparent reason. On a day like today, when Isaiah and Peter's words remind us that "the grass withereth, the flower fadeth," we feel as though we are eyewitnesses to the plucking of a barely budded rose. But what would we do without their concluding assurance that "the word of our God [still] stand[s] for ever" (Isa. 40:8 KJV; see 1 Peter 1:24b)?

THE LIFE OF CHILDREN

God's Attitude

Despite our sorrow today, we are encouraged to remember that God loves children. How else can we understand Solomon's words when he writes, "Children are an heritage of the LORD" (Ps. 127:3 KJV)? Not just some children but all children. Not just offspring born "perfect"

233

but even our kin born with disabilities. Not just sons and daughters destined to live long lives but little boys and girls who are here only for a moment and then vanish away (James 4:14).

Christ's Atonement

How else can we read God's heart but to sense His tender compassion toward children? When Hannah and Elkanah brought little Samuel into the mentoring of Eli's priesthood, the Scripture says, "Samuel did not yet know the LORD" (1 Sam. 3:7 KJV); but, by placing children in good families, such as the Kesslers here, God has shown us His commitment to surround children with love and goodness.

When Jesus drew little children onto His lap (Matt. 18:1–14), He not only showed us that it takes childlike faith to enter the kingdom but also that spiritual greatness is measured less by who notices us and more by whom we notice: the little ones. Indeed, in His homily about children, Jesus teaches us something about departed children: "Their [Gr., *angeloi*—not angels but departed spirits] do always behold the face of my father in heaven" (Matt. 18:10 KJV; see Acts 12:15). Although children might die physically—that's their connection to Adam and Eve— a child such as Andrew David, at seven weeks, never lived long enough to sin knowingly or to believe savingly. He, it seems, would be covered by the atonement of Christ: "Behold the Lamb of God, which taketh away the sin of the world" (John 1:29 KJV); "not for our [sins] only, but also for the sins of the whole world" (1 John 2:2 KJV).

THE LOSS OF CHILDREN

Rob's Tragic Morning

Three days ago, when Rob got up to go to work at 4:30 A.M., he was expecting to shuffle into Andy's room and watch him sleeping quietly. If the baby stirred, Rob was expecting to hold him for a few minutes and maybe give him a bottle, the same routine in which they had been for nearly two months. Instead, he was shocked to find death. Calling out for Monica to call 911, he already knew that it was too late. As a paramedic, he knew that death had occurred probably hours before: "SIDS death," they call it—"Sudden Infant Death Syndrome." Typical of these cases, the autopsy gave us no clues.

Clapton's Lyric Mourning

Monica and Robert are not the first parents to bury a baby and, sadly, they will not be the last. Last year, legendary guitarist Eric Clapton was rocked by the death of his son, Connor. In a freak accident, Connor had fallen forty-nine stories from the balcony of their Manhattan high-rise. In a grief-stricken tribute to their son, daddy Clapton wrote the song that will now be sung for you: "Tears in Heaven."

[Special Music]

Didn't you hear that melancholic yearning in this song, a yearning for reunion?

[quote song lyrics]

If anything good comes out of these tragedies, it is that God bends our knees, brings us closer to Himself. Although Clapton won a Grammy for that single and album, he reached back farther than that, all the way to another album, the book of Revelation. Clapton wrote that he knew there would be no more tears in heaven. In an apostolic vision of the future, the near-martyr John had written, "And I saw a new heaven and a new earth: for the first heaven and the first earth were passed away. . . . And God shall wipe away all tears from their eyes; and there shall be no more death, neither sorrow, nor crying, neither shall there be any more pain: for the former things are passed away. . . . Behold, I make all things new" (Rev. 21:1, 4–5 KJV).

But the British musician leaves open one dramatic question: not whether our babies are welcomed into heaven but will older children and adults be?

. . . .

David's Future Morning

Another grief-stricken father sharpens that point. When King David buried his one-week old son, David's insides felt as though they were exploding (2 Sam. 12); yet, in his lyrics there was hope: "I shall go to him, but he shall not return to me" (v. 23b KJV). That old warrior knew that death was final on this side, but he had rock-solid hope of re-union with his boy. Why? Because David had admitted his sin to God: "Against thee, thee only, have I sinned" (Ps. 51:4 KJV).

David knew that all of his spiritual regrets—thoughts, words, and actions that should never have been, as well as all of the good that should have been—needed an atonement beyond him. He cried to God for forgiveness: "Have mercy upon me, O God . . . cleanse me from my sin . . . and I shall be whiter than snow" (vv. 1a, 2b, 7b KJV). Daddy David, who had received the gift of salvation some years before, asked God to renew that gift upon the death of his son: "Restore unto me the joy of thy salvation" (v. 12a KJV).

CONCLUSION

The Butterfly Analogy

It all comes down to faith. Do you believe that death ends it all, or might little Andy have launched away from this veil of tears, like a beautiful new butterfly wrestling free from its incubating chrysalis? Can you embrace the idea that this little lad, who left the warmth and safety of his mother's womb seven weeks ago, has now blossomed again into a fuller life amid the angels, the saints, and his grandparents?

Flying Blind

A few years ago, I was reminded what it means to live by faith. On board a little seven-passenger plane, I was casually speeding toward a two-bit airstrip on the side of a mountain near eastern Tennessee. As we approached Bluefield, Virginia, a thunderous summer shower overtook our sky. The sun disappeared and the little plane was whipped like the front car on a world-class roller coaster. Our cabin became anxiously silent, as every passenger leaned toward the aisle to look through the cockpit into the ominous airspace ahead.

With windshield wipers in high gear, I felt more like I was on a submarine plunging through ocean depths than on a Cessna hurdling toward a mountain town. Rather than panicking, the pilot picked up the radio and began talking to a control tower miles away. The copilot pulled out a black, spiral-bound notebook and laid it open against the control panel. There, in black-and-white, was a diagram of the airstrip: our destination. Someone, who had been there ahead of us, had laid out everything we needed to know: altitude, angle, approach speed, everything. By now, the pilots were no longer looking through the windshield; they were staring at the diagram of an unseen place, talking to invisible friends. For fifteen minutes, the plane continued in its sober silence, slowing, descending, and angling, until at the last minute the ground appeared just before we touched down.

That's our life: learning to believe there's a land unseen; not panicking but charting our course by the good book written by one who's gone before; and learning to reorient our approach through two-way communication with the control tower of heaven.

The Passport Analogy

Over the years when C. Everett Koop was earning his worldwide reputation as a pediatric surgeon at the Children's Hospital in Philadelphia, he talked to hundreds of kids about passports. He explained that death was not the end; it was a transition. Using concrete illustrations, he taught them that death meant travel. "The key question," he would say, "is whether you have the passport—faith in Jesus—to enter that new land called heaven." Do you have it today? Are you ready to travel home?

. . . .

The Boy and the Bridge

What would it be like to travel home today by faith? Would it hurt? Would it make you lonely? I think it would be like the experience of a little European boy from several generations ago. The dad in this home had weekly business in a distant town, requiring him to take a very long walk through the Alps. These trips would cover such a great distance that the father would leave before dawn and return after dark. As his son grew up, the boy used to beg to go along on these weekly trips, but his dad knew that his little legs could not keep up.

After years of refusing, the father finally gave in, reluctantly. As the two spent their morning walking, they crossed a high, rope bridge, with a few missing wooden slats, suspended over a rocky valley. With the daylight on their side and the father leading the way, the two crossed the ravine easily. But, as the day wore on and their business was complete, the little boy began to worry. He could picture the bridge but began to fear the bridge after dusk. As the two walked silently toward home, the boy kept punctuating their silence with worries about the bridge and the missing slats, worries about the impending darkness and the deep gorge below. Unable to cross the bridge before they came to it, the dad was unable to give the boy full assurance. With strong arms and a loving confidence, the father finally scooped up the boy and began carrying him piggyback.

The next thing the boy remembered, his eyes were blinking open with the early rays of sunlight. Uncertain, he made out the silhouette of his father, standing in a doorway. "Dad, what happened?" the boy puzzled. "What about the bridge?" he worried out loud. "Well, son, you fell asleep with your arms around my neck. I carried you across the bridge and laid you safely in your own bed. You've just awakened on the other side."

Two Sets of Plans

Memorial Service Following a Community Tragedy

Bill Oudemolen

EDITORS' NOTE: The tragedy at Columbine High School took place on April 20, 1999, in Littleton, Colorado. Fourteen students and one teacher were killed in a shooting spree. Foothills Bible Church hosted two of the funerals where hundreds of family members, students, and teachers gathered to mourn the losses. Pastor Bill's words, "What Satan intended for evil, God intended for good," helped people to put the tragedy into perspective and encouraged them to place their hope and trust in God.

INTRODUCTION

I, like many of you, have been overwhelmed this week. I think what has been particularly overwhelming for me, in addition to the obvious, has been the requirement to stand and speak publicly in the midst of a crisis like this, and to speak hope, and healing, and comfort into a situation that is so obviously devastating, and disruptive to us. Like many of you, in the early hours of this I was in a state of shock. And then in downtimes, at night when I wasn't sleeping, I'd turn to God and say, "God, You know what we need right now? We need You to speak. We need You to talk." There are a lot of people talking, and believe me, we've just seen the tip of the iceberg on conversations and discussions that will take place about the events that have unfolded here in our city this week. So I suppose at some level we all say, "Is there a word from God?" and I come today to tell you that there is. I have some fears. My fear is that I appear glib, or too articulate, or trite. Let me tell you something.

There's one reason I can even be standing here today, and that is the power of God and the prayers of His people. I knew we would be in church on Sunday, and I knew we would want a word from God. Most of you would probably predict that this would not be like every other Sunday for us today, and that's true. I've been searching the Scriptures in my mind and my heart in those sleepless hours in the middle of the night, "Lord what is Your Word for us now? What do You have to say to us today?" One of the stories I've landed on is the story of the life of Joseph in the book of Genesis. I want to turn to this first as our starting point for today, under some thoughts I want to share with you that I've entitled "Two Sets of Plans." Let's pray together:

> Father, we've been doing a lot of praying in these days, and we're going to continue. We pray for the service that will be held just a few hours from now over at the Mann Theatre parking lot. God, we ask that You will lift up Your Word and Your name at that service. From the names of the people that we've heard will be there, Lord we know that they know You, and would You allow that they will have great strength to take the time to talk about Jesus in this place. For other churches across our city, our sister churches that are going through the same thing we are, God, we lift them up. We're all saying the same thing to You. We need a word from You. We want to hear You speak today, and our hearts and our minds, quite obviously, are turned directly toward You today. As You speak, we will listen, and I pray that we'll listen in a way that will last. In Jesus' name we pray. Amen.

Joseph: Satan's Plan Versus God's Plan

All of you know the story of Joseph in the Old Testament, the book of Genesis. His story is about rejection, imprisonment, brokenness, and abandonment. He is sold into slavery by his brothers, he ends up in Egypt in the house of Pharaoh as a servant, and assumes maybe things will go well there. Of course they don't. In fact, he's accused of trying to seduce Potaphar's wife. Because of that he's put in prison. He's sitting in a prison cell contemplating what God told him all the way back at the beginning of the story—that there would be a great thing that would happen in his life, and there would be great things that would flow, and he would be a great leader for God—and there he is sitting in prison. As the story goes, one of the people who was in prison with him was connected to the Pharaoh, and as a result of that connection, Joseph ends up before Pharaoh interpreting a dream that he had. The next thing you know, Pharaoh has a right-hand man, his vice president, his second in charge. Joseph's family, of course, doesn't know this, but they eventually find out. They go to Egypt because there is a famine in their land, and upon finding their brother, they're filled with fear. The Bible makes it very clear that the fear was pervasive, and here's what they feared. They feared that their brother Joseph would somehow unleash his vengeance against them because of what they had done to him. Well, while their father was living, it didn't seem quite as serious, or at least it seemed they may be in some sort of a protected environment, but, as you know, it comes to the time right at the end of the book of Genesis when Joseph's father dies. It says in chapter 50 of Genesis,

> When Joseph's brothers saw that their father was dead, they said, "What if Joseph holds a grudge against us and pays us back for all the wrongs we did to him?" So they sent word to Joseph, saying, "Your father left these instructions before he died: 'This is what you are to say to Joseph: I ask you to forgive your brothers the sins and the wrongs they committed in treating you so badly.' Now please forgive the sins of the servants of the God of your father." When their message came to him, Joseph wept. His brothers then came and threw themselves down before him. "We are your slaves," they said. But Joseph said to them, "Don't be afraid. Am I in the place of God?" (vv. 15–19)

Now listen to the next verse, and particularly listen to it in light of the tragedy of this past Tuesday. Genesis 50:20–21 reads, "'You intended to harm me, but God intended it for good to accomplish what is now being done, the saving of many lives. So then, don't be afraid. I will provide for you and your children.' And he reassured them and spoke kindly to them." Let me repeat verse 20. "You intended to harm me, but God intended it for good."

LITTLETON: SATAN'S PLAN

On Tuesday morning at Columbine High School, the forces of evil converged to unleash a violent and bloody spring holocaust on teens and their teachers. Two suicides, as we all know, followed thirteen homicides. The morning of mayhem led to a horrific afternoon and evening of waiting. We have parents sitting here today who were part of that waiting, and we watched as riveting reunions between parents and kids brought tearful relief to hundreds throughout that dark day. But as we all know, sadly, some parents left Leewood Elementary School that night without a reunion, and their reunions took place in hospitals and funeral homes across our community. One of those families who first saw their son in a funeral home are John and Doreen Tomlin. Friday morning they said good-bye to their sixteen-year-old son, John Robert Tomlin. Men and women, on April 20, 1999, Satan had a plan for Littleton. Coincidentally or not, Satan's plan unfolded on Hitler's birthday, and we know that it was Satan who gained a grip on those two boys whose names we all know, and we know that it was Satan because he left his calling cards: death, destruction, and dread. Make no mistake, Tuesday's atrocity is not simply about black trench coats or purported parental failure, or anemic gun laws, or inattentive teachers, or kids in cliques, or racial prejudice, or Marilyn Manson. Ultimately, what we saw on Tuesday came from Satan's home office, the pit of hell. In fact, you know what? I believe I smelled hell on Tuesday right there at the corner of Pierce and Bowles.

Pastor Boone and I were actually out together for a morning of meetings, and we were on our way back, coming down C-470. If you were out on the roads, then you certainly heard the sirens, and within ten minutes of driving we saw between fifteen and twenty emergency vehicles racing past us. Of course, we were well aware something huge was going on. We got off C-470, came down Bowles, kept heading in that direction, cars continued to pass us with emergency lights flashing, and we were actually able to drive all the way up to the corner of Pierce and Bowles right now where they have it blocked off. We pulled into the lot of the apartments right across the street. We had rolled down the window right before we pulled in, and one of the kids that was running said there's someone with a gun inside and he's shooting everybody. We got out of the car, walked across the street, and joined literally hundreds of others who were arriving at the scene—both law enforcement and others—and there was a huge group of kids coming around the edge, making their way up toward the public library, which became a kind of command post. It was utter chaos. Many of you know, because you were a part of it. We began talking to the kids and asked them what they knew, what had happened. Many of them needed to call their parents. I got my cell phone out and encouraged the kids to call their parents to let them know that they're OK. I saw a teacher who attends Foothills here and prayed with him. Saw another one, prayed with him. In the early moments of this thing we were on the hillside where now you see the incredible memorial that's been put up. There was terror on every face, and, I want you to know, I smelled the presence of Satan in that place. You could see it and smell it and taste it. On Tuesday, April 20, 1999, Satan had a plan for Littleton. His plan had some very clear goals. Here's what I believe he wanted for Littleton.

Fear

First, he wanted fear. Some of you have had trouble sleeping. Some of you have kids who are having nightmares. Some of you are waking up in the middle of the night with a start because you've been dreaming about guns and shootings and killings, and I have joined you in that. Every time I have been interrupted by a wave of fear, I find my heart and mind being drawn to 2 Timothy 1:7 (NKJV), which says, "God has not given us a spirit of fear." If God's not given us a spirit of fear, then where's it coming from? We know where it's coming from; it's coming from Satan, and Satan's plan is that this community will be consumed by our fear. See, Satan wants us to operate with fear. He wants us to be afraid; he wants us to be afraid to go to bed at night. One of the nights—it's all a blur now, believe me—I looked out my front window because I heard something. There was someone sitting out there in a car with a light on inside the car. I looked out the window and just kind of stayed there watching, and all of a sudden I just became overwhelmed by this fear of why this person was out there. Believe me, if you haven't felt it yet, you probably will, and I know where that's coming from. That's coming from the pit of hell. That was a part of Satan's plan for Littleton on Tuesday.

Hate

He has another thing that he would like to see in our community. He would love to see us not only characterized by fear but by hate. Today I prayed for the families of the two boys who were responsible for this mayhem on Tuesday. That might have been hard for some of you, the fact that we're actually praying for them. I'm not an expert on grief, but I know that anger is a very normal part of the process, and if you felt anger, or had anger, I'm not surprised. It's predictable. I've had my share. Satan wants us to stay there. He wants us to live with anger.

Some of you, perhaps, watched on Thursday night of this week *Nightline*—"Special Edition" with Ted Koppel. They were in Jonesborough, Arkansas, where thirteen months ago they had a similar tragedy. The title, interestingly, was, "Lessons Learned." But I don't think the evening went the way they planned it. I think they were hoping that people from Jonesborough would say, "Here's how we learned to walk through this, Littleton, let us comfort and encourage you." But believe me, that's not the message that came through. The message that came through from the small sample of the population interviewed is that thirteen months later there is still incredible hostility between those who were victimized, and those who are the family of the victimizers. The mom of the young boy Mitchell Johnson was actually there, and many in the room did not know. They were meeting in a church, and many of them did not know she was going to be there. In particular one of the men who lost his wife, one of the teachers in that tragedy, was, you could tell, pretty close to out of control with rage. I'm not critiquing his response or hers, I'm just saying this: I know what Satan wants Littleton to look like at thirteen months. He wants us to be hateful and spiteful. He wants us to see people wearing black trench coats and the gothic demeanor and attire, and he wants us to unleash our anger and our energy against them. As I said at the memorial service on Friday, he wants evil to be repaid by evil. He wants hatred to be repaid by hatred. Satan had a plan for Littleton, and his plan was that we would be overcome by fear, and overcome by hatred, and finally overcome by inconsolable grief.

Grief

I don't know if you know this, but inconsolable grief can ruin your life. That's not to say that there's not a place for grieving, and I believe five days after this episode we are all still in a state of shock, and we are still grieving. Here I am talking while grieving. It's so intriguing to me, everyone handles his or her grief differently. Some people laugh and giggle during their grief. Some people can't stop crying. Some people like to make silly little jokes. Some people get irritable. Some people get so tired they can't stay awake. Some people stare at the wall and become immobilized. Some people become angry, and call in to talk shows, and scream about this situation and all their solutions. We are a community in grief, and I'm the first to acknowledge that. But Satan wants us to stay right here, like this, with our inconsolable grief. That's how he wants us to be. I don't know if you were here on Wednesday night or not, but if you were, you heard Gerry Shemmal, who is one of our church family here, and a survivor of the plane crash, United 232, Sioux City, Iowa, back in July 1989. Gerry had some incredible words. I'm not sure they were all heard, and maybe we weren't even ready to hear them, but one of the things he said is, "You're never going to get over this," and secondly, "There are some from their particular tragedy who are in mental health facilities today, ten years later, because they were not able to process their grief." I'm telling you right now, friends, Satan loves it. He loves the scene that plays over and over again in my mind like a video recording, of standing on the side of that hill trying to help kids with phones and prayer. Of hearing and seeing a number of law enforcement officers across the way with their weapons drawn, and taking beat on someone they didn't know across the parking lot who could have been a suspect, for all we knew. We heard it, and everyone said, "Get down, get down." And we all crouched there on the side of the hill. I can still remember that feeling. Many of you can do the same. You remember your feelings in the middle of that episode, and Satan wants you to live right there constantly.

Satan had plans for Littleton on April 20, 1999. We read disturbing articles about copycat episodes since this has unfolded. A fifteen-year-old boy who leaves a suicide note expressing grief over the Columbine tragedy. I want to tell you something, friends: Satan loves it.

LITTLETON: GOD'S PLAN

Satan had a plan on Tuesday, but I don't think it worked. Why? Because God also had a plan. Remember when I said, "two sets of plans"? Satan had a plan, but God also had a plan. Proverbs 19:21 says, "Many are the plans in a man's heart, but it is the LORD's purpose that prevails." In Genesis 50, the story of Joseph comes together kind of like the last five minutes of a movie, and you know what we learn? We learn that what they intended for evil, what they intended for harm, what they intended for hate, God intended for good. I love those words: "But God." We read the newspapers and we see the news and we appear in interviews and all the rest, and we talk about this tragedy, and in the midst of it are these words: "But God . . . but God . . . but God." And in the early moments of that episode, by the way, God wasn't taken by surprise at all. Someone in this room gave me a plaque two or three years ago; I don't remember exactly when, and I want to thank them for it. It has ministered to me in ways that you would never realize. It's on the wall in my study at home right next to my computer screen, and every time I glance toward the door, I see it. It's personalized. It says, "Bill, I have everything under control. Jesus." But God . . .

God has plans for Littleton. These young men became gripped by the power of Satan, and their goal was to ruin this community and bring us to a place of fear and hate and inconsolable grief. Then God steps in, and the light begins to shine in the first seconds of this episode. If it's true that Satan has a plan, then we ask the question: What could God's plan for us possibly be? I want to go back to 2 Timothy 1:7 (NKJV) where we read, "[But] God has not given us a spirit of fear, but [a spirit] of power and of love and of a sound mind," or self-disciplined, or right thinking. See, Satan's plan for Littleton was fear, hate, and inconsolable grief. God's plan, which went into action immediately, is for power and love and sound thinking. Oh, I love this.

Now, I said earlier, I don't want to appear glib or preachy today. But men and women, if we're going to turn to God in this crisis, we have to turn to God believing that He is able to do exceeding abundantly above and beyond anything that we could ask or think, and I want to be one voice in this community, talking to reporters or anyone else, who is saying, "God is still in control, and God is good. God has plans for us that could amaze us, and could last us until the time Jesus Christ returns to this earth." Where are those plans?

Power

God wants people of Littleton, and the world, to see and experience His power—God's power. I want to tell you God's power was evident in the middle of this bloodbath. All of us have read about Cassie Bernall, whose memorial service is going to be right down the road at West Bowles Community Church tomorrow. Seventeen years of age. As Pastor Burns mentioned, a number of these kids were strong Christian witnesses. Not just kids who went to church but strong Christian witnesses. I think I heard this morning that Rachel Scott, the girl who was buried yesterday, wanted to be a missionary. John Tomlin had been on missionary trips and was interested in our clinic in Ecuador.

These kids were on fire for God. Back in March when we were talking about the persecuted church, could you ever have imagined that just a few weeks later, in Columbine High School, a precious seventeen-year-old girl would be asked, "Do you believe in God?" And perhaps in the microseconds that she processed her thoughts she may have thought, "If I say no, they might spare me." I don't know that. But what I do know is she, according to the eyewitness, said "Yes." She was gone in an instant; she was in the presence of the Lord. We talk about the power of God. This past Wednesday night a group of kids was having a meeting, friends of John Tomlin in particular, and a group that he had been involved with. John had been witnessing to one of his friends Brandon, and maybe you heard about this if you were at the memorial service on Friday morning. John had been talking to Brandon about Jesus. Kids talk to other kids about Jesus and the power of God. And Brandon had not yet accepted Christ as his Savior, until Wednesday night when the man leading the meeting said, "Would anyone like to receive Christ?" Brandon replied, "I want to." The leader said, "I want to be very sure. I don't want this to be an emotional decision. I know you're all stirred up by everything that's going on." Then Brandon said, "John has been talking to me about this. I know exactly what the gospel is, and this has made my decision for me. I'm going to receive Christ tonight."

On Friday morning, John and Doreen said to me, "We want John Robert Tomlin's service to be an evangelistic service. We want you to give an invitation. We want you to ask if there's anybody there who wants to be saved. Oh, we know that that won't erase the pain of the loss of our son, but please present the gospel." What an incredible opportunity not only here but also through the live feed that we had. We were able to stand here and say, "The Lord Jesus Christ is first, and He was first in John's life. If you'd like to put your faith and trust in Him and receive Him as your Savior, then I want you to raise your hand right now." And across this very room five hands went into the air as five people said, "Yes, I want to receive Jesus Christ as my Savior."

Now I know I'm probably being a little paranoid about this, but I want to say this because I know what some of you are thinking: "Bill, we're still grieving. How can you be so loud, and how can you be so positive about what's going on with this? This is a horrible tragedy." I know. I think I feel it as deeply as anyone who didn't have someone in the school can feel it. We had our kids from here in that school. There's Mom and Dad in the front here, who know exactly what I'm talking about. What I'm wanting to say to you is, God has a plan. His plan is to turn evil to good. John and Doreen have amazed me. I know they're in the early hours and days of this. Their constant and abiding faith in the Lord has amazed me. The father of Rachel Scott has amazed me. When asked if he has any anger toward the boys who have done this and their families, he said, "I don't, and I probably should. But I feel like I'm covered; I'm blanketed by a covering of grace. God's grace." I saw an interview with the parents of Cassie Bernall. They've been very bold in saying, "We believe the Lord can use this for His glory." Men and women, none of us, no sane person sitting in this room would ever have chosen what happened on Tuesday. That was Satan's plan. But don't miss this truth in the midst of this horrendous tragedy: God also has a plan, and God's light is bringing people to the truth, and God's power is real.

Before we leave today, I'm going to ask you if you've not put your faith and trust in Him, then maybe you've been moved to a place where you have decided, "Today is the day for me. I need Jesus in my life." You see, God wants Littleton to be a place right now where His power is displayed to the whole world.

Love

He wants us to be a place where His love is being displayed. God's plan is not fear and hate and inconsolable grief. God's plan is power and love. Can you feel the love in this community? I want to tell you something. I've lived in this community for sixteen years, and I've gone to the restaurants, been in the malls, gone to and fro and bought gasoline. It's palpable; it's in the air. Think about the area over at the corner of Pierce and Bowles, where the makeshift memorial has been erected. Do you feel a love when you go over there? Oh, I feel pain and I have tears, but there is such a surge of love. That's God's love. How can a precious family sit right down on this row on Friday morning after the service was over and be interviewed by both local and national media, and say, "We're praying for the families who have lost their kids, and for the families of the boys who were responsible for this." I hate what happened on Tuesday, but I love what's happened since. God's love reigns. I feel it in this room. I don't think I've been hugged as much in the last five years as I have been in the last five days. And let me tell you something. It feels fantastic. I've had people come up to me and say, "We're praying for you. Just want you to know we've watched you kind of go through this week, and we're praying for you." And the love is just tangible. Let me ask you a question. If that love continues, what do you think this community is going to look like in thirteen months?

Clear Thinking

God's plan for Littleton would be that we would see His power, His love, and then I want to add this one. Again, it comes out of verse 7 in 2 Timothy chapter 1. It says a "sound mind" (NKJV). That word means "clear thinking." And you know who seems to me to have the clearest thinking right now? The kids who went through the tragedy or have friends who went through it—that's who seems to be thinking most clearly. You know the verse that says the little children shall lead them? The kids are leading our community, and you know why I say they are leading us? Let me ask you where they're going. Are they going to the malls primarily? No way. Are they talking about designer labels and designer clothes? Are they obsessing over MTV or computers? No! Are they turning to keg parties and all-out blasts? Are they finding the sports events really meeting their needs? Are they trying to find places where they can get involved in sexual immorality or drugs? Men and women, open your eyes. City of Denver, open your eyes. State of Colorado, open your eyes. The world, open your eyes. The kids are turning to God. They're going to churches. They're saying we went to one service, and then we tried to quickly find another because we needed to go to church. Why are they going to church? They know they need God. And oh, how I pray that out of this devastating evil, dark, horrible tragedy, the eyes of the world will be opened up, and we will begin to think with sound minds, clear thinking, and right priorities. What matters now? What you wear, where you live, what you drive, how much you earn? No. What matters now is God and God alone. I know I'm under the influence of something good right now. God is at work in our city, and again, I probably shouldn't apologize quite as much as I am, but I just want to make sure I am not demeaning or diminishing this tragedy one bit. I'm not saying, "Oh, wow, I'm so glad that happened on Tuesday." No, no, no, no, no. But there is evil in this world, and the evil flows out of the pit of hell, and there will continue to be evil until Satan is cast into the lake of fire. In the midst of it all, brothers and sisters, let us look to the plan that God has. He wants us to be known for His power and His love and clear thinking for His glory. That's what we want to see, that's where we want to turn, and that's where we want to look. To the true and living God.

CONCLUSION

I don't know about you, but I have resolved I will never be the same. And in some respects I don't think I have any choice. We are being shaped by a tragedy that will mark us for the rest of our lives. Only time will tell whether the city of Littleton will be known for God's power, God's love, and clear thinking as a result of this tragedy. I pray we choose God's plan over the plan of our enemy, for God's glory and in His name.

Let's bow together for prayer.

Our Father, we've been praying throughout the week, throughout this day, and as we come to the end of our service this morning, God, I pray for You to move in Foothills Bible Church right now, that this community will never be the same because people will see in us God's power, God's love, and clear thinking. Lord, what they intended for evil, You intend for good. We want to give You the praise today. We want to give You the glory, and once again we tell You, we need You, O Lord. In Jesus' powerful name, we pray. Amen.

[The hymn "Amazing Grace" was sung.]

A Memorial Service for Commander Patrick Dunn, United States Navy

National Tragedy

Jeff Watson

EDITORS' NOTE: This memorial service was conducted for Commander Dunn after the tragic terrorist events in New York City and Washington, D.C., September 11, 2001.

INTRODUCTION

On consecutive days last week, our nation mourned one of many fallen heroes. Amid marble and stained glass, flowers and flickering candles, hundreds gathered in Annapolis and Arlington to rehearse one clear truth: darkness can never overcome the light!

NAVAL ACADEMY

On Wednesday, at the chapel of the United States Naval Academy, we were surrounded by an ocean of dress-white uniforms, from seamen to admirals, all filled with honor for a fallen shipmate. Under the same roof where John Paul Jones, the father of the modern American Navy, is buried, a band of brothers began to rehearse the character of their fallen friend from the Class of '85, Fifteenth Company, recognizing in him that unmistakable tenor of leadership that was born in an

. . . .

earlier era when ships were made of wood and men were made of steel.

Had you been able to join us, you would have been drawn to the words of an earlier Navy man, President John F. Kennedy, who spoke on those Academy grounds when Patrick was but a boy, "Any man who may be asked in this century what he did to make his life worthwhile . . . can respond with a good deal of pride and satisfaction . . . , 'I served in the United States Navy.'"

ARLINGTON

On Thursday, at Arlington National Cemetery, not far from the grave of the hero of PT 109, we stood two and three deep inside Fort Myer's Old Post Chapel, this while six gray horses—one riderless—stood outside waiting to carry the silver-and-gray casket of a thirty-nine-year-old patriot on our sorrowing walk into resurrection ground.

PAT'S LIFE

On these two days of mournful celebration, Navy Commander Patrick Dunn brought us to attention and said through his shipmates on Wednesday, "I am proud to be an American; specifically, I am very proud to be an American who serves in the United States Navy."

On Thursday, Pat's sentiments echoed to us from beyond the horizon, when he said through his friends, the Navy chaplains, "I am comforted to be a Christian; specifically, I draw deep hope from the death, burial, and resurrection of Jesus Christ."

On Thursday, not far from the Tomb of the Unknown Soldier, we all thanked God that we had known this soldier, this sailor. In memories, public and private, Pat's portrait was painted with the oils of admiration. We heard him described as: "Sensitive . . . smart . . . funny . . . loving and lovable . . . a storyteller to rival all Irishmen . . . a reflection of the best in all of us . . . a wonderful uncle . . . a peacemaker . . . the baby of the family . . . confident but not cocky . . . a great son and grandson . . . a joyful husband and father-to-be . . . Stephanie's perfect knight . . . a magnificent influence on the ship . . . known for hard work well done . . . among the happiest men on earth . . . having the purest heart of any man I know."

Patrick Dunn now belongs to history, but we were proud to have known him. As a decorated engineer and executive officer, he showed us that he could master the heavy equipment of modern fleet operations; as a recruiter, he showed us that he had mastered the rich personality of the U.S. Navy; as a member of the strategy branch for the Chief of Naval Operations at the Pentagon, he graduated to glory on September 11, doing what he loved best, blending an excellence of mind and body in service to this great nation.

A company mate who survived September 11 said, "We gave some, but Patrick gave all." On behalf of a grateful nation, President George W. Bush, through an admiral, has now conveyed on Pat two posthumous awards: the Purple Heart and the Meritorious Service Medal.

CONCLUSION

As Thursday's ceremony came to a close, the *Washington Post* reported, "[F]or a moment, Stephanie . . . stood under a threatening sky in Arlington National Cemetery, at the center of national grief."

As the Navy band fell silent, the twenty-one guns fired their farewell, and a sailor played taps in the distance. We were all struck as we wheeled to our right and were confronted through a natural opening in the nearby trees by the specter of the scorched hole where the hijacked 757 slammed into the Navy watch at the Pentagon.

Unwilling to foul today's air by pronouncing the names of those new Hitlers of the twenty-first century, we have steadfastly purposed to lift up the name of one good man, in love with one good woman, together in service to one great nation with a great future.

Were Pat standing with us as we wheeled away from the grave, I believe he would not have stared at the hole or cursed the terrorists; he would have rendered a smart salute to the grand American flag, equally visible there through the trees.

Patrick has weighed anchor one last time, but I know, Stephanie,

. . . .

that you are still waving your flag of undying love toward that horizon that separates this world from the next.

On Eagle's Wings

Our prayer for you and your baby, for the whole Ross and Dunn families, comes from the great Hebrew patriarchs Isaiah, Daniel, and Jeremiah, promising words about the love and presence of God, sung upon you both in Annapolis and Arlington. Stephanie . . .

[quote refrain from "On Eagle's Wings" by Michael Joncas]

[Here the speaker quoted from a prayer of Max Lucado, entitled "Do It Again, Lord," originally spoken at America Prays, September 15, 2001.]

Why Doesn't God Do Something?

Andy McQuitty

SCRIPTURE READING

John 11:1–21, 32

INTRODUCTION

1. When tragedy strikes, many of us are tempted to ask tragedy's question: "Why doesn't God do something?"
2. There are numerous possible answers to tragedy's question, "Why doesn't God do something?"

MESSAGE

I. He could but He won't—the assumption of God's apathy (vv. 1–21, 32).
    A. Tragedy makes many people assume God's aloofness (vv. 6, 21, 32).
    B. This was not a rebuke. "Don't you love us?"
    C. We are tempted sometimes to assume that God's love is incompatible with tragedy ("yet," v. 6).
    D. When bad things happen because a bad God stood by and did nothing ("He could but He won't").

II. But God loves us (vv. 3, 5, 33–36).
    A. What a wonderful affirmation of Christ's love (vv. 3–5, 33–36).
    B. Jesus was "deeply moved," literally "groaning." And He wept.

C. Thus, love is not incompatible with pain. But this shows us that pain comes with a purpose.

D. The great expositor Alexander Maclaren described it well:

Christ's delays are the delays of love. If we could once get that conviction into our hearts, how quietly we should go about our work! What patience we would have if we recognized that the only reason that moves God in His choice of when to fulfill our desires and lift away burdens is our own good! Nothing but the purest, simplest love sways Him in all that He does.

III. Therefore, we can trust in God's purpose (vv. 4, 15, 39–42).

A. As always, Jesus seeks God's glory, a revelation of God's attributes: goodness, grace, love, judgment, and wrath.

B. Under what circumstances is God's glory revealed? When the storm is raging? When the crucible is white-hot.

C. Peter told us of the long-term perspective we need for suffering.

D. "In this you greatly rejoice, though now for a little while you may have had to suffer grief in all kinds of trials" (1 Peter 1:6).

E. No, in tragedy we must not cave in to the temptation of believing that God is apathetic. He loves us!

IV. "He would but He can't"—the admission of God's weakness (vv. 33–37).

A. Tragedy makes many people assume God's weakness (v. 37).

B. OK, so maybe God isn't apathetic. Maybe He really does love us but just couldn't act (v. 37).

C. Rabbi Harold Kushner tried to explain it this way in his book, *Why Bad Things Happen to Good People.*

D. Yet, repeatedly, the Bible tells us that God is sovereign, all-powerful, and able to do whatever He pleases and whatever pleases Him.

    E.   Nevertheless, people often think of God as weak when He doesn't seem to perform the miracle.

Show me somebody who is always smiling, always cheerful, always optimistic, and I will show you somebody who hasn't the faintest idea what the heck is really going on.

                  —Mike Royko, syndicated columnist

V.   But God is omnipotent (vv. 25–26, 38–44).
    A.   Jesus claimed to be the embodiment of the power of God that could raise her dead brother. And He backed those claims.
    B.   Nobody wanted that stone rolled away. The fourth day had come. The stench of death emanated from within. "Lazarus, come out!" Only an omnipotent God could do such a thing!

VI.   Therefore, we can trust in His plan (vv. 6, 9–10).
    A.   If Jesus is the purposeful, loving, and omnipotent God, then we can trust His plan.

In him we were also chosen, having been predestined according to the plan of him who works out everything in conformity with the purpose of his will, in order that we, who were the first to hope in Christ, might be for the praise of his glory. (Ephesians 1:11–12)

    B.   That was why Jesus waited two days: "already had in mind what he was going to do" (John 6:6).

Your eyes saw my unformed body. All the days ordained for me were written in your books before one of them came to be. (Psalm 139:16)

VII.   "He can and He will"—the adoption of God's perspective (v. 4a).

. . . .

    A. The Lazarus story raises the age-old human cry, "Why doesn't God do something?"

    B. "Be patient," Jesus is saying. "He can and He will."

Therefore we do not lose heart. Though outwardly we are wasting away, yet inwardly we are being renewed day by day. For our light and momentary troubles are achieving for us an eternal glory that far outweighs them all. So we fix our eyes not on what is seen, but on what is unseen. For what is seen is temporary, but what is unseen is eternal. (2 Corinthians 4:16–18)

VIII. "So we fix our eyes"—perspective and commitment to seeing life the way God does. There are two aspects.

    A. Eternity—not time—is ultimately important!

    B. "Our momentary troubles": our life is but a blip on the eternal radar screen.

Why, you do not even know what will happen tomorrow. What is your life? You are a mist that appears for a little while and then vanishes. (James 4:14)

    C. Negative? "Life is hard, then you die!" But "Life may be hard, then comes heaven."

Death is not the end of all. The end of the natural body is death. But resurrection is the end of death. Death is a terrible enemy, but death is a defeated enemy.

—John G. Mitchell

    D. That's why I imagine Lazarus had tears in his eyes when he walked out of that tomb. Bummer!

    E. Jesus didn't bring Lazarus out of that tomb for Lazarus's benefit but for ours; not to give Lazarus life again on this earth but to give us confidence for life again in heaven.

Someday you will read in the papers that D. L. Moody of East Northfield is dead. Don't you believe a word of it. At that moment I shall be more alive than now. I shall have gone up higher, that is all—out of this clay tenement into a house that is immortal; a body that death cannot touch, that sin cannot taint, a body fashioned like unto his glorious body. That which is born of Spirit will live forever.

—Dwight L. Moody

F. Glory—not grief—is ultimately important!
G. Tragedy is a part of life in a sin-cursed world. But coming glory, not present grief, is important.

For our light and momentary troubles are achieving for us an eternal glory that far outweighs them all. (2 Corinthians 4:17)

H. What could outweigh the pain of paralysis? Unwanted singleness? Loss of a child? Bombs and tornadoes?
I. The eternal weight of glory for the young mother, single woman, and those who suffer in wheelchairs.
J. Someday, pain will be erased by a greater understanding, eclipsed by a glorious result. Something so superb, so grandiose is going to happen at the world's finale that it will suffice for every hurt, atone for every heartache, and make right every injustice.
K. Jesus' raising of Lazarus was just a small sample of the glory to come. Therefore, it's OK to grieve life's hurts—but not without hope. Pain is God's megaphone to rouse our heart's desire for a better world that He has promised to create. Thus, as Joni Eareckson Tada wrote so well,

· ·

It is to our benefit that we are not satisfied in a world destined for decay.

Conclusion

Why doesn't God do something? He can. He will. And He is!

Seek Jesus, the Shepherd of Love

Psalm 23

John W. Reed

Introduction

We live in a violent, sinful world. It is easy to feel vulnerable and insecure. In the face of the loss of a loved one, we feel empty and drained of strength to go forward. We have inner fear that our basic needs might not be met in the future. Where can we look for the meeting of our temporal and eternal needs?

In Psalm 23, the shepherd points us to the greatest of all Shepherds. Then he gives us a big surprise. The Shepherd becomes more than a shepherd. But let's look at the text.

Where should we look for satisfaction? The first verse reveals the Source.

Message

   I.   Seek satisfaction from Jesus (vv. 2–3).
      A. Find rest.
      B. Find refreshment.
      C. Find renewal from the pain of sorrow.

  II.   Seek life guidance from Jesus (v. 3b).
      A. Experience righteous living.
      B. Honor the reputation of God.

. . . .

III. Seek inner peace from Jesus in the presence of grave danger (evil) (vv. 4–5).

    A. Verses 4 and 5 form an interesting transition. The shepherd becomes a gracious host and welcomes us from the grassy fields to the banquet hall of his kingly castle.

    B. Know comfort and protection through Jesus, the loving Shepherd.

    C. Enjoy provision through Jesus, the gracious host.

CONCLUSION

The response of faith in the loving Shepherd is to dwell securely under His care (v. 6). Apparently, David was separated from access to the house of God (the tabernacle). He longed for restoration to that sacred place. This world is not our true home. We are longing for the full fellowship of our eternal home, where we will enjoy an eternal banquet with God and our loved ones who have gone ahead of us.

Jesus, the Shepherd of Love, is the gracious host of our perpetual dwelling. If you do not know Jesus as your Shepherd of Love, would you trust Him today?

Postabortion Memorial Service

Judy Elliott and Rob Harrell

I.   Scripture Readings, in order
    A. Deuteronomy 33:27
    B. Deuteronomy 31:8
    C. Isaiah 40:28–31
    D. Matthew 19:13–16

II. Opening Prayer

III. Hymn: "A Mighty Fortress Is Our God"

IV. Scripture Readings, in order
    A. Psalm 139:1–16
    B. Psalm 130
    C. Matthew 11:28–30
    D. John 11:25-26

V.   Obituaries

VI. Hymn: "Children of the Heavenly Father"

VII. Meditation by the Minister

VIII. Postsermon Prayer Leading into the Lord's Prayer

. . . .

PART TWO:

IX. Hymn: "Savior, Like a Shepherd Lead Us"

X. Read John 14:1–4, 6

XI. Benediction

Memorial Message for a Devoted Father

Spoken by His Son

John Breneman

A FEW MOMENTS AGO, THE CASKET was closed for the final time. Later today, the casket will be lowered into the ground, bringing to an end the final chapter in Glen Breneman's earthly life. But it is not the end of his story because the memory of his life will continue to have an impact on those of us who have been touched by his life in one way or another. I would like to take a few minutes to share some personal reflections based on a parable that most of you know well. Let's take a look at the parable of the prodigal son in Luke 15. Often when we read the story or listen to a message on this parable, the focus is on the son. But as I read the parable, think about it from the perspective of the father.

The first perspective is found in verses 11–12. What would be the normal reaction if the son came to the father and asked for his full share of the inheritance and the father knew full well that he would squander it? The father would probably say, "I'm not going to give it to you. You have not learned how to handle money." Yet, the text says that the father divided his wealth between the two sons. Here was a father who was willing to allow his son to make mistakes and to fail. That is a wise father.

And that is the kind of father we experienced as we were growing up in our family. He was a father who allowed his children to make their own choices and to take responsibility for those choices. He gave us the freedom to make decisions. When a decision turned out to be a mistake or led to failure, there was never a word of judgment or condemnation from our father. We are thankful for a father who gave us space to grow and mature.

We see the second perspective in verses 13–19. I take it that the father was not aware of all of the events in his son's life at this point; but as we think of the perspective of the father, what we do know is that the son had left him and gone on a journey. We can imagine the pain that the father must have felt. That pain can be very real at times. It's the pain of knowing that things have not turned out the way we have dreamed or anticipated or desired. The father's dream for a close father-son relationship had been shattered. What was left was the painful reality of a son who was lost.

We had a father who knew and experienced pain and was very much aware of it. He was in physical pain much of his adult life. In 1936, doctors discovered a tumor on his elbow and another on his back. He was told that the only thing that could possibly save his life was radiation treatments. Dad also suffered epileptic seizures in the 1930s, one of which left him with a kink in his neck. That pain is something that he felt for sixty-five years. In the last years of his life, he suffered from other diseases that brought even more pain.

As much as he suffered physically, one would think that this was his primary pain. But the truth of the matter is that what he felt more intensely was personal pain. The first instance of this pain was when his mother died giving birth to his youngest brother when he was three years of age. Dad's father was an alcoholic and did not want anything to do with the three boys. Dad's older and younger brothers were adopted by one of the relatives while a couple outside the family adopted Dad.

The rejection that he felt in his first years of childhood marked him for the rest of his life. Several examples could be cited from his adult life as well, but perhaps the event that inflicted the most pain was the tragic death of our brother Terry in a motorcycle accident on his twenty-third birthday.

How does one handle pain? Some people respond with anger and bitterness because of the way they have been treated. Others respond with tremendous self-pity. Then there are those who respond by turning against and hurting other people.

Despite the great pain he experienced in his life, our dad kept his focus on his family, on his farm, and his fellowman. Dad was a fighter. He did not give up. He did not quit. He persevered when the pain could have controlled his life. This is one of the traits that we have seen modeled by our father and that has become a quality in our lives as well. Each of us children could share examples of when we have encountered severe adversity in our life experience. But we, like our father, have not backed off but rather have kept on keeping on.

We are thankful for our father's legacy. But there is also a backside that must be considered. It has been said that our greatest strength is our greatest weakness. Clearly, one of Dad's strengths was his determination to persevere in his pain. But his weakness was that he did not share his pain with others. He wanted to go it alone. As a result, he was a very private person. Much of what I know about his life comes from other people who have been with him in life. I am thankful for a father who was aware of his pain and in many respects handled that pain well.

The third and final perspective is the attitude of the father found in verses 20–24. The perspective is of a father who was compassionate and loves and forgives. The father did not focus on the pain that his son caused him, nor did he allow the pain and hurt to keep him from reconciling with his son. His focus was on their relationship then and there. When his son returned home, the father received him with open arms, forgave him, and affirmed him, and initiated a time of celebration.

Our father expressed those qualities in his own way. Each of us siblings has his own stories to tell in terms of how we experienced that affirmation from our father. A number of years ago, our year of home ministry had come to an end and we were saying our final good-byes before returning to our ministry in Sweden. Judy and our two children drove away first in one of the two cars we were taking back with us. I had a few moments alone with my dad. The words that he spoke to me that morning influenced and affirmed me in a way that I had never experienced earlier: "I am proud to have you as my son." I think I cried halfway to New York after giving him a parting hug.

This reminds me also of a time when Dad came to hear me preach. After the service, in the back of the church, a neighbor said to Dad, "You must be very proud of your son."

As fast as lightning, as if he had been anticipating the remark, Dad replied, "Which one? I have four sons of whom I am proud."

As children, we longed to hear those affirming words from our fathers. The mark of a wise father is to set aside his hurt and pain and to love his children unconditionally.

There is another perspective here as Jesus tells the story, and that is the perspective of the heavenly Father. This particular story tells us what God is like. He is the God who loves unconditionally; the God who demonstrates grace, mercy, and compassion without fail; and the God who extends His forgiveness to those who have turned their back on Him, walked away from Him, and wasted their lives on the empty pleasures of this world. The question is, do we want to be forgiven? If so, how do we receive His forgiveness?

Jesus gives us an invitation in verse 21. "Father, I have sinned against heaven and against you. I am no longer worthy to be called your son." We receive His forgiveness by acknowledging that we have turned away from our Father and gone our own way. Our sinful ways and words have separated us from God. The only way to experience forgiveness is to place our trust in Jesus Christ, who paid the penalty for our sins through His death on the Cross.

Many years ago, someone had a conversation with Dad in which concern was expressed about his relationship with God. Dad replied, "I get up every morning and go out and milk the cows and then go out to the field to work. I see the variation of God. I experience God in all that He has created, and I enjoy His presence." That is one of the reasons we as a family have chosen the hymn "Great Is Thy Faithfulness" as a part of this service for Dad.

Unfortunately, the recording by Steve Green that we are going to listen to in a few moments has omitted the second verse. Instead, we have included the words on the card that each of you has received. The verse reads as follows:

> Summer and winter, springtime and harvest,
> Sun, moon, and stars in their courses above
> Join with all nature in manifold witness
> To Thy great faithfulness, mercy, and love.

What a faithful Father!

Personalized Service with Eulogy and Message

Spoken by a Son-in-Law

Brent Strawsburg

I WOULD LIKE TO WELCOME YOU HERE this morning for the funeral of Regina Curtiss. On behalf of the family, I would like to express my appreciation for your being here to remember Reggie and to demonstrate your love for the family. On behalf of the family, I want to thank those of you who've sent lovely cards and flowers and those of you who've brought food. Your tangible expressions of love have been appreciated greatly.

I have the privilege to speak to you not only as a minister of the Good News of Jesus Christ but also as Reggie's son-in-law. As part of the family, I was regularly touched by her life.

EULOGY

The purpose of a funeral is to help family and friends in the process of coming to grips with their loss and with the sense of the finality of death. Each of us needs this opportunity. It's an appropriate time for people to express their genuine emotion at the homecoming of a mom, grandma, or close friend. With the shocking nature of her death, we all sense our need to say and to feel many of the things that time did not afford us to tell Reggie.

[obituary notice read]

As we prepare to remember Reggie's life and to be reminded of the fragileness of our lives here on earth, would you join me as we turn to God, who is eager to invade our moment of hurt and pain and touch us with His comfort.

[Prayer followed by song, "How Great Thou Art"]

Our loss this morning is very deep. We are mourning the loss of a wife, mother, sister, grandmother, cousin, aunt, friend, and neighbor. What makes our loss this morning so deep is our memory of what a great person Reggie was. Through her care and thoughtfulness, she regularly touched people wherever she went.

Reggie was a giver. Whether it was through her profession as a nurse or her role as a good neighbor, lifelong friend, wife, mother, or grandparent, Reggie was always giving. She was always picking something up or putting something aside for the grandchildren. She was extending herself to her four children, assuming a positive parenting role, and ensuring that everything was right even when each of her kids were fully grown with families of their own.

She was quite unusual in her capacity to give. I remember that on those occasions when Cheri, the kids, and I would come up on a Saturday to visit, she would ask me if I wanted anything out of the fridge. Usually, I would say no, I was fine. But she wouldn't stop. She'd say, "Well, I have leftover chicken, some ham, brisket, luncheon meats, crackers, three kinds of bread, different kinds of soda, and more."

"No, Reggie, I'm fine."

"Well, I also have some ice cream, one last piece of cheesecake or Bon Bons." She was unusually concerned that everyone had what they needed. Each of you knows that to be true. Most of you benefited from her giving nature.

Reggie showed this giving attitude in everything she did. In her chosen profession as a nurse, during her years at Daniel Freeman, through her involvement with the Elks, she found a way to extend herself to those around her, shut-ins who were going through hard times. It was Reggie who would reach out a helping hand. She was a

. . . .

giver. She had an unusual capacity to give. At those rare times when she didn't give, it was most likely because she didn't know about the need because, if she had known, she would have been there. That was Reggie.

One of Reggie's best friends, Jo Wilks, wanted to share her comments:

> I first met Reggie when our family moved to Vicksburg Ave, across from the Curtiss family. She came bringing cookies and Kool-Aid, and our four small children to her yard so that Ken and I could unpack! That was thirty-five years ago, and we've been friends all of these years. We have raised our children together and shared lunches, shopping trips, birthdays, and many talks over cups of tea! She was always there in times of crisis. Being nurses, we consulted with each other before we saw a doctor. We laughed, recently, about the evening I felt ill and called her to come over. We diagnosed it as "stomach flu" and I went to bed. At 2 A.M. I was in surgery having an emergency appendectomy! Early in the morning, we opened our front doors to signal to each other we were up and it was time to talk and have coffee. She was my best friend and I will miss her terribly. But I have years of happy memories.

Reggie kept people informed. In many ways, she was the center of information. I know that in our family she was the centerpiece for finding out what was going on. She wanted to know the good so that she could be excited, and she wanted to know the hard stuff so that she could be a support. Most of you here benefited directly from Reggie in this way. She would call you, bring over a meal to a family in need, or jot a note.

Cheri, the kids, and I were always getting cards from Reggie. Her family was so important to her that she wanted to stay in touch and let you know that she was always thinking about you. I need to tell you that she never missed a holiday, not just Christmas and birthdays but New Years, Thanksgiving, Halloween, and Easter. She had cards for every occasion. I sometimes laughed because she never forgot a holiday. In fact, I didn't even think they made cards for some of the holidays, but Reggie knew.

Each of us benefited in one way or another from Reggie's life. Her ability to care for people and to accept other people with very little qualification was a trait that has always stood out. Yet, it's for the family that Reggie's life took on even greater dimensions.

It's for you that I have some very personal and important things to say. Each of us feels her loss in different ways. We will each mourn different aspects of our relationship with her. At different times, we will feel the pain of her absence. At times, we will laugh out loud, remembering something funny that she used to do. At different times we will long for her listening ear, her acts of kindness, or her supportive attitude. I'd like to say something to each of you.

Curt, you will feel the most unique sense of loss because you are losing your mate of forty-six years. It was hard initially for Reggie to move out to California from Pennsylvania, but two things kept her here—the palm trees and you. She was your companion on cruises and other trips. She was the one who worried about you constantly, especially on your long hunting trips. You and Reggie brought four wonderful children into this world, giving them memories for a lifetime. Curt, I cannot predict all of the adjustments that will come into your life, but I can say this: your family will continue to need you—your kids and especially your grandkids. They will need to see some of Nana in you. I will also tell you that you'll need us as a family to remind you of what you and Reggie were so proud of. Your family pledges our continued support and love for you.

To the four adult children of Reggie—Kathee, Ken, Keith, and Cheri—I can barely express my sense of hurt and loss for each of you. You have lost your mother; no words can remove its reality or lessen its awful sting. In the weeks and months and even years to come, you will face situations that will remind you of her love, memories that will make you smile, or memories that will make you cry.

You'll remember how she always wanted to take a family picture at the holidays. We'd be ready to eat, but Reggie would make us all stop

· ·

for a picture. I remember that it always took her so long to take the picture. Many times, the flash wouldn't work. Ken would often say that Mom owned three cameras, two of which didn't work. You'll remember her acts of kindness, her genuine concern, her helpful advice, and her unconditional love for you. You'll remember that she was always sending you into the garage to get some of Dad's elk meat or to the other freezer that was packed full of breads and rolls. She knew when you didn't have much money and wanted to help in any way she could. Let those memories remind you of her kindness. As you remember your mother, as you sense your heartache, don't forget each other. Listen to each other's hurt, and do what your mom did so well— listen and show tangible acts of love.

In this moment of sorrow, the children wanted me to express some of their comments about their mom.

My mom was the best mom, Nana, and friend you could ever ask for. She was always giving to and thinking of others before herself. She loved to cook, eat, and talk about both. She would always critique the restaurant or social function she had just gone to with Dad. There was always a casserole in the freezer, food in the fridge for an army, cookbooks to give away, and recipes cut from articles in papers or magazines that she clipped especially for you. The grandkids would get the See's candy novelties at all the holidays, which I remember her giving us as kids. There was always a pile of stuff on the TV for us to go through. Oh, she had some funny quirks, like having lots of camera problems, giving me knives, flashlights, and gadgets at Christmas, and worrying about us all the time. We didn't tell each other often enough, but I know she loved us, and she knew we loved her. Although I don't go to church, I sometimes pray when others are in need. The only thing I prayed for myself was that Mom and Dad would live long enough to spoil our children. I regret that prayer wasn't answered, but thank God for letting Katrina and me see her that one last time before He took her to His world. I am comforted in knowing that she was proud of us kids. She knew that we were all happy, and she got to play with her nine grandchildren.

I have two bits of advice for you here today. One is to appreciate what you have now because you never know when it will be taken away. The other is to think about and communicate your wishes for when you pass on. You needn't buy a plot or prepare your cremation. Just make sure that your loved ones know your wishes. They will be comforted in knowing that the last thing they did for you was done the way you wanted. We know that Kathee and Dad picked a good place for Mom, here in Los Angeles, where she raised our family, and overlooking Daniel Freeman Towers, where she worked for many years. We love her a lot, miss her much, and will never forget all of the love and caring that she has given us.

—Love Ken, Marcela, Katrina, and Cameron

[Then, Linda Curtiss shares:]

Reggie was one of the most giving women that I know. She gave of her time and her love. She accepted me unconditionally, as her daughter, when I married Keith. Mom always made me feel welcome, loved, and part of her family.

She loved her grandchildren and was the center of information for me about them. Whenever we spoke on the phone, she would give me updates on what was happening with them all. As Nana, she enjoyed reading night night stories and giving them back rubs. Mom's legacy is her four grown children—Kathee, Ken, Cheri, and Keith. They have all inherited her thoughtful, kind, and loving spirit. The other day, someone said to me, "This doesn't seem real. I can't believe she's gone." Well, she isn't gone. She'll always be alive in our hearts and memories.

[And Cheri Strawsburg comments:]

My mom always loved and accepted me for who I was. Mom was a servant not only to our family but also to many others. She genuinely cared for people. My mom gave to others from her heart, and she was generous to everyone. Whenever I needed someone to listen, she was available. I will miss my mom.

To the nine grandchildren—four of whom are here, three are in Australia, and two younger ones are at home—I want to say something very simple to each of you. It's OK to be sad. It's OK to remember and feel very sad for missing your Nana today or next week or four months from now when you think about Nana and miss her. As your parents, we will be there for you as you miss Nana because you had a unique bond with her that no one else had.

Try to remember the things that Nana gave you, the special See's candy at all of the holidays, how she loved you, and how much she made you feel like you were the center of attention. You should never forget how special she made you feel. You're each special, not because of what you do but because of who you are.

To other family members, you knew her as a sister, as a cousin, or as Aunt Reggie. Some of you have known Reggie for so long that the thought of her absence is beyond "difficult." You've grown accustomed to her thoughtfulness, her kindness. My sorrow for you is genuine. I pray that the pleasant and happy memories of time you spent with Reggie and the joys of your children and grandchildren will soften some of your hurt.

Our family will never be quite the same, but now, more than ever, we must continue to support, love, and communicate as a family. In many ways, Reggie was the focal point of our family, either by meeting at her home, getting a phone call from her asking if we could get together, or extending herself in acts of kindness that somehow drew the family to her. In her absence, each of us must remember her legacy.

MESSAGE

This morning, we not only remember and honor the special life of Reggie Curtiss but also remind ourselves of the fragility of life. This week has been a painful reminder that life here on earth will not always go on. Life is all too fragile. None of us was fully prepared to say "good-bye." However, I want to remind every person here that you can be prepared for when life here on earth stops.

Over the years, society has become increasingly uncomfortable with the subject of death. It has been ignored or its implication carefully avoided. For many people, death is seen as just the final chapter; to others, heaven is seen as a catchall for just about everyone who is a good person. But such views do not amply prepare anyone for death.

Preparing yourself starts by realizing that there is more to life than just what you can see. People are more than just simply the by-products of some evolutionary process. We are not, as Carl Sagan would say, "just a highly complex mobile computer." When you view someone who has died, don't you sense that something vital to that person's life on earth is absent? What's missing? It's their soul. People have souls, something above and beyond this body. It's that part of mankind that makes us unique. It allows us to have a relationship with God.

In these painful moments, each of us has a unique opportunity to understand and evaluate our relationship with God. Unfortunately, our world has either diminished the significance of God's role in our life or it has complicated it. Allow me to simplify it for you. You and I were made to have God as a part of our lives. It's the only perspective that makes any true sense out of life. To illustrate this, I'd like to tell you about an event from the life of Jesus.

Jesus, facing one of the most difficult situations in His life, came to the funeral of His good friend Lazarus. As He came to console the family, Martha, Lazarus's sister, came to Jesus, saying, "Lord, if You had been here, my brother would not have died" (John 11:21 NASB).

Jesus responded, "Your brother shall rise again" (v. 23 NASB). Martha didn't know what that meant. It was then that Jesus distinguished Himself from all people at all times when He said, "I am the resurrection and the life; he who believes in Me shall live even if he dies, and everyone who lives and believes in Me shall never die" (vv. 25–26 NASB).

What was Jesus saying? He promised that people have the opportunity to live on even if they die physically. What Jesus says here makes

. . . .

sense only if our souls live on even after we die here on earth. If we have souls, we must prepare ourselves for the most important issue of life. Are we prepared to stand before a perfect God? Jesus wanted His good friends to know that it all came down to whether they placed their trust in Him. A few chapters later, Jesus made it even clearer when He said, "I am the way, and the truth, and the life; no one can come to the Father, but through Me" (14:6 NASB).

My belief in the God of the Bible dictates that every person is ultimately accountable to God for his or her life. People don't just die and that's it. It's important that, as we face the fragile nature of life here on earth, we look to where our souls stand before God.

Listen once more to Jesus' response. Jesus came upon another of Lazarus's sisters, Mary, who immediately fell at His feet and said, "Lord, if You had been here, my brother would not have died" (11:32 NASB). And when Jesus saw all of the people weeping and heard Mary's comment, the Bible tells us that Jesus Himself wept.

Why do I mention that? Jesus understands our loss when someone we love dies. He longs for us to have the kind of relationship with Him that is deeply personal, a relationship in which we can benefit from His presence. But I also mention it for another reason. Jesus wept because, for a brief moment, Mary was seeing things from a purely physical level—"Jesus, You could have prevented my brother from dying"—instead of seeing the far more pressing question, "Will you believe in Me and guarantee an eternal relationship with the God of this whole world?" Jesus has the same concern for people today.

In the midst of the realities of life, even when we face the reality of death, He's concerned that we not miss the spiritual dimension. Where do we stand with God? Why is life so fragile? It's because we only have life here to determine our hope for living in the presence of God. Your life on earth will inevitably come to an end. Before it ends, you must ask yourself, "Have I prepared myself to live forever in the presence of God?"

I hold out this hope, the only hope that I believe makes sense out of life. It's the hope that you can place your trust in what Jesus Christ did on the Cross. Jesus did something for you and me that we could never do for ourselves.

You and I will never be good enough to enter into the presence of a perfect God. So He's provided the way.

Jesus took your sin and my sin, and, as a perfect man, gave His life so that, by trusting in what He did, you and I could have a real and genuine relationship with God. The only way to prepare yourself to live forever in the presence of God is to depend on what God has done for you. Our efforts are simply not good enough. Thankfully, His love has provided the way. It's only by trusting in what He did that you can prepare your soul for the finality of death. Don't miss this opportunity to prepare yourself to stand before God!

Would you bow your heads as we talk with the One who understands our plight and understands our grief? At this moment, He also wants to extend His incredible love to each of us.

[Prayer followed by song, "Amazing Grace"]

This concludes our service. The family would like to invite you to a brief service at the graveside, which will be followed by a reception for Curt and the family at the Westchester Elks.

Memorial Service for a Godly Man

Spoken by His Protégés

EDITORS' NOTE: This very touching memorial service was developed by two younger men who spoke in honor of their deceased friend, father, uncle, and spiritual mentor, Ralph Zorn. We had the privilege of knowing Ralph personally. His memorial service was fitting, honoring, and memorable. A minister gave very brief words of introduction, explaining that these men would speak. Their testimonies of their love for Ralph and his love for them spoke volumes more than most funeral messages could have said.

Doug Thompson:

For those of you who don't know me, my name is Doug Thompson. My mother is Donna Thompson, Kay's sister; so Ralph was my uncle. I'm the oldest of all of the children born between the two sisters, so I have had the privilege of knowing Ralph longer than any of the others.

My family and I live in St. Louis, Missouri, and we all drove down here yesterday. This is a very hard time for all of us because Ralph and Kay have been very special to our family. Since my parents live quite a way from St. Louis, Ralph and Kay were like grandparents to my kids as they grew up. They were not only an aunt and uncle for me but also very good friends for my wife and me.

As we drove down here yesterday, I was thinking that my children have probably never seen me cry or be emotional for any reason. I'm not particularly proud of that. I'm just not a very emotional person. However, it might be difficult for me to say some of the things I'd like to say today. So if I get a little choked up along the way, please be patient and we'll all get through it OK.

I have to confess that there have been some times that I have cried. I cry when the St. Louis Rams lose games. I cry when my eighty-year-old dad beats me at golf. And I've cried many times at my Uncle Ralph's corny jokes.

Last Thursday night, I got a phone call from my cousin Sandy telling me that Ralph had had a heart attack. She was calling from her car on the way to the hospital and naturally was very upset. She asked me to please call all of our family and have everyone pray for her dad.

I was at home by myself, working in my office, when I got the call. My whole family was at church that night practicing for our church's Christmas musical. Now I'd like to say at this point that I am not a singer. This was not a regular church night, so there was no reason why I should have been at church with them.

After we hung up, I went upstairs to a quiet room in our house and got on my knees to pray. And, of course, I prayed a selfish prayer that God would work a miracle, heal Ralph, and spare his life so that all would go on happily ever after. Well, we all know from life's experiences that things don't always work out the way we want them to. Now this doesn't mean that God doesn't love or care about us. It's just that God has His own plan for each of our lives. And, in this case, it was God's plan for my Uncle Ralph to come home this week.

So I began to pray for the family, that all of us would have the strength and courage to get through this difficult time. Now some people might say, "How can a prayer like this comfort or encourage you in such a dark time?" It's a time when your hurt is so great that you don't know if you can endure it.

Well, I can tell you how it helps: because I know that someday I'll see my Uncle Ralph again. By God's grace, we'll meet again in heaven.

When I was twelve years old, I was sitting in the balcony of a small Methodist church in southern Illinois on a Sunday evening. And on that night two miracles happened. The first is that I was listening to the message being preached. The second is that my life was changed forever.

. . . .

The pastor preached a message about the salvation that was available to each of us through Jesus Christ and of the hope of eternal life that came with it. And it was perfectly clear to me that if I wanted the salvation being talked about and the promise of eternal life, I needed to make a decision. That decision was to acknowledge the fact that Jesus Christ was the Son of God, that He did die to save me from my sins, and that He was raised from the grave to overcome death.

Well, I made that decision that night, and I'd like to thank God publicly for saving my soul, and I also thank my mom and dad for being fine Christian parents to point me in the right direction.

At some point, Ralph had also made that decision; therefore, I know that, no matter how much I'll miss my uncle, I also know that someday I'll see him again.

So I'm not saying good-bye tonight; instead, I'm saying, "I'll see you later, Uncle Ralph."

I'd like to share with you a poem that my wife and I wrote nine years ago for Kay and Ralph's fortieth wedding anniversary. It's not the best piece of poetry you'll find, but it will give you an idea of what Kay and Ralph meant to our family.

You've Always Been There

Aunt Kay, Uncle Ralph . . . YOU'VE ALWAYS BEEN THERE,
And here are a few times that we'd like to share:
YOU WERE THERE when Doug needed a second home,
YOU WERE THERE when the army called him to roam,
YOU WERE THERE when Doug married his beautiful wife,
(This is my favorite line)
YOU WERE THERE when we struggled with apartment life.
YOU WERE THERE when we moved into our first home,
YOU WERE THERE letting us borrow, always willing to loan,
YOU WERE THERE when our family began to grow,
You watched as Jennifer's grandparents adored her so.
YOU WERE THERE when Gina burst into our life,
And, thank God, you're still there helping us handle her strife!

YOU WERE THERE when Jacqueline arrived in the fall,
YOU WERE THERE probably wondering if this surely was all!
YOU WERE THERE when they danced,
YOU WERE THERE when they sang,
YOU WERE THERE when they cheered,
YOU WERE THERE when the boys rang,
YOU WERE THERE just as any grandparents would be,
And they grew to love you so much, you're who they are
anxious to see,
I hear, "Is Aunt Katie coming?"
I hear, "Will Uncle Ralph be there?"
YOU WERE always THERE to support them and give loving care.
As children, they remember your family gatherings and the pool,
They loved coming over, playing "Marco Polo" and being "COOL!"
YOU WERE THERE when we moved into the old "money pit,"
YOU WERE THERE every Christmas bringing generous gifts,
YOU WERE THERE when we needed help with the attic fan,
YOU WERE THERE when we couldn't afford the plumber man.
YOU WERE THERE so that the hot water would run,
YOU WERE THERE when the old water heater had to be undone,
YOU WERE THERE when the garage needed finishing and stuff,
And you knew we'd call you when the wiring got tough.
YOU WERE THERE through the fun times and the
stressful times too.
God sent you to be there when Gina came out of ICU,
YOU'VE BEEN THERE every time that we've needed you most
And this, for twenty years, we can boast!
It's amazing to us that you're always around . . .
How you've ALWAYS BEEN THERE when you're always
out of town!
We Love You
Happy Fortieth Anniversary!

When we got the news about Ralph, my wife and I were certain that
we'd be coming to Dallas to be with the family. I wasn't so sure about

all of my daughters, though. My oldest daughter, Jennifer, had two sick children at home. In fact, one of them had just gotten out of the hospital Thursday morning.

My daughter, Gina, is a single parent with two small children, and she just started a new job. I was sure it would be almost impossible for her to work things out.

And my youngest daughter, Jacqueline, had a major part in our church's Christmas program, with a performance tonight. So her attendance was doubtful too.

Well, believe it or not, they were all able to work something out, and they're all here today. Thursday night, we were together talking about how great it was that we were all going to be here. My son-in-law, whom we unintentionally left out of our plans, said, "I'd like to go. Ralph was my uncle too." After he made that comment, it dawned on me that that's how it was with Ralph. If you were fortunate enough to have met him, you couldn't help but love him.

We love you, Uncle Ralph, and we'll miss you.

Ken Zorn:

I'm Ken Zorn, and I am here to celebrate my dad's glorious home going. What a blessing and joy it is to have all of you here to share in this celebration!

You've already heard how Dad reached and touched several lives. I know that each of you could come up here and tell how Dad touched each of your lives. Over the past several days, I have heard a number of you recount these incidents.

> For Mom, memories of a loving husband. A great dad who loved all of his children deeply. A papaw who loved to play games, tell corny jokes, and loved to tease. A breakfast buddy. He fondly addressed the youth of our family as "you crazy kids."

As a brother-in-law, he was "so special." "Good old Ralphie." He had that great sense of humor that put people at ease.

Dad modeled well these words that the apostle Paul wrote to his protégé, Titus:

> Similarly, encourage the young men to be self-controlled. In everything set them an example by doing what is good. In your teaching show integrity, seriousness and soundness of speech that cannot be condemned, so that those who oppose you may be ashamed because they have nothing bad to say about us. (Titus 2:6–8)

A Daughter's Love

Written by Denise Willhite,
for the Memorial Service of Her Mother,
Janet L. Hibberd, December 13, 2000

"I HAVE SOME GOOD NEWS FOR YOU!" This is the way Mom wanted her family to be told that she had gone on to be with the Lord. She wished that her death would not be just a time of grief but also a time of hope. She wants us to be encouraged that she has been freed from any pain or tears, has completed her days, has completed her work, and now is present with God.

There will be hard times when we will feel an emptiness and will need the comfort of each other and the comfort of God. Mom anticipated this and longed to comfort in advance those who hurt now. Her last talks with me focused on the love that she was experiencing and how she desired for all of us to experience and share with one another that same love. Along with the hard times of missing Mom, we will have moments of warmth when we remember special times with her and when we remember who she was.

Mom was a woman of deep faith, a woman of strength, and a woman who valued order, kindness, and service to others. Mom had a gentleness that attracted many people to her. She exhibited a sacrificial, servant's heart.

She was a loving daughter who treasured her mother's love and comfort and the memory of a closeness with her father. She loved her brothers and sisters, and her life was enriched by many shared times with them. She loved to remember old times with them at the Hughes' place, Marshall High School, riding ponies with her sister, and of course, her trumpet.

Mom was a good wife and homemaker, first with Dad and then with Gary. Both marriages helped to fill Mom's life with many blessings. Mom was greatly comforted by Gary and his faithful attentiveness during her illness. She loved being a homemaker. Three children first blessed her life—David, Dale, and Denise—and then later three dear stepchildren blessed her life—Wendy, Rob, and Dean.

Mom was a great mother. She loved us with an undying love. She was fiercely loyal and unselfishly gave all that she could give. She believed in us.

We will miss you, Mom. We will see you in the ordinary when we reach for a dish and remember the apple pie you used to make. We will miss you in the essential when we are teaching our own children the principles of life and remember a mother of integrity who taught us those principles. Mom, you will live on through us and through your grandchildren.

Her crowning joy of life was her grandchildren: Katie, David, Christopher, Sarah, Nicholas, Conner, Jeremy, Blake, and Anastasia. She loved her grandchildren, and each of them has been touched by her teaching and nurture.

Mom's hope for the future is that her life would still be used by God; that her influence of faith would be imprinted on her children and grandchildren and those who knew her; and that we all would be drawn to her Lord, the One in whom she had complete faith and trust.

Mom desired that we would not think of her during this last fragment of life but that we would picture her stepping on the shore of heaven and know that she is finally home.

When the Roll Is Called Down Here

EDITORS' NOTE: Dr. Bryan Chapell records the practice of some South American churches who remind themselves of the reunion with loved ones in the future. He explains their practice thus:

> [These churches] keep alive the reality of our ultimate union with loved ones in annual services in which the names of departed Christians are read to the congregation. After a reader voices each name, the congregation responds in unison with the word *presenté*, which means "present!"
>
> "Jose Gonzales."
>
> "Present."
>
> "Maria Rodrigues."
>
> "Present."
>
> In this way, the family of God reminds itself of the heavenly reality that grants hope in the face of our greatest trial. Those now present with the Lord in spirit will be present with us in body at the Resurrection, and, as a result, they never ultimately depart from us.[3]

A Prayer of Hope

Source Unknown

Our Father, You are a God of comfort and security. We would not pretend today, our God, that we do not hurt. You know the agony of grief and we do grieve. But we do not grieve as those who have no hope. We have great hope. Our hope is assurance. Assurance of eternal life with You, only because of the work of the Blessed Hope Himself, the Lord Jesus. And so, our Father, we call upon You in this time of pain and loss to bring comfort and hope to these whom You love. We ask this not because we are deserving but because You are a God of mercy and comfort. Make Your strength known in this time, O God. And, in turn, we shall praise You! We ask this in the name that is above all names, the name that has conquered death, the name of Jesus. Amen.

A Prayerful Perspective on Death

The Most Difficult Prayer I've Ever Prayed

Keith Willhite

EDITORS' NOTE: This is the prayer that I (Keith) wrote in my journal just after returning from the doctor's office, having learned that I had a baseball-size brain tumor, Monday, August 25, 1997.

Father, I know (and believe) that You are both sovereign and good. You know, Father, that my life is surrendered to Your will. But this brain tumor scares me, and it scares my family.

I cannot imagine why You would call me home when I have two young kids who need a dad, or why You might require Denise to be a single mom. So Lord, You know that my desire is that this will not be cancer and that You will touch my body with Your healing hand. Please give me a doctor who is a fighter.

I'm not sure I can say this with complete honesty, Lord, but if it is Your will to call me home, I want to come. But Lord, if that is Your will, please be gracious to Denise, Katie, and David. Be a better father for Katie and David than I could ever have been. And let them know how much I loved them and how much You love them. May they walk close to You all the days of their lives.

And please give Denise the strength to persevere. Keep her heart close to You. Thank You so much for the wonderful wife she has been. Help her to forgive me for my shortfalls. Give her family and close Christian friends for support. If it's Your

· ·

will for her to marry, give her a godly man who will love and cherish her as well as love and cherish Katie and David.

You know my heart Lord, so only You know if I really mean these words. They are hard to say. But whatever Your will is, Father, glorify Yourself! In Jesus' precious name. Amen.

The Shadow of Death

Psalm 23:4

Source Unknown

THE MASTER PREACHER DONALD BARNHOUSE became a widower at a young age. The death of his wife left him and a six-year-old daughter in the home. He had real difficulty working through his own grief, but the hardest part was comforting and explaining the death to his daughter. He later recalled that all of his education and theological training left him at a loss.

One day, he and the little girl were standing on a busy corner at a downtown intersection waiting for a light to change. Suddenly, a very large truck sped by the corner, briefly blocking out the sun and frightening the little girl. To comfort her, Dr. Barnhouse picked her up, and, in a moment, the wisdom of God broke through and he was able to explain to his daughter: "When you saw the truck pass, it scared you, but let me ask you, had you rather be struck by the truck or the shadow of the truck?" She replied, "Of course, the shadow." He went on to explain that "when your mother died, she was only hit by the shadow of death because Jesus was hit by the truck (death)." The psalmist reminds us that God is with us even though we walk through the valley of the *shadow* of death.

The Cleft of the Rock

Keith Willhite

WHEN I HAD THE PRIVILEGE OF visiting Israel, I saw the "dry, thirsty land" about which Fanny Crosby wrote in her beautiful hymn "He Hideth My Soul." As the hymn came to mind, I could not help but observe that high above the dry, thirsty land is exactly where God hides our souls in protection. Where? "He hideth my soul in the cleft of the rock."

The rock is way up there, a long way from the dry, thirsty land. And as she wrote in the chorus of the song, that cleft is a symbol for something: "He hideth my life in the depths of His love, and covers me there with His hand."

That's the situation today. Yes, physical death seems to have won a battle. But the security of God's loving grasp has not been breached.

Only God Is Great!

Haddon W. Robinson

In 1717, Louis XIV of France died. Louis, who called himself "the Great," was the monarch who declared, "I am the State!" His court was the most magnificent in Europe and his funeral the most spectacular. His body lay in a golden coffin. To dramatize his greatness, orders had been given that the cathedral would be very dimly lit with only a special candle set above the coffin. Thousands waited in hushed silence. Then, Bishop Massillon began to speak. Reaching down slowly, he snuffed out the candle and said, "Only God is great!"

The Cross

Light Versus Darkness

Keith Willhite

I BELIEVE I HAVE NEVER SEEN A more stark contrast between light and darkness than when I was in the city of Bucharest, Romania, in 1997. On my way to a teaching ministry in Moldova, my partners and I spent a night in Bucharest to adapt to the change in time zones. On the morning before we flew to Kishinev, Moldova, we had an hour or so to do a little sightseeing in Bucharest.

Our guide took us first to the palace that Nicolae Ceausescu built as his new home. Because of the revolution, this was one of Ceausescu's last acts, and he never occupied the palace. It was absolutely the epitome of opulence. Not only is the building huge but also beautiful hardwood walls, inlaid with gold and other precious metals, filled the conference rooms. Wall hangings of ivory and silk decorated other rooms.

Few dictators have committed worse crimes against their citizens than did Nicolae Ceausescu and his wife, Elena. Ceausescu rebutted all criticism of his rule and of the hardships inflicted by his government. In an extraordinary outburst, he declared, "I will tell you that for the first time a cooperative worker received 200 kg of wheat per person, not per family, but per person . . . there has never been such a level of development in the villages as there is today. We have built schools, ensured that there are doctors, ensured that there is everything for a dignified life." As for the industrial workers, Ceausescu asked the members of the court whether they had not witnessed "how the people cheered when I went to the factories?"

As the military prosecutor commented, a rational dialogue with the Ceausescus was impossible. Indeed, he went on to say, it was hard to sentence people who failed to appreciate that they had committed any crimes at all. Nevertheless, the prearranged verdict was given: confiscation of all the defendants' property and capital punishment. There then followed an unseemly scuffle as the hands of Nicolae and Elena Ceausescu were bound and they were led out to a courtyard. When Elena saw the firing squad drawn up in readiness for the execution, she is alleged to have cried out in disbelief, "And I was like a mother to you!" This last fond delusion failed to sway the firing squad. Indeed, even before the Ceausescus and a cameraman recording the event could assume position, the members of the execution squad, together with other soldiers present in the courtyard, had opened fire.

The bodies of both Ceausescus were kept at Tirgoviste for several more days before being transferred to the capital. On December 30, the Ceausescus were interred without ceremony beneath wooden crosses in Bucharest's Ghencea cemetery. Nicolae Ceausescu's grave was marked "Col. Popa Dan 1920–1989" and Elena's with the equally commonplace "Col. Enescu Vasile 1921–1989." The secrecy with which the Ceausescus were buried derived from a concern in the government that their final resting place should not become a shrine or place of pilgrimage.

When we left the palace, our guide drove us through the city to the small Ghencea Cemetery where both Ceausescus are buried in commoners' graves. On the way, he proudly showed us the "walls of the revolution," marked by hundreds of bullet holes. Then came the contrast. As we walked into the small, common cemetery, our guide led us directly to Nicolae Ceausescu's grave. Yes, as reported, it was a very common grave, with nothing to indicate that the person buried here was a former head of state. Ironically, at the head of the grave was a wooden cross. What a stark contrast between the darkness of this man and the light of Jesus' cross. We could not help but feel a sense of "God is in control; and, ultimately, He will judge."

In Whose Hands Are You?

A basketball in my hands is worth about $19.
A basketball in Michael Jordan's hands is worth about $33 million.
It depends on whose hands it's in.

A baseball in my hands is worth about $6.
A baseball in Mark McGuire's hands is worth $19 million.
It depends on whose hands it's in.

A tennis racket is useless in my hands.
A tennis racket in Pete Sampras's hands is a Wimbledon
    Championship.
It depends on whose hands it's in.

A rod in my hands will keep away a wild animal.
A rod in Moses' hands will part the mighty sea.
It depends on whose hands it's in.

A slingshot in my hands is a kid's toy.
A slingshot in David's hand is a mighty weapon.
It depends on whose hands it's in.

Two fish and five loaves of bread in my hands is a couple of fish
    sandwiches.
Two fish and five loaves of bread in God's hands will feed thousands.
It depends on whose hands it's in.

Nails in my hands might produce a birdhouse.
Nails in Jesus Christ's hands will produce salvation for the entire world.
It depends on whose hands it's in.

As you see now, *it depends on whose hands it's in.* So put your concerns, your worries, your fears, your hopes, your dreams, your families, and your relationships in God's hands because, you see, it depends on whose hands it's in.

—Author Unknown

Emergency Numbers

Source Unknown

When you are in danger, call Psalm 91.

When you are lonely and fearful, call Psalm 23.

When you want Christian assurance, call Romans 8:1–30.

When you want courage for a task, call Joshua 1.

When you want peace and rest, call Matthew 11:25–30.

When you have sinned, call Psalm 51.

When you worry, call Matthew 6:19–34.

When you grow bitter and critical, call 1 Corinthians 13.

When you feel down-and-out, call Romans 8:31–37.

When you leave home for labor or travel, call Psalm 121.

When you think of investments and returns, call Mark 10.

When your faith needs stirring, call Hebrews 11.

When your prayers grow narrow and selfish, call Psalm 67.

When in sorrow, call John 14.

When man fails you, call Psalm 27.

When God seems far away, call Psalm 139.

When the world seems bigger than God, call Psalm 90.

If you want to be fruitful, call John 15.

If you are depressed, call Psalm 27.

If you find the world growing small and yourself great, call Psalm 19.

If you are losing confidence in people, call 1 Corinthians 13.

If your pocketbook is empty, call Psalm 37.

If people seem unkind, call John 15.

If you are discouraged about your work, call Psalm 126.

For Paul's secret to happiness, call Colossians 3:12–17.

For an idea of Christianity, call 1 Corinthians 5:15–19.

For a great intervention or opportunity, call Isaiah 55.

To get along with your fellowmen, call Romans 12.

Emergency numbers may be dialed direct. No operator assistance is necessary. All lines to heaven are open twenty-four hours a day, seven days a week.

Drinking from My Saucer

Encouraging Description of a Faithful Life

I've never made a fortune
And it's probably too late now.
But I don't worry about that much,
I'm happy anyhow.

And as I go along life's way,
I'm reaping better than I sowed.
I'm drinking from my saucer,
'Cause my cup has overflowed.

Haven't got a lot of riches,
And sometimes the going's tough,
But I've loved ones around me,
And that makes me rich enough.

I thank God for His blessings,
And the mercies He's bestowed.
I'm drinking from my saucer,
'Cause my cup has overflowed.

O! Remember times when things went wrong,
My faith wore somewhat thin.
But all at once the dark clouds broke,
And the sun peeped through again.

So, Lord, help me not to gripe
About the tough rows that I've hoed.
I'm drinking from my saucer,
'Cause my cup has overflowed.

If God gives me strength and courage,
When the way grows steep and rough,
I'll not ask for other blessings,
I'm already blessed enough.

And may I never be too busy
To help others bear their loads.
Then I'll keep drinking from my saucer,
'Cause my cup has overflowed.

I do hope this prayer finds its way
To brighten up your day.
I pass it along to all my friends
In hopes that our friendship never ends.

—Author Unknown

Let Me Get Home Before Dark

Robertson McQuilkin

It's sundown, Lord.
The shadows of my life stretch back
into the dimness of the years long spent.
I fear not death, for that grim foe betrays himself at last,
thrusting me forever into life:
Life with You, unsoiled and free.

But I do fear.
I fear the Dark Spectre may come too soon—
or do I mean, too late?
That I should end before I finish or
finish, but not well.
That I should stain Your honor, shame Your name,
grieve Your loving heart.
Few, they tell me, finish well. . . .
Lord, let me get home before dark.

The darkness of a spirit
grown mean and small, fruit shriveled on the vine,
bitter to the taste of my companions,
burden to be borne by those brave few who love me still.
No, Lord. Let the fruit grow lush and sweet,
A joy to all who taste;
Spirit-sign of God at work,
stronger, fuller, brighter at the end.
Lord, let me get home before dark.

. . . .

The darkness of tattered gifts,
rust-locked, half-spent or ill-spent,
A life that once was used of God
now set aside.
Grief for glories gone or
Fretting for a task God never gave.
Mourning in the hollow chambers of memory,
Gazing on the faded banners of victories long gone.
Cannot I run well unto the end?
Lord, let me get home before dark.

The outer me decays—
I do not fret or ask reprieve.
The ebbing strength but weans me from mother earth
and grows me up for heaven.
I do not cling to shadows cast by immortality.
I do not patch the scaffold lent to build the real, eternal me.
I do not clutch about me my cocoon,
vainly struggling to hold hostage
a free spirit pressing to be born.

But will I reach the gate
in lingering pain, body distorted, grotesque?
Or will it be a mind
wandering undeterred among light fantasies or
grim terrors?
Of Your grace, Father, I humbly ask . . .
Let me get home before dark.

My First Christmas in Heaven

EDITORS' NOTE: This poem was found in E. W. Cavender's room when he died. Mr. Cavender was a godly layman who lived in Dallas, Texas. The author of the poem is unknown.

I see the countless Christmas trees around the world below
With tiny lights, like heaven's stars, reflecting on the snow.
The sight is so spectacular! Please wipe away that tear,
For I am spending Christmas with Jesus Christ this year.

I hear the many Christmas songs that people hold so dear,
But the sounds of music can't compare with the Christmas choir up
    here.
I have no words to tell you the joy their voices bring,
For it is beyond description to hear the angels sing.

I know how much you miss me; I see the pain inside your heart.
Even though I am so far away, we really aren't apart.
So be happy for me, loved ones. You know I hold you dear.
Be glad I'm spending Christmas with Jesus Christ this year.

I hear the many Christmas songs that people hold so dear,
But the sounds of music can't compare with the Christmas choir up
    here.
I have no words to tell you the joy their voices bring,
For it is beyond description to hear the angels sing.

. . . .

I send you each a special gift from my heavenly home above.
I send you each a memory of my undying love.
After all, "LOVE" is the gift more precious than gold.
It was always most important in the stories Jesus told.

Please love and keep each other, as my Father said to do,
For I can't count the blessing or the love He has for you.
So, have a Merry Christmas and wipe away that tear!
Remember, I'm spending Christmas with Jesus Christ this year.

Mother Is Another Word for Love

When it comes to knowing how to give and how to love,
Mother, you've always been a true inspiration.
Your love has been at the heart of our family harmony and happiness.
And the warmth and welcome of our home have always been a reflection of your kindness and your caring.
Your love has been there whether you're keeping a confidence, healing a hurt, or sharing a dream.
Through the "sown" times your love and concern have been here in a comforting hug or a reassuring word.
And the little loving touches you put into a day have made a happy difference more often than you know.
No matter what, your love is always there—And that means more than anything!
So often and in so many special ways, you make it so easy to see . . .
That mother is another word for love!

—Author Unknown

Safely Home

I am home in heaven, dear ones;
Oh, so happy and so bright!
There is perfect joy and beauty
In this everlasting light.

All the pain and grief is over,
Every restless tossing passed;
I am now a peach forever,
Safely home in heaven at last.

Did you wonder I so calmly
Trod the valley of the shade?
Oh! But Jesus' love illumined
Every dark and fearful glade.

And He came Himself to meet me
In that way so hard to tread;
And with Jesus' arm to lean on,
Could I have one doubt or dread?

Then you must not grieve so sorely,
For I love you dearly still:
Try to look beyond earth's shadows,
Pray to trust our Father's will.

There is work still waiting for you,
So you must not idly stand;
Do it now, while life remaineth—
Ours shall rest in Jesus' land.

. . . .

When that work is all completed,
He will gently call you home;
Oh, the rapture of that meeting,
Oh, the joy to see you come!
                    —Author Unknown

The Dash

I read of a man who stood
To speak at the funeral of his friend.
He referred to the dates on her tombstone
From the beginning—to the end.

He noted that first came the date of her birth
And spoke of the second with tears,
But he said that what mattered most of all
Was the dash between those years.

For that dash represents all the time
That she spent alive on earth,
And now only those who loved her know
What that little line is worth.

For it matters not, how much we own;
The cars, the house, the cash.
What matters is how we live and love
When we're living out the dash.

If we could just slow down enough to consider
What's true and what is real
And always try to understand
The way other people feel.

And be less quick to anger
And show appreciation more,
And love the people in our lives
Like we've never loved before.

. . . .

If we treat each other with respect,
And more often wear a smile,
Remember that this special dash
Might only last a while.

So, when your eulogy is being read
With your life's actions to rehash
Will you be pleased with what there's to say
About how you spent your dash?

—Author Unknown

"The Worst Day of My Life"

A Mother's Reflective Poem on the Death of a Child

EDITORS' NOTE: A day that a mother describes as "the worst day of my life" started when she awakened realizing that it was the morning of her young son's funeral. This poem, written at that moment, expresses her thoughts.

You lie there sleeping, my little son,
with long dark hair
and your play clothes on.

How many times I'd pray that you'd sleep
one more hour—a day—a week,
so I could wash, or clean, or bake
a pie—some cookies—or a cake.

How many times when the house was clean,
I'd get upset because you'd spill your juice—
or crumble a cookie—or drip your bottle
all over the steps.

If only you'd wake up
in my bad dream and
throw your bottle
or stand there and scream.

If only we could
see you smile—
or spill your cereal
on our new tile.

. . . .

Dear God—give me strength to forget
the bad days I had—
when I got upset
with this little lad.

With his long dark hair,
with his curls and his smiles
who lies there sleeping
with his play clothes on.

If We Could See Beyond Today

EDITORS' NOTE: This hymn, written by Norman J. Clayton, often is very appropriate for reading to give perspective in a memorial service.

If we could see beyond today,
As God can see,
If the clouds should roll away,
The shadows flee;
O'er present griefs we would not fret,
Each sorrow we would soon forget,
For many joys are waiting yet,
For you and me.

If we could know beyond today
As God doth know
Why dearest treasures pass away,
And tears must flow,
And why the darkness leads to light,
Why dreary days will soon grow bright,
Some day life's wrongs will be made right,
Faith tells us so.

If we could see, if we could know
We often say,
But God in love a veil doth throw,
Across our way.
We cannot see what lies before,

. . . .

And so we cling to Him the more,
He leads us till this life is o'er;
Trust and obey.[4]

TAPS

EDITORS' NOTE: Although we have verified this story, we cannot locate the original source.

It all began in 1862 during the Civil War, when Union Army Captain Robert Ellicombe was with his men near Harrison's Landing in Virginia. The Confederate Army was on the other side of the narrow strip of land. During the night, Captain Ellicombe heard the moan of a soldier who lay mortally wounded on the field. Not knowing if it was a Union or Confederate soldier, the captain decided to risk his life and bring the stricken man back for medical attention.

Crawling on his stomach through the gunfire, the captain reached the stricken soldier and began pulling him toward his encampment. When the captain finally reached his own lines, he discovered the uniform of the soldier was actually a Confederate one, and the soldier was dead. The captain lit a lantern.

Suddenly, he caught his breath and went numb with shock. In the dim light, he saw the face of the soldier. It was his own son. The boy had been studying music in the South when the war broke out. Without telling his father, he enlisted in the Confederate Army.

The following morning, heartbroken, Captain Ellicombe asked permission of his superiors to give his son a full military burial despite his enemy status. His request was partially granted. The captain had asked if he could have a group of army band members play a funeral dirge for the son at the service. That request was turned down since the soldier was a Confederate.

Out of respect for the father, however, they did grant his request, saying that they could give him only one musician. The captain chose a bugler. He asked the bugler to play a series of musical notes he had

. . . .

found on a piece of paper in the pocket of his dead son's uniform. This wish was granted.

The music was the haunting melody we now know as "TAPS"; today this melody is used at all military funerals.

These are the words to "TAPS":

> Day is done,
> Gone the sun,
> From the lakes,
> From the hills,
> From the sky.
> All is well.
> Safely rest.
> God is nigh.

Additional Resources for Funerals

EDITORS' NOTE: Denominations often publish or print funeral guidelines or resources.

Berkeley, James D., ed. *Leadership Handbook of Preaching and Worship*. Grand Rapids: Baker/Christianity Today, 1997.

Cadenhead, Al. *The Minister's Manual for Funerals*. Nashville: Broadman and Holman, 1988.

Choice Hymns of the Faith. Fort Dodge, Iowa: Gospel Perpetuating Fund, 1952.

Christensen, James L. *Difficult Funeral Services*. Old Tappan, N.J.: Revell, 1985.

Criswell, W. A. *Criswell's Guidebook for Pastors*. Nashville: Broadman, 1980.

Funeral Ideas and Illustrations. On floppy disk. Swan Lake Communications, P.O. Box 6687, Jackson, MS 39282.

Gibson, Scott M. *Preaching for Special Services*. Grand Rapids: Baker, 2001.

Lloyd, Dan S. *Leading Today's Funeral*. Grand Rapids: Baker, 1997.

Peterson, Eugene H., and Calvin Miller., eds. *Weddings, Funerals, and Special Events*. Carol Stream, Ill.: Christianity Today, 1987.

Richmond, Kent D. *A Time to Die: A Handbook for Funeral Sermons*. Nashville: Abingdon, 1990.

Wallis, Charles L. *The Funeral Encyclopedia*. New York: Harper and Row, 1953.

Wiersbe, Warren W. *Be Quoted from A to Z with Warren W. Wiersbe*. Ed. James R. Adair. Grand Rapids: Baker, 2000.

part three

OTHER OCCASIONS

Introduction

THE PASTOR MUST BE ABLE TO STEP with confidence into a number of different speaking venues or situations. Some of these situations are "special occasions." What makes an occasion "special" might not be the fact that it is unique or new. For example, a church might baptize many people within the year, but "my" baptism is special because it is mine. Or a person's *first* communion might be special. Other occasions are more rare, such as the dedication of the new public library or the dedication of a new division of a business.

Because other books have supplied the texts of messages for holidays and special occasions, we have sought to provide only a few creative ideas and a few supporting materials that may be adapted or used to spawn other creative ideas. Hence, we hope that this collection of varied resources for special occasions will be useful and will stimulate ideas for other materials. For an excellent discussion of what constitutes a "special occasion," see chapter one of Scott M. Gibson's fine book, *Preaching for Special Services*.[1]

Some "special occasions" are special because they invite celebration. Others do not invite celebration but perhaps even disappointment or shame. As with any setting, the pastor must ask, "What does the Word of God say about this situation, and how do I best communicate God's Word?"

THE LORD'S TABLE

Communion with a Bread Machine

Jeffrey D. Arthurs

FOR COMMUNION, SET A BREAD (baking) machine in the back of the church to bake at a certain time so that the bread is done by the end of your sermon. As you preach on the body of Christ and how we are "one loaf," or how our prayers are a sweet aroma to God, the smell of the bread permeates the room. After the message, use that loaf for Communion.

Communion with Congregational Responsive Singing

"Nothing but the Blood"

Richard Allen Farmer

As THE CUP IS BEING DISTRIBUTED, the pastor or worship leader turns to the congregation:

PASTOR:	Please respond in song to the following.
PASTOR:	What can take away our sins?
	[Sings the opening line of the hymn.]
CONGREGATION:	Nothing but the blood of Jesus.
	[Sings response.]
PASTOR:	What can make us whole again?
CONGREGATION:	Nothing but the blood of Jesus.
ALL:	Oh! Precious is the flow that makes me white as snow;
	No other fount I know, nothing but the blood of Jesus.

EDITORS' NOTE: If the cup is still being passed at this point, repeat the verse of the hymn. If the hymn is unknown to the majority of the people, put the words and designations up on a screen. However, spontaneity in the response is valuable.

An Affirmation of God's Love

Communion Meditation

John W. Reed

ONE OF THE MANY BENEFITS OF coming to the Lord's Table is being reminded of God's everlasting love. In a world filled with suffering and trials and, at times, persecution, we need this reminder regularly.

SCRIPTURE READING

1 John 3:1–3

It is not unusual for us to experience the feeling of rejection in this life. There are "big" rejections and some rejections that are not quite so "big." We might feel the smaller rejections when someone does not notice a new hairstyle or a friend does not even stop to say "hello" in the church foyer. Other "rejections" in this life hurt even more deeply. The student overlooked for medical school might feel rejected from his "chosen profession" for the rest of his life. A child feels "rejected" when her father died just before her birth. Cognitively, she knows that it was no fault of hers, but inside she feels guilty and rejected.

It is in the face of such feelings that Jesus poured out His blood to save and redeem us from not only spiritual death but also the heartaches and injustices of this present life. In his first letter in the New Testament, the apostle John reminded us of God's love and how significantly different it is from the rejections of this life.

1. How great is God's love for us (1 John 3:1a).

2. Because of God's great love, we are children of God (1 John 3:1b–2).
3. Because of our great hope in what we will be with God, we should purify ourselves (1 John 3:3).

Baby Dedications with a Large Number of Children

Steve Stroope

EDITORS' NOTE: Follow Pastor Steve Stroope's procedure to make these dedications both personal and quick. In this case, "large number" refers to seven to twenty-five children. Obviously, for this process to work well, parents have to be instructed ahead of time as to when and where to walk.

1. The parents and children come single file onto the platform.
2. Someone on an off-platform microphone announces the names (e.g., "This is John and Mary Smith and their daughter Jessica Lynn.").
3. Pastor Steve then has a sheet of paper (nicely printed and fit for framing) with the child's name and a "life verse." He reads the life verse to the child.

Jessica Lynn, God's Word tells us in Proverbs 3:5–6:

> Trust in the LORD with all your heart,
> And lean not on your own understanding;
> In all your ways acknowledge Him,
> And He shall direct your paths. (NKJV)

4. Then, he hands the sheet to the parents as they walk off the platform.

5. He does the same with each child but using a different verse.
6. When the line is complete, the pastor leads the congregation in a prayer of dedication for the parents to raise these children in accordance with God's Word and with the support of their local church.

Parent Dedication

An Affirmation of God's Love

Brent Strawsburg

OUR PURPOSE THIS MORNING IS TO dedicate each of these parents to the task of being a godly influence in the lives of their children.

I'll remind you that this ceremony doesn't confer upon these children any spiritual or religious benefit. It doesn't give them a foot inside the door of heaven. Rather, it's a somber time of dedication for each parent to commit to or renew their commitment to raising their children with a godly influence.

The Bible teaches that children are a blessing from the Lord. Psalm 127:3–5 says,

> Sons are a heritage from the LORD, children a reward from him. Like arrows in the hands of a warrior are sons born in one's youth. Blessed is the man whose quiver is full of them.

At the same time, the Bible teaches that parenting is a spiritual act that requires absolute dependence upon the Lord:

> Unless the LORD builds the house, its builders labor in vain. (Psalm 127:1)

Before we ask to hear your parental vows, it's only proper that we read to you the following parental job description.

Position: Mom and Dad Job Description

Description

Long-term team players needed for challenging permanent work in an often-chaotic environment. Candidates must possess excellent communication and organizational skills and be willing to work variable hours, which will include some evenings and weekends and frequent twenty-four-hour shifts on call. Some overnight travel required, including trips to primitive camping sites on rainy weekends and endless sports tournaments in distant cities. Travel expenses not reimbursed. Extensive courier duties also required.

Responsibilities

For the rest of your life, you must be willing to be hated, at least temporarily, until someone needs $5 to go skating. Must be willing to bite tongue repeatedly. Also, must possess the physical stamina of a pack mule and be able to go from zero to sixty miles an hour in three seconds flat in case, this time, the screams from the backyard are not someone just crying wolf.

Must be willing to face stimulating technical challenges, such as small gadget repair, mysteriously sluggish toilets, and stuck zippers. Must screen phone calls, maintain calendars, and coordinate production of multiple homework projects. Must have ability to plan and organize social gatherings for clients of all ages and mental outlooks.

Must be willing to be indispensable one minute and an embarrassment the next. Must handle assembly and product safety testing of a half million cheap, plastic toys and battery-operated devices. Must always hope for the best but be prepared for the worst. Must assume final, complete accountability for the quality of the end product. Responsibilities also include floor maintenance and janitorial work throughout the facility.

Possibility for Advancement and Promotion

Virtually none. Your job is to remain in the same position for years, without complaining, constantly retraining and updating your skills, so that those in your charge can ultimately surpass you.

Previous Experience

None required, unfortunately. On-the-job training offered on a continually exhausting basis.

Wages and Compensation

You pay them, offering frequent raises and bonuses. A balloon payment is due when they turn eighteen because of the assumption that college will help them become financially independent. When you die, you give them whatever is left. The oddest thing about this reverse-salary scheme is that you actually enjoy it and wish you could only do more.

Benefits

While no health or dental insurance, no pension, no tuition reimbursement, no paid holidays, and no stock options are offered, job supplies limitless opportunities for personal growth and free hugs for life if you play your cards right.

Now that you've heard the job description, we can ask for your vow. I'd like each of you to affirm your willingness to be the kind of parents that depends upon God to raise your children the way He envisions.

- Will you raise your children in an atmosphere of love and discipline, knowing that the best hope for a healthy childhood is one of unconditional love and clear standards? If so, please respond "I will."

Parents: I will.

- Will you communicate to your child the necessity of placing his or her faith in Jesus Christ at an age when he or she can understand the need and His sacrifice on the Cross? If so, please respond "I will."

Parents: I will.

- Finally, will you regularly pray for your child? Will you pray that God would use your child for His glory? Will you also pray that God will use you to develop his or her talents and passions to be used by Him? If so, please respond "I will."

Parents: I will.

I'd like to ask for each family, one at a time, to come to the center of the platform so that you can introduce your child to the church and introduce any extended family who might be with you this morning. After that brief introduction, I want to pray for each family.

1. Jeff and Sheila Whittmeyer bring their son, *Josiah Samuel* . . .
2. Dennis and Karen Morgan present their son, *Logan Trent* . . .
3. Zachary and Monica Lewis introduce their son, *Collin Zachary* . . .

Child's Dedication Letter from Pastor

Rick Reed

Matthew Christian Phillips
[Date]
Dear Matthew,
[Insert date] was a big day for your family. On this day, your mom and dad dedicated you to the Lord.

Your mom and dad think that you are a very special boy, Matthew. They know that you are a gift from God to them, and that's one of the reasons they wanted to dedicate you to the Lord.

Let me tell you what happened on the day that you were dedicated. After all, you were pretty little that day! Your mom and dad brought you to the front of the church. I told everyone that your parents wanted to dedicate you to the Lord Jesus. This meant that they wanted to raise you so that you'd grow up knowing that Jesus loves you very much. They wanted you to grow up knowing how you could have Jesus as your Savior and your Friend. In a sense, they dedicated themselves to helping you come to know Jesus as you got older.

Matthew, your being dedicated to the Lord didn't make you a Christian. Becoming a Christian is something you must do for yourself. I hope that by the time you read this letter you will already have decided to believe in Jesus as the only One who can forgive you and give you eternal life *(life that goes on forever!)*. If you haven't already made the decision to believe in Jesus and become a Christian, I hope that you will do that soon. I became a Christian when I was seven years old; it was the *best decision* I ever made.

Matthew, one more thing: I want you to know that I felt honored to be the pastor who got to pray for you and your parents. I prayed that God would help you grow into a young man who really loves Jesus and who loves people. I prayed that you would be a courageous and kind person. I prayed that you would bring much joy to your family and to the Lord.

Happy tenth birthday!

Sincerely,

Pastor Rick Reed

Parent/Child Dedication Reminder

Randy Frazee

TO COMMEMORATE THE PARENT/CHILD dedication, the church prints the following commemoration on a small (only 3 x 5 inches) parchment and gives it to the parents in a beautiful polished brass frame. For example:

Pantego Bible Church

Parent/Child Dedication

[Insert date]

Jonathan David Green

*Believing that Jonathan David was given to us as a priceless
treasure from the Lord, we are dedicating him back to our God,
knowing that he belongs to Him. In acknowledging this,
we are dedicating ourselves, as his parents,
to raise him according to biblical standards and to do our best
always to be a godly example for him to observe all of the days
that God would allow us to be together here on this earth.*

Caleb and Brittney Green

Celebration Service

Creative and Evangelistic Baptisms

Dale Hummel

WE HOLD OUR BAPTISMAL SERVICES ON Sunday evenings and call them a "Celebration Service." We also include baby dedications. We wait until we have at least eight candidates and two or more babies. The families give us the names of anyone they want to invite. We encourage them to invite as many nonbelievers as possible. We send out very nice invitations to the people whose names they give us. On Celebration Sunday, we host a special reception afterward just for the candidates and their invited guests. Staff and key leaders also join in to meet the new people.

During the service, each candidate is asked to give a brief testimony. All family and friends of that particular candidate stand while they are baptized; as each candidate rises from the water, the whole church cheers.

This practice has become very popular, and we always end up with an overflow crowd. I give a brief (ten minute) evangelistic story at the close of the service. We have seen many nonbelievers influenced positively, and the service opens the door for their family and friends to witness.

A Bright, Shining Light

Source Unknown

CHRISTMAS LIGHTS. HOW FITTING THAT our homes and our cities should become ablaze with lights in observance of Christmas because the first Christmas was marked by the shining forth of the radiance of the Shechinah glory of God, as Luke testifies, "The glory of the Lord shone round about them" (Luke 2:9 KJV).

To our eternal God belongs an infinite weight of glory. It was this glory that moved Abram out of Chaldea to embark on a journey of faith into a promised land (Acts 7:2). It was this revelation of glory that brought Moses out of the wilderness to become Israel's deliverer (Exod. 3:2). It was this glory that transformed the tabernacle at the time of its erection (40:34) and filled the temple at the time of its dedication (1 Kings 8:10).

This was the light that penetrated the world's darkness through the coming of the One in whom and from whom God's glory was displayed (John 1:9). We celebrate the coming of the One who is "the brightness of his glory" (Heb. 1:3) by illuminating our homes with Christmas lights today.

One day, the world will be dazzled by the display of His glory for "the Son of man shall come in his glory . . . then shall he sit upon the throne of his glory" (Matt. 25:31 KJV).

So until the time comes when it can be said "the glory of God did lighten it, and the Lamb is the light thereof" (Rev. 21:23 KJV), turn on the Christmas lights as a reminder that the Light of the World has come.

Christmas in Perspective

Howard G. Hendricks and John F. Walvoord

For me, Christmas is my personal pause that refreshes, a time to bow my heart and reflect on the truth that all the wonderful activities and gifts—and even people—are nothing compared with Him, my Savior and Lord. How can it be that He humbled Himself as the Baby in the manger?

—Howard G. Hendricks
A Collection of Christmas Memories
from Your Friends at Dallas Seminary, 1998

Christmas should be understood as an exchange of gifts, God's loving gift to us of His Son and the gifts of ourselves as we surrender to the Lord in faith and obedience.

—John F. Walvoord
A Collection of Christmas Memories
from Your Friends at Dallas Seminary, 1998

The Truth About Christmas

Keith Willhite

INTRODUCTION

1. It's not difficult, really, to understand why people get so confused about what Christmas is really about.
2. Most people know at least that it began as a religious holiday, but then Santa Claus began getting so much attention, and the retail sales were what we heard about on the news broadcasts and spent our time doing.
3. I suppose that if we're ever going to understand the truth about Christmas, we need to return to the source of the event, the Word of God. Only there can we find reliable theological reflection on Christmas.
4. To do that, let's open our Bibles to the first chapter of the gospel of John.
5. You might wonder, of course, why we're turning to John 1. It is not an account of Jesus' birth, such as we have in the familiar Luke 2. No, but John 1 takes a "big picture" perspective to begin to unfold the theology of Christmas; hence, in John 1, we can learn the truth about Christmas.

SCRIPTURE READING

John 1:1–13

Message

In this chapter, we observe at least three critical views of the coming of Jesus. The first is an eternal view. The second is a view of anticipation. The third is a view of record. We're not going to make a detailed study of John 1, but let's observe these views as we begin to study this great chapter. Even these brief observations will tell us the truth about Christmas. First, we see an eternal perspective or view.

I. Jesus has always existed (vv. 1–5).
  A. Jesus is eternal
    Eternal = never ending; never beginning
  B. The reason that Jesus is eternal is that Jesus is God.
    1. These verses declare that Jesus is the *logos,* the Word.
      a. In Hebrew Scripture: agent of creation; the source of God's message to His people.
      b. In Greek philosophy: the principle or reason that governed the world.
      c. In Hebrew philosophy: another term for God.
      d. John's understanding: God in the flesh, gospel, and the Good News of Jesus Christ.
    2. The *logos* is Christ. He *is* the Word.
      a. He is not the Word because He spoke the Word of God.
      b. To the contrary, He spoke the Word of God because He Himself is the Word.
  C. There is a well-known translation problem at the end of verse 1.
    1. It's well known because of its erroneous use by the Jehovah's Witnesses to try to deny the deity of Jesus.
    2. There are three ways of translating the noun *God* in verse 1.
      a. It could be a definite noun ("*the* God").
      b. It could be an indefinite noun ("*a* God").
      c. It could be a qualitative noun. A qualitative noun

. . . .

does not stress identity or definiteness; rather, it stresses a quality, nature, or essence.

3. Greek does not have an indefinite article, such as *a* in English.

4. Thus, it seems best to conclude that the noun is qualitative rather than definite or indefinite.

5. In no way does this militate against the deity of Christ.

6. Rather, it emphasizes that although the person of the Father is not the person of the Son, their essence is identical.

= one God/two persons

This is the Jesus who is eternal. He is eternal God! (In verse 3, then, we find that Jesus has always been even more than the Word.)

D. Jesus is the Creator.

1. Most of the time, we probably think of the Father as the only Creator because creating seems more Father-like than Son-like.

2. But Jesus is just as much the Creator!

(Congruent with what we might think of a Creator doing, verses 4–5 tell us that Jesus also does something else.)

E. Jesus is the Giver of Life and Light (vv. 4–5).

1. John used the word "life" to point to knowledge of God and relationship with Him. (Another way to say this is "genuine life in Christ.")

2. This life is said to be the "light of men" (v. 4).

a. And the light is contrasted with darkness.

b. Life and light are twins.

c. With life comes an awareness of righteousness.

d. If you see one who claims to have life in Christ but there's no righteousness, look again.

e. Light and darkness cannot coexist.

f. But, as we notice at the end of verse 5, darkness did not comprehend or overpower the light.

I can appreciate good photos only from a distance, because I know very little about taking good pictures. I do know, however, that you have to have good light. No matter how carefully designed the lens, how quick the shutter, or how steady the hand, or even if you insist on Kodak paper, you cannot get the picture without light. That's the way it is with Jesus! We must have Him, for He is the light!

> That's the way it is with Jesus Christ!
> And surely, someone that exclusive in relationship with God deserves to be celebrated!

Summary: Jesus has always existed. Jesus is eternal God. Jesus is the Creator. Jesus is the Giver of life and light.

(But very soon in this passage, we notice another view of Jesus, and it seems quite different from the view that Jesus has always existed. It comes primarily from the one known to us as John the Baptist. What view does John give us?)

II. Jesus is coming (vv. 6–8).
    A. This might seem to contradict the statement that Jesus has always existed.
        1. But there is a difference in the Jesus who has always existed and the Jesus who is coming.
        2. They are the same person, but the Jesus whom John announces as coming is going to be Jesus in the flesh! (In verse 6, we're introduced to the announcer of Jesus in the flesh.)
    B. John the Baptizer had a very definite function, mission, and purpose (v. 7).
        1. John's function was to be a witness.
            = another key term in the gospel of John
        2. A witness is one who speaks the truth about something.
        3. In this case, John foretold the truth about someone.

4. Verse 8 declares that John was not the light, but he came to bear witness of the light!

   a. When we witness, we must be careful not to substitute ourselves for the Light.

   b. Those who bear witness have little, if any, following.

   c. But the *Light* should have a great following.

On these cool December nights, perhaps you have noticed the brilliance of the moon, as I have. You realize, of course, that the light of the moon is not the light of the moon at all; it is the light of the sun. The moon merely reflects the sun's light. We are to reflect the light of Jesus Christ (that is, to bear witness).

(The heart of John's witness was that "Jesus is coming." But the heart of your and my witness is found in our third statement or point of view.)

III. Jesus has come (vv. 9–13).

   A. When Jesus came into the world in the flesh, He was the true Light.

      1. As Light, John tells us later, Jesus came to reveal the darkness of our sin and to dispel darkness.

      2. But when we come to verses 10–11, we read what are, in many ways, the saddest verses in the Bible.

      3. Jesus' life on the earth is summarized in these two verses. His own people rejected Him. But had it not been for this truth, all we Gentiles might never have known the *Light* of the world!

Let's say that you arrive home on Christmas Day. You look through the window of the house and there they are: your parents, your brothers and sisters, presents, a Christmas tree, cookies, and even hot chocolate. There's only one problem. No one will let you in. You realize that it's a Bob Eucker

Christmas! There you are with your own family, but they despise you; they hate you; they reject you. Then, they send you away. That's what Jesus faced!

      4. Thankfully, the rejection was not universal.
  B. To receive Jesus Christ is to believe or trust in Him with your faith.
      1. Are you sure that He alone is the object of your faith?
      2. Verse 13 reminds us that all of this is possible only by God's will.

CONCLUSION

Do you know the truth about Christmas?

1. Jesus has always existed.
2. John the Baptizer proclaimed, "Jesus is coming."
3. We know that Jesus has come. Why?
4. *Jesus became a child so that those who believe in Him can become children of God!*
5. It's truth worth reviewing time and time again.
6. It's truth worth sharing.
7. It's truth worthy of our praise to God!
8. *Jesus became a child so that those who believe in Him can become children of God!*

A Service of Ordination

Source Unknown

The Biblical Basis

For the purpose of inducting properly appointed leaders into the offices of the church, the New Testament reveals the use of a solemn ceremony that we call "Ordination." The essential elements of this ceremony were (1) the imposition of hands and (2) prayer (see Acts 6:6; 13:3; 1 Tim. 5:22). It is also appropriate to read the biblical qualifications and require the making of public vows. Such a service does not confer on the candidate any spiritual authority or gifts but is simply the church's public recognition of spiritual fitness in its properly chosen officers and servants and also their public induction into the church's service. (See Acts 6:3–6, where the men chosen were full of wisdom and the Holy Spirit *before* ordination, not by virtue of it.)

Because the office of elder is within the power of the local church, it is the right of the electing church (in consultation with the candidate) to determine the time, place, and manner of the ordination service. However, the actual service should be in the charge of other elders. Compare 1 Timothy 4:14, which speaks of the "laying on of the hands of the presbytery [elders]" (KJV). If the electing church has no elders, they may be called in from other churches. It should always be remembered that the elders thus engaged are temporarily authorized.

Opening Remarks

[The presiding minister will address the congregation:]

We have gathered today in obedience to the Word of God and in the presence of our Master and Lord, to set apart for the sacred office of the Christian ministry, by prayer and the laying on of hands, a Brother who has ("Brethren who have," if more than one is being ordained) been called to the gospel ministry and has proved by his life (have proved by their lives) and work that he is (they are) fitted to be a true shepherd (shepherds) of the flock of God, and has (have) been found acceptable by the local examining council. We pledge to him (them) our prayers and material support, that we may be laborers together as faithful stewards of the manifold grace of God.

CONFESSION OF FAITH

[The presiding minister will address the candidate(s):]
Brother (Brethren), you have heard the Word of God concerning the sacred office of the minister. I now call upon you in the presence of God and this company of believers to declare your faith.

[The candidate(s) will confess his (their) faith in whatever manner he has (they have) been requested by the ordaining council.]

QUESTIONING THE CANDIDATE(S)

[The presiding officer will question the candidate(s):]
Do you believe the Bible to be the Word of God, the only perfect standard for faith and conduct?

Candidate(s): *I do.*

Do you believe that God has called you into the sacred office of a minister of the gospel, and do you willingly dedicate your life to this service?

Candidate(s): *I do.*

Do you promise, by the grace of God, to discharge faithfully the duties of a minister of the gospel, proclaim the Word of God in all sincerity at home or abroad, administer the ordinances in accordance with the Scriptures, comfort the sick and the sorrowing, shepherd the flock of the Lord, and seek to reclaim those who are lost?

Candidate(s): *I do.*

Do you resolve, in humble dependence on God, to fulfill your ministry and in word and deed serve as a worthy example to God's people?

Candidate(s): *I do.*

Do you purpose to work in harmony with the (name of church, association, or denomination)?

Candidate(s): *I do.*

Bow your knees and lift up your hearts to God.

[Prayer]

CHARGE TO THE CANDIDATE(S)

[The charge consists of Scripture passages that are applicable to candidates to the ministry, usually ending with the commission of Matthew 28:19.]

PRAYER OF ORDINATION

[The candidate(s) should kneel facing the congregation. The officiating ministers should stand, or kneel, behind him (them) placing their hands upon his (their) head(s) while the prayer of ordination is offered.]

· ·

Presentation of Ordination

[The presiding minister will now present the candidate(s) the Certificate of Ordination and by name to the congregation.]

[Include a hymn of dedication.]

Benediction

The Suffering and the Glory of Ministry

Ordination Message Outline

John W. Reed

SCRIPTURE READING

1 Peter 5:1–11

INTRODUCTION

The road to glory is the trail of tears: verse 1 = the patterns (Peter and Jesus).

MESSAGE

I. Suffer willing *self-sacrifice* and experience Christ's crown of glory (vv. 2–4).
   A. *Suffer* self-sacrificing shepherd service. Jacob to Laban (heat and cold). Wages changed ten times (see Gen. 31:40).
   B. *Glory* of Chief Shepherd's crown of glory.

II. Suffer humble *self-rejection* and experience God's *exaltation* (vv. 5–7).
   A. *Suffer* self-rejection—submit to elders, one another, and God. Submit cares to God.
   B. *Glory*—God will lift you up when He is ready.

. . . .

III. Suffer vigilant *self-controlled* spiritual warfare and experience
the God-honoring *performance of a seasoned veteran* (vv. 8–
11).
   A. *Suffer* self-controlled vigilant warfare against Satan. Alert
and vigilant as a shepherd (e.g., David—before Goliath,
lion, and bear). Remember that you are not alone (v. 9).
   B. The *glory* of the God-honoring performance of a seasoned
veteran.

Restore/establish/strengthen/settle—bedrock foundation.

CONCLUSION

See verse 11 for the conclusion.

How to Have a Powerful Ministry

Keith Willhite

INTRODUCTION

1. Today, we can look around and see many pastors who have "successful" ministries, at least by the traditional benchmarks. Churches are growing in attendance and membership, several converts are added regularly, the budget is being met, attendance is increasing, etc.

2. We can also observe many pastors who are not doing so well. They are discouraged, even depressed perhaps, and feel as though nothing is happening. There's just no peace or power in their ministry.

3. What's the difference?

4. More specifically, how can you have a powerful ministry?

5. That's exactly the question that the apostle Paul answered for his young protégé, Timothy, and others in the ministry at the close of his first letter to Timothy.

6. Let's turn together to 1 Timothy 6:20–21 to see Paul's answer to this question, "How can you have a powerful ministry?" Read: 1 Timothy 6:20–21.

7. In Paul's answer to the question of how to have a powerful ministry, we find two commands and a benediction.

MESSAGE

I. First command: guard what has been entrusted to your care.
   A. Similar to Paul's command in 2 Timothy 1:14, which has

been entrusted to Timothy is the gospel—the truth of the Good News of Jesus Christ.

B. Nothing is more critical to the power of your ministry than the guarding of the gospel.

1. Preserve its purity (no salt and pepper).
2. Pass it on to others (2 Tim. 2:2).
3. Preach it (2 Tim. 4:2)!

(The importance of guarding what has been entrusted to your care becomes even more obvious as we see the second command. How can you have a powerful ministry? First, guard the gospel of Jesus Christ!)

II. Second command: turn away from godless chatter and false teachings.

A. "Turn away" has the sense of intentionally moving in a different (or opposite) direction.

1. Paraphrase: "Avoid godless chatter like the plague!"
2. "Godless chatter" might point to the false teachings prevalent in Ephesus and Asia Minor or, more generally, to speculations that were not necessarily anti-God but were at least *without* God.

B. Paul went on to instruct Timothy to turn away from "the opposing idea of what is falsely called knowledge."

1. Here, Timothy would have recognized Paul's more specific references to the heresy of Gnosticism, one form of which taught that people could be saved by knowledge.
2. Thus, the importance of guarding the truth of the gospel becomes all the clearer.
3. In Timothy's day, as in our day, false teachings existed (v. 21).
4. So, the apostle was very concerned about the message—guard its veracity and turn away from false teaching.

(These are his two commands for a powerful ministry—guard the gospel and turn away from things that threaten it. But in one final phrase, he gives a benediction to Timothy and the Ephesian leaders.)

III. A benediction: minister in God's grace.
   A. A "benediction." The word translated "you" in verse 21 is in the plural and probably indicates Paul's intent that this is not a piece of private correspondence for Timothy. But the letter should be read to all of the Ephesian Christians.
      1. This is part of my rationale for choosing this passage for the installation service.
      2. Not only the new minister but also the congregation needs to know how to have a powerful ministry.
      3. Hopefully, this will keep us from the "success questions."
         a. "Why don't we do it like that church over there?"
         b. "Should we be growing like that?"
         c. "This preaching isn't related to life enough, is it?" etc.
   B. More importantly, as in all other things in this life, especially the ministry, when we are without God's grace, we are without hope.
      1. Peter explained this point to the elders when he reminded them that they could minister only as the Great Shepherd ministers through them. He reminded them:

      Young men, in the same way be submissive to those who are older. All of you, clothe yourselves with humility toward one another, because "God opposes the proud but gives grace to the humble." (1 Peter 5:5)

   C. Remember, if you have any power in your ministry and see genuine fruit in your ministry, it will come only through the grace of God.

CONCLUSION

1. The *biblical* benchmarks for "success" in ministry involve faithfulness in guarding the truth of the gospel, turning away from false teachings, and ministering in God's grace.
2. Avoid the numbers game, the ego temptations, or the opportunities to build your own name, or even this church's name, instead of exalting the name of Jesus.
3. To have a powerful ministry, guard the gospel, turn away from false teachings, and minister in God's grace.

Letters from the Bean Field

The 1995 State of the Church Message

Ray Pritchard

SOMETIMES YOU STUMBLE ACROSS A new idea in the most unlikely places. Mine came from a little note that a friend wrote when he explained why he had decided to become a prayer warrior. He did it because of "Shammah, the Philistines, and the bean field." I had absolutely no idea what he was talking about. His next sentence confused me even more. He said that, in his opinion, "931 Lake Street is a bean field." That didn't help because, although you can find many things up and down Lake Street, you can't find a bean field within miles of here.

So I asked him later to explain what he meant. He wrote a nice letter referring me to an obscure passage in 2 Samuel 23, the chapter that tells of David and his mighty men. It is from that unlikely spot that I begin my 1995 state of the church message.

DAVID'S SPECIAL FORCES

We all know that King David was a great leader of men. He combined in himself those qualities of bravery, compassion, and integrity that made other men rally to his cause. The Bible tells us that within his army of soldiers were thirty warriors who might in today's terms be called his "special forces." These men were the best of the best, the strongest of the strong, the bravest of the brave, the ones who would not flinch under fire, and the men on whom you could depend if you were surrounded by the enemy. To put it in another context, these thirty men combined the best aspects of Sylvester Stallone, Bruce Lee, Chuck Norris, Jean-Claude van Damme, and Arnold Schwarzenegger. They were David's "go-to" guys when things got tough. Second Samuel 23 lists their names.

Above the Thirty were the Three. These were the three soldiers who were leaders of the Thirty. In all Israel you could not find better men than the men called "the Three." One man was named Josheb-Basshebeth, another was named Eleazar, and the third was named Shammah. Each man had risen to fame by virtue of a great victory won against overwhelming odds.

Let's look at the third man, Shammah, for a moment. The record, though brief, tells an amazing story:

> Next to him was Shammah son of Agee the Hararite. When the Philistines banded together at a place where there was a field full of lentils, Israel's troops fled from them. But Shammah took his stand in the middle of the field. He defended it and struck the Philistines down, and the LORD brought about a great victory. (2 Samuel 23:11–12)

At first glance, fighting the Philistines in a bean field ("a field full of lentils") doesn't seem to rank up there with landing with the rangers on Omaha Beach or with the marines on the sands of Iwo Jima. What was so significant about this encounter in the bean field? Was it something about Shammah, the bean field, or something else?

Why Fight in a Bean Field?

We begin with the simple observation that Shammah was a soldier. Every soldier knows that when you are outnumbered, you either retreat or seek another position that will allow you to even the odds. This usually means finding a place that is easily defensible, such as a mountaintop, a cave, or a valley with a very narrow opening. That way, even though you are outnumbered, you can make the terrain work to your advantage.

It seems that some of the Israelites didn't like the idea of fighting the Philistines in the middle of a bean field. They favored making a "strategic withdrawal" to a better location. But not Shammah; he was one of David's best warriors. He wasn't stupid, but neither did he "give ground" to this host of Philistines. Why?

Think about the bean field for a moment. It's a large, flat field with no cover, no place to hide, with the bean vines almost knee-deep. Your feet get tangled every time you move. Whenever you stand, the enemy sees you, and you're an instant target. The enemy can attack from all sides at once, in whatever numbers he can muster, so it's easy to find yourself surrounded by people who would rather kill you than say hello. Therefore, the bean field was a difficult place to fight a battle, and the situation was worsened by the fact that most of Shammah's brothers had hightailed it to the hills where they could establish a "proper" defensive position. There doesn't appear to be much here that would encourage Shammah (or anyone else) to take a stand and defend the ground against the army of the Philistines.

O Little Town of Gettysburg

But students of warfare know that you can't always choose your preferred battleground. Historians tell us that the Battle of Gettysburg happened by accident. A chance meeting turned into a skirmish that became a battle that eventually drew the Army of Northern Virginia into mortal combat with the Army of the Potomac. The whole course of the Civil War (and ultimately of America itself) hung on that chance meeting in early July 1863. Sometimes you choose your battles; sometimes your battles choose you. David chose Shammah as one of "the Three" because, when the battle chose him, he didn't run away. He stood and defended the ground even though it wasn't a good place to fight a battle.

On Friday, I ate lunch here in Oak Park with some friends from my days in Texas. As we walked down Lake Street toward the restaurant, we talked about how the history of this village is tied up in two names—Frank Lloyd Wright and Ernest Hemingway. Many people consider Frank Lloyd Wright the greatest architect America has ever produced. He lived and worked three blocks from here for twenty years. There are more Wright-designed homes in Oak Park and River Forest than anywhere in the world. Although he left Oak Park eighty-five years ago, he remains our number one tourist attraction. Ernest Hemingway was born four blocks from here, grew up seven blocks from here, went to church one block from here, and graduated in 1917 from Oak Park High School, about eight blocks from here. By all accounts Mr. Hemingway is one of the two greatest American writers of the twentieth century, winner of both the Nobel Prize and the Pulitzer Prize for literature.

Voices from the Past

The heroes we choose tell much about us. Go to Washington and you will find monuments to Abraham Lincoln, George Washington, and Thomas Jefferson. Come to Oak Park and you will hear about Wright and Hemingway. Both men were brilliant, extraordinarily gifted in their respective fields, and unquestioned geniuses. Yet, while he was here, Frank Lloyd Wright had an affair with a married woman, for whom he designed a beautiful home that we today call the Cheney Mansion. That torrid affair, which ended in fiery tragedy, has been called Oak Park's most famous romance.

When Ernest Hemingway graduated from Oak Park High School, he went off to World War I, came back with false stories regarding his war record, left Oak Park again, leaving behind his Christian upbringing, and moved to Paris, where he met F. Scott Fitzgerald, John Dos Passos, Gertrude Stein, and others who would form "the lost generation." He married, divorced, remarried, divorced, married again, had innumerable affairs, wrote brilliant novels, fell into deep despair, and in 1961 took a shotgun and blew his brains out in Idaho.

We have chosen as our heroes deeply flawed men, men of great brilliance who epitomize the term "secular humanism." They represent both sides of the great truth about the image of God in man. All men are made in God's image. That means that every human being has inherent worth because they reflect the handiwork of God who made them. It is because of the image of God that men are able to write great novels and design world-renowned buildings.

But ever since the fall of man, when Adam knowingly ate the fruit, that image of God inside all of us has been deeply marred by sin. Thus you have men like Wright and Hemingway who were capable of great works of art and yet lived in complete disregard of the Christian faith. Wright wanted nothing to do with biblical Christianity, which he regarded as narrow and sectarian, and Hemingway knowingly rejected his Christian upbringing.

The Way We Were

When I explained this to my friends on Friday, they asked if Oak Park had always been that way. Oh, no, I said, Oak Park was founded by families that moved here from New York State in the 1830s. They came primarily from Scotch-Irish Presbyterian and Congregational backgrounds. In those days, when Joseph Kettlestrings settled here, Oak Park represented the first bit of high ground after you left Chicago and traveled west across the marshland that eventually became the West Side of Chicago.

Those early settlers saw more than symbolism in the high ground. They were Christian people who wanted Oak Park to be a Christian village, a "city set on a hill" that would shine its light into the darkness of Chicago. That's why there are so many churches built around Scoville Park. They were sending a message that the church was to be at the heart of the village, the moral conscience of Oak Park. The founders of Oak Park wanted this village to be built upon the enlightened teaching of the Bible as the guide of moral and civic life.

Things have changed in the last 150 years. Oak Park started out on the high ground. We're a bean field now.

. . . .

SOONER OR LATER, YOU HAVE TO FIGHT

So what was left for Shammah? Most of his army had fled, the area was infested with Philistines, and even the terrain favored the enemy. Why did Shammah take a stand against the Philistines when everything he could see, hear, and touch was clearly against him?

Many possible answers to that question exist, but I favor this one: I think that Shammah stood and fought because he knew that if he gave up the bean field, he'd have to fight the Philistines later anyway. The more territory you give up now, the more you're going to have take back later. Somewhere along the way, you have to stop retreating. Sooner or later, you have to join the battle. Why not here? Why not now?

If they take the bean field, pretty soon they'll go after the barley. If they take the barley, they'll also take the corn. If they take the corn, they'll come after sheep. Once they have the sheep, they'll slaughter the cattle. The Philistines weren't nice people, and they didn't make war according to *Robert's Rules of Order*. They attacked and attacked until someone started to fight back.

VICTORY COMES WHEN WE STAND OUR GROUND!

That's what Shammah did. Instead of running and hiding, he decided to fight back. From a worldly point of view, what Shammah did was foolish at best. He dared to stand his ground amid challenges from every side. He did not compromise with the enemy, did not retreat from them, and did not establish a "multicultural discussion team" to help iron out the differences between the Israelites and the Philistines. He stood his ground, striking down the attacks of the enemy, and the Lord brought about a great victory in that bean field.

It has always been that way for the people of God. Victory comes when we stand our ground. Note the perfect balance between our part and God's part. What Shammah did required courage, faithfulness, and initiative:

- **Courage:** "He took his stand in the middle of the field."
- **Faithfulness:** "He defended it."
- **Initiative:** "He struck the Philistines down."

Then comes the victory: "And the LORD brought about a great victory." What made the difference? One man who refused to run away. One man turned the tide of battle, and through him God brought about a great victory.

One question remains. What's the hardest part of winning a battle like that? Answer: having the courage to take your stand in the middle of the field.

If you can do that, the rest is easy. The hard part is not running away.

A MODERN BEAN FIELD

In many respects, 931 Lake Street is like that bean field. It's located in an area that attracts all types of modern Philistines who neither acknowledge the true God nor desire to obey His commandments. They have either not accepted or have outright rejected the King of kings and Lord of lords. The moral and spiritual landscape here is relatively flat with no real "high ground" recognized by all participants as being generally defensible. We're knee-deep in regulations and ordinances that can trip us up if we're not careful.

Some people look at the situation and prefer to head for high ground elsewhere. Faced with such a situation, Calvary Memorial Church has chosen, like Shammah, to take a stand against the attacks that threaten the Christian values intended by God, Jesus, and America's Founding Fathers. We're out in the open, the battle is very real, and we need to rely on God to bring about another great victory through us.

(I am very grateful to a good friend for his penetrating analysis of the story of Shammah in 2 Samuel 23. It was his cryptic note to me that led me to this intriguing story.)

· ·

Never a Dull Moment

I suppose that one fair question would be, "Pastor Ray, how do you feel about things right now?" I realize that some people might not enjoy living in a bean field, but after six years, it feels like home to me. There is much to enjoy about Oak Park—the arts, the music, the culture, and the educational opportunities—and one thing is for sure: life in Oak Park might be many things, but it is never dull.

The banners on the wall behind me proclaim that 1995 is "The Year of Celebration." That refers to the fact that this is our eightieth anniversary as a church. Eightieth birthdays always call for a special celebration, and this one is no different. Eighty years ago this month, a small group of people formally began Sunday worship services in a Chinese laundry on Madison Street. When they started, they had less than one hundred dollars among them, most of which they spent on wooden chairs and hymnals. But they had a vision of building an independent, Bible-believing church here in Oak Park that would be interdenominational in its outreach and evangelical in its theology. Our founders wanted to establish a church that would do three things very well: teach the Bible, win the lost, and support world missions. You can trace those three concerns from that small beginning across the decades to the great church that God has given us today.

What Would They Think?

As I think about the size of our congregation and all that God has given us, and when I reflect on our humble beginnings in 1915, it occurs to me that our founders would be amazed to see what God has done with the church they started, *but they wouldn't be surprised that God has done it.* They knew all along that God was bigger than their plans and that He had dreams for this church that they couldn't begin to imagine.

I don't know what our first pastor would say about our contemporary worship service, but I think he would be delighted to see a sanctuary filled to overflowing. I don't know what one of our first missionaries would say about our spending $200,000 on world missions this year, but he'd be delighted that one of our couples is going to Nigeria this summer as full-time missionaries. None of our founders would understand the words or the music of our teenagers, but they would recognize the gospel that our youth pastor preaches, and they would rejoice to know that our youth group today is seven times larger than the church they founded eighty years ago.

THE SAWDUST TRAIL

In 1921, our church built its first building on the corner of Madison and Wisconsin streets. They decided to celebrate by inviting a famous evangelist named Homer Hammontree to conduct a two-week revival. They invited a sixteen-year-old boy to play the piano for those services. That was seventy-four years ago.

I don't have to wonder what that precocious teenager thinks about Calvary because, when I saw him three weeks ago, he told me how thrilled he is with our redesigned sanctuary platform and our new grand piano.

When he was here a few months ago to play for the senior adults, he told me that he remembered attending the Billy Sunday Crusade in 1918 in the huge wooden auditorium at the corner of Clark Street and North Avenue in Chicago. A few weeks ago, while I was preaching in Florida, I met a man who told me about hearing Billy Sunday preach at the Temple Baptist Church in Philadelphia. Six months ago, I had the privilege of portraying Billy Sunday standing in front of his grave at Forest Home Cemetery in Forest Park. With the help of a few friends and some gifted actors and actresses, we spread sawdust in front of his grave and re-created the sawdust trail.

That day I told the story of Billy Sunday's life and preached the gospel to nearly four hundred people. One woman came out of the crowd to shake my hand and say that she was trusting Christ as Savior. Most people appreciated it, but not all did. One of our workers heard a woman ask her husband who was the man portraying Billy Sunday. "It's Ray Pritchard from Calvary Memorial Church."

"It figures," she huffed.

That's life in the bean field, and, frankly, I love it. To me, this is the most exciting place in the world, the most exciting church, the most exciting village, and for all of its problems, it's a great place to live and raise a family for the glory of God.

We Ought to Be Grateful

As I look to the future, I find many things that encourage me. God has been so good to us. If we aren't grateful, we ought to be because God has given us so much. We have a wonderful location; an inspiring history; a beautiful building (nearly paid for too); more than a thousand people in worship every Sunday; gifted men and women who serve on the staff; godly elders, deacons, and deaconesses who exemplify the meaning of the word *servant*; more than two hundred prayer warriors; a vast army of Sunday school teachers, AWANA workers, and Caraway Street leaders and workers; a growing small group ministry; a burgeoning family ministry; gifted lay counselors; our wonderful choir; the brand-new church orchestra; our contemporary worship teams; and the college students who come each Sunday from Moody, Wheaton, Trinity, University of Illinois, Concordia, Rosary, Triton, and Morton, to name only a few schools. We ought to be grateful for Power Connection and Allied Force and for the opportunity to work with ministries such as the Near West Chicago Care Crisis Pregnancy Center, Circle Urban Ministries, and Inner City Impact. In addition to all of that, God is opening the door for us to play a leading role in the upcoming Luis Palau Chicago Campaign.

Last year, I shared that my greatest dream is to see a first-class, evangelical Christian day school established here in Oak Park. In less than twelve months, God has brought us to the east bank of the Jordan River. By God's grace, the waters will part, and on Monday, August 28, the Oak Park Christian Academy will open its doors for the very first time.

In October, when I visited Jerusalem, we spent a few minutes at the Western Wall, the holiest site in the world to Judaism. It is the only remaining part of Herod's temple, the temple that Jesus visited during His ministry. People come from around the world to write their prayer requests on little pieces of paper and place them in the crevices of those massive foundation stones. When I was there, I wrote my prayer request on a piece of paper and placed it in the wall—"For the foundation of a Christian school in Oak Park, Illinois, by the fall of 1995." With all of my heart, I believe that God is going to answer that prayer.

THE MOST IMPORTANT THING

The most important thing is that, after eighty years, people are still coming to Christ. Although much has changed, our heart for people remains the same. We preach the same gospel today that Louis Talbot and the founders of this church preached eighty years ago. We have the same Lord, the same Bible, and the same message that they had. Those things have not changed at all. Everything we do as a church is geared toward one goal: seeing men and women find salvation and the forgiveness of sins through the Lord Jesus Christ.

This week I received a letter from someone who told me about a friend who accepted Christ in our services last Sunday morning. Let me share part of her letter with you.

> When I first met him I learned he had attended another church for most of his life. He was fairly active with his mom during his youth, but only casually attended lately. He told me he was a Christian and we agreed to attend Calvary. Recently I began to realize that what he thought made him a Christian and what I thought did were two different things. I tried to explain what we believed, as did my brother and family. He struggled with things he had done in his past and with the concern that he had to be perfect before God would accept him. He believed he was going to heaven because he was baptized as a child. Well, each week he would go to church and I would pray for you to speak directly to his heart. Your sermon on regeneration

I think is what did it!!! You said you can be baptized one hundred times and attend church every week, but you still won't go to heaven. In another sermon you said God will take us as we are. I tried to reassure him that he did not have to never sin again to be loved by God.

Well on Easter Sunday he accepted Christ into his heart. He told me in my Easter card and said that if you asked him where he was born, he would say Melrose Park the first time and Easter Sunday in Oak Park the second time. I was so happy I cried.

At the end of the letter, she added this sentence: "I just thought you should know the positive impact you have on people's lives but may not always know it or hear the stories." It's not me or my sermons; it's the Holy Spirit working through all of us to create an atmosphere where seekers can find the Lord.

Five Years from Now

There is much work that needs to be done. Yesterday, at the New Members Seminar, I was asked to share my vision for this church. Specifically, I was asked to share where I thought Calvary would be in five years. Well, I don't know the future, but I hope that we are all right here together, still serving the Lord, still preaching God's Word, still sharing the gospel, still loving each other, and still willing to take new risks for the sake of Jesus Christ and His kingdom.

I do believe God has more people for us to reach, more missionaries to send, more children to teach, more families to help, and more broken lives to mend through the power of the gospel. I have no doubt that the challenges before us are in many ways greater than anything we have faced in the past. I fully expect that we will be challenged by the community because of our stand for the gospel, and we might find ourselves crucified by the local papers, and we might see pickets show up in front of our church again. But that's OK. Our founders weren't trying to win a popularity contest in Oak Park, and neither are we.

Exciting Days

I believe that God has called us to take our stand right here in Oak Park. Like Shammah of old, this is our bean field. It's not the easiest place to serve the Lord, but it's the only place we have. We might as well stand and fight right here because if we run away, we'll just have to fight somewhere else.

Exciting things are ahead for us. We have new services to begin, new ministries to form, and new opportunities to reach across ethnic and racial lines with the love of Jesus Christ. In the years to come, we're going to find new ways to fellowship with evangelical Christians in many other churches. I believe that God has called us to become a regional church for the near-western suburbs of Chicago. Already people drive great distances to attend our services. That trend will continue in the next few years as our congregation grows increasingly far-flung. I also predict that in the next ten years we will expand by starting five new churches in areas north, south, east, and west of here.

Four Images of the Church

I close now by sharing four images of the church that God is calling us to build. I believe that God has called us to be

- a lighthouse of truth in the prevailing moral darkness,
- a hospital of grace where the sick can find healing,
- a school of discipleship where we can all grow spiritually, and
- an army of God marching forth with the gospel to the ends of the earth.

I have been your pastor for nearly six years now. When I mentioned that to one of my friends from Texas, he said, "No, it seems like you've been gone for only two or three years." On the other hand, someone told me Friday night that he could see a lot of gray hair mixed in with the brown. Which is right? They both are. These have been wonderful years—not always easy but greatly rewarding.

Someone has said that the future is as bright as the promises of God. I believe that, and because I believe that, I am excited about tomorrow. These are great days to be alive, great days to serve the Lord, and great days to be part of God's family at Calvary Memorial Church. Welcome to the bean field!

REENACTMENT OF AN INFLUENTIAL CHRISTIAN

Billy Sunday Monologue

As Presented at Forest Home Cemetery,
Forest Home, Illinois, October 30, 1994

Ray Pritchard

EDITORS' NOTE: Pastor Ray Pritchard performed this reenactment of Billy Sunday in the cemetery where Mr. Sunday is buried. This cemetery has several other famous people buried in it, and the city hosts an annual reenactment, in which Pastor Pritchard has been a regular participant.

GREETING

Hello, folks. My name is Billy Sunday. Welcome to the Sawdust Trail.

Most of you know me as a preaching evangelist. But before I was an evangelist, I was a pretty fair baseball player. And that's where the story of my life really begins.

CHILDHOOD

I was born in 1862 in a little two-room log cabin near Ames, Iowa. I never knew my father because he died in the Civil War. My mom did the best she could for me and my brothers and sisters, but those years in Iowa were tough. So, when I was about eight or nine, my mom sent my brother Paul and me to the Soldier Orphanage in southwestern Iowa. I didn't much like the place. The rules were strict and the food wasn't so good, but I'm grateful for one thing. I learned how to play baseball at the orphanage.

. . . .

When I was about sixteen years old, my brother and I moved to Marshalltown, Iowa, where we got a reputation as pretty good ballplayers. One day, a man named Cap Anson came to see me play. He was a player with the famous Chicago White Stockings. I think you know them today as the Chicago Cubs.

Well, his father lived in Marshalltown and told him, "Son, there's a pretty fair ballplayer named Billy Sunday you need to meet." So Cap Anson came to watch me play. He said, "Sunday, you're a pretty fair country ballplayer, but I don't know how you'd do in the big city. Why don't you come to Chicago for a tryout?"

That was all I needed. So I packed all my clothes in a suitcase and hopped on the train for Chicago. When I got there, I had my suitcase and one dollar in my pocket. That same day, I went out to the ballpark. Wow! It was bigger than anything I had ever seen in Iowa.

Cap Anson decided to see how good I was, so he had me run a race with Fred Pfeffer, the fastest man on the White Stockings and reputedly the fastest man in the National League. So we lined up, me and old Fred Pfeffer. He had on his running shoes, but I was barefooted. Someone yelled out, "Hey, Sunday, where's your running shoes?"

"Ain't got no running shoes. Never heard of anything like that."

Off we went, and when the race was over, I had beat Fred Pfeffer by ten whole feet.

Cap Anson said, "Boy, I don't know whether you can play baseball or not, but I want you on my team."

Baseball Years

I played with the White Stockings for about six years. Never could hit much, but I was a speed demon on the bases. One year I stole ninety-four bases. I was also the first man to run the bases in fourteen seconds flat from a standing start. My greatest game came the day that I stole four bases off Connie Mack, who pitched for the Philadelphia team.

CONVERSION

The turning point of my life came in June of 1886 when our catcher, Mike Kelly, and I, and some of the boys were going out drinking in the saloons on State Street. We were just having a big time, carousing and carrying on, when we came to the corner of State and Van Buren Streets. There I saw something I had never seen before. It was a Gospel Wagon coming straight toward us. On the wagon was a group of men and women playing trombones, cornets, drums, and flutes. They were playing and singing the old gospel songs my godly momma used to sing to me back in that old two-room log cabin in Ames, Iowa. As I listened, the words to those songs came to my mind. The one that tore my heart out was a gospel song called "Where Is My Wandering Boy To-night?" When I heard it, I remembered what my mother had taught me and how far I had gone from my Christian upbringing.

Right then and there I said, "Boys, I've come to the end of the line. I'm through with the old life, and I'm heading in a new direction." That night, I went to the Pacific Garden Mission and heard Harry Monroe preach the gospel. I went back the next night and the next and the next. Finally, on about the fourth night, I was under such conviction of sin that I didn't know what to do. Mrs. Clark, wife of the founder of the mission, came and put her arm around my shoulders. "Billy, don't you think it's time you gave your heart to Jesus?"

I jumped up and ran down front, knocking over some chairs in the process. Then I knelt at the altar and prayed a prayer that went something like this: "Jesus, I believe You are the Son of God. I believe You died for my sins. Jesus, if You can do anything with an old country boy from Iowa, I'll give You my heart." When I stood up after that prayer, I was new man. I had been saved and redeemed by the blood of Jesus Christ.

CALL TO THE MINISTRY

I played ball for about five more years. Then, in 1891, I faced a big decision. The Philadelphia club offered me $500 a month—an enormous sum of money. But the YMCA offered me $83 a month to become their religious director. I didn't know what to do. $500 . . . $83 . . . $500 . . . $83. Finally, I prayed all night, and at 5:00 in the morning I said, "Lord, if You'll take care of my family, I'll be glad to give You my life." So I decided to take the YMCA job.

That ended my baseball career.

Five years later, I preached my first crusade in Garner, Iowa. I only had eight sermons (most of them borrowed from a man named J. Wilbur Chapman). When I preached those eight sermons, I preached them all over again. I was embarrassed to preach them a third time, so I closed the meetings. But I had seen three hundred people walk the sawdust trail.

Evangelistic Career

And so began a forty-year evangelistic ministry that took me to every part of America. During those years, I preached in three hundred crusades to more than one hundred million people. And that was before the days of radio, TV, VCRs, tape recorders, or public address systems. I saw more than a million people hit the sawdust trail and claim Jesus Christ as Lord and Savior.

Late in my life, I held a crusade in Charlotte, North Carolina. A little six-year-old boy heard me preach and went home scared to death. After the crusade was over, some folks in Charlotte organized a Billy Sunday Club to continue the work of evangelism. Ten years later, they invited a man named Mordecai Ham to come to Charlotte for a great tent revival. That young boy—by then sixteen years old—went forward at the invitation and gave his heart to Christ. His name was Billy Graham. Between us, we preached to more people than anyone in the history of Christianity.

Closing

I'm about done now. Before we go, I'd like to invite you to walk the sawdust trail and shake my hand and say, "Billy, I'm ready to follow

. . . .

Jesus Christ." Who will be the first? Just shake my hand and say, "I'm going to follow Jesus wherever He leads me."

I'd like to leave you with one final word to ponder.

When the Great Umpire of the Universe makes the Final Call, will He find you "safe at home" or "out for all eternity?"

Additional Resources for Other Occasions

Adams, Jay E. *Shepherding God's Flock*. Grand Rapids: Zondervan, 1975.

Berkley, James D. *Leadership Handbooks of Practical Theology*. Vol. 1: *Word and Worship*. Grand Rapids: Baker, 1992.

Blackwood, Andrew W. *Special-Day Sermons for Evangelicals*. Great Neck, N.Y.: Channel Press, 1961.

Cox, James W. *The Minister's Manual*. San Francisco: Harper and Row, 1988.

Criswell, W. A. *Criswell's Guidebook for Pastors*. Nashville: Broadman, 1980.

Gibson, Scott M. *Preaching for Special Services*. Grand Rapids: Baker, 2001.

Sanborn, Hugh W. *Celebrating Passages in the Church: Reflections and Resources*. St Louis: Chalice Press, 1999.

Thielen, Martin. *Getting Ready for Special Sundays: A Practical Guide for Worship and Preaching Preparation*. Nashville: Broadman, 1991.

Tidwell, Derek J. *Skillful Shepherds*. Grand Rapids: Zondervan, 1986.

Vassallo, Wanda. *The Church Communications Handbook: A Complete Guide to Developing a Strategy, Using Technology, Writing Effectively, Reaching the Unchurched*. Grand Rapids: Kregel, 1998.

Endnotes

PART 1: WEDDINGS

1. W. A. Criswell, *Criswell's Guidebook for Pastors* (Nashville: Broadman, 1983), 283. While Dr. Criswell's words regarding premarital counseling are certainly endorsed here, we have not included resources for premarital counseling because a number of good resources already exist.
2. Scott M. Gibson, *Preaching for Special Services* (Grand Rapids: Baker, 2001), 26–27.

PART 2: FUNERALS

1. Haddon Robinson, James Means, and Paul Borden, "How to Prepare a Funeral Sermon," *Expositapes* (Denver: Denver Seminary, 1984), audiocassette.
2. Bryan Chapell, *The Wonder of It All: Rediscovering the Treasures of Your Faith* (Wheaton: Crossway Books, 1999), 196.
3. Chapell, *The Wonder of It All*, 197–98.
4. "If We Could See Beyond Today." Norman J. Clayton © 1943 Wordspring Music, Inc. All rights reserved. Used by permission.

PART 3: OTHER OCCASIONS

1. Scott M. Gibson, *Preaching for Special Services* (Grand Rapids: Baker, 2001).

About the Editors

Dr. Aubrey Malphurs serves as Department Chairman and Professor of Field Education at Dallas Theological Seminary. He is a visionary with a deep desire to influence a new generation of leaders through his classroom, pulpit, consulting, and writing ministries. He is heavily involved in a number of ministries from church planting and growth to leadership development. He has pastored three churches and is the author of numerous books and articles on leadership and church ministry. He earned both Th.M. and Ph.D. degrees from Dallas Theological Seminary. He is the president of the Malphurs Group and is a trainer and consultant to churches, denominations, and ministry organizations throughout North America and Europe. Dr. Malphurs and his wife, Susan, have four children.

Dr. Keith Willhite served as Professor of Pastoral Ministries at Dallas Theological Seminary. Before joining the faculty of Dallas Seminary in 1996, he served ten years in pastoral ministry and then as Chairman of the Department of Homiletics and Director of the D.Min. Program at Denver Seminary. He earned the Ph.D. degree in communication from Purdue University and the Th.M. degree from Dallas Seminary. In addition to his teaching, Dr. Willhite was founder and president of *Strategenuity*, a ministry consulting firm. Dr. Willhite and his wife, Denise, have two children.

Scripture Index

. . . .